I.

POLITICS AND DEVELOPMENT

POLITICS AND DEVELOPMENT

A Critical Introduction

Olle Törnquist

SAGE Publications
London • Thousand Oaks • New Delhi

This edition is a revised and expanded version of a work originally published in Swedish as *Politik och utveckling i tredje världen* by Studentlitteratur, Lund. The original book was translated into English by Peter Mayers. Chapter 13 of this edition is a revised version of the author's contribution to *Democratisation in the Third World*, edited by Lars Rudebeck, Olle Törnquist and Virgilio Rojas (Macmillan, 1998).

SAGE Publications Ltd
6 Bonhill Street
London EC2A 4PU

SAGE Publications Inc
2455 Teller Road
Thousand Oaks, California 91320

SAGE Publications India Pvt Ltd
32, M-Block Market
Greater Kailash – I
New Delhi 110 048

British Library Cataloguing in Publication data

A catalogue record for this book is available from the British Library.

ISBN 0 7619 5933 5
ISBN 0 7619 5934 3 (pbk)

Library of Congress catalog record available

Typeset by Photoprint, Torquay
Printed and bound in Great Britain by
Athenaeum Press, Gateshead

Contents

Preface

What seemed at first would be a fairly simple task of writing an introductory text – something to be accomplished in my spare time and on the basis of already existing knowledge – has proved to require much in the way of rethinking and new intellectual analysis, together with a considerable effort to present the material in (I hope) a telling fashion. To begin with, it would have been impossible to complete the original book in Swedish without devoting a part of my previous so-called higher research appointment in political science – with a focus on developing countries (1991–97) – to the performance of the task. (An acknowledgement is therefore in order of my debt to SAREC, the department for research co-operation within the Swedish Development Aid Authority, Sida, which financed my research appointment.) Thereafter, moreover, much of the extensively revised and expanded English edition has been written within the stimulating milieu of the Department of Political Science and Centre for Development and the Environment at the University of Oslo, to which I shifted in mid-1997.

A first draft was ready in the autumn of 1994. Students taking the basic course on development studies at Uppsala University offered valuable comments on the text, and inspired me to introduce extensive changes. The same goes for the Masters and Ph.D. students at Uppsala who attended the yearly course on 'State, Development and Democratisation', as well as several students at Oslo with similar interests. My thanks to all of you! I have also received encouragement and critical suggestions from Peter Mayers, who translated the original book into English, the editors and readers at Sage, and many colleagues. My special thanks to Maria Edin (who has both taken and taught the very course for which this book was originally intended), Lars Rudebeck (who has considered these questions since publishing a book in 1970 on a related topic), Ishtiaq Ahmed, Björn Beckman, Henrik Berglund and Lars Lindström (who instruct and advise students on similar questions at the Department of Political Science at Stockholm University), Anders Uhlin (who first performed similar duties at the Department of Political Science at Lund University and now continues to do so at the new University College of South Stockholm), many of the participants in the Skytteanum research seminar at the Department of Government at Uppsala University, and several of my new colleagues at Oslo.

Olle Törnquist
Kungshamn and Oslo

Introduction

This is a book for students of politics who are also interested in addressing problems of development in the so-called Third World (and for students of development who also wish to consider in depth its political aspects); for students, that is, who may need an introduction to the subject, to the main schools of thought, and to how one can go about planning a critical study of one's own – a study which questions the conventional truth.

In other words, this is not a book in favour of universal studies of 'political development' (which usually take experiences in the West as the point of departure), of specific studies of Third World politics as such, or of interdisciplinary studies of the politics of development. Rather, it is a book that reviews relevant work within the dominant frameworks in order to help us bridge and go beyond them; to bridge and go beyond those frameworks by *first* defining the general questions in relation to the interdisciplinary politics of development, *then* focusing on the political agents, processes, institutions and structures that affect (and are affected by) the development problems, and only *thereafter* (on the basis of solid empirical knowledge of the Third World itself) opening up for broad and even universal generalisations. Actually, such specific studies of politics related to problems of development in the Third World may be thought of as a new sub-discipline within political science, tentatively labelled 'politics and development'. (We shall return in Chapter 1 to a critical discussion on the notion of the 'Third World'.)

Studying the politics and development of the Third World is important and rewarding – but demanding. To begin with one must know (and probably also be concerned about) the problems of development and the role of politics. For political scientists, this implies broadening one's competence to include interdisciplinary co-operation and knowledge of how different factors interrelate in processes of development. Thereafter (once the way in which politics relates to this process has been defined), there is a need for empirically well-grounded studies of the political ingredients themselves; studies which despite their solid empirical character do not lose track of comparative and theoretical perspectives. For most of us, this implies time-consuming searching for necessary information in the field, in addition to reading relevant literature. Finally, one must be able to position the study in a comparative perspective and open up for generalisations; and this, of course, implies knowledge of other theories, contexts and cases as well.

Having to combine all this is a dilemma, but there are no short cuts. Those wishing to study 'politics and development' in a serious way must be able to sit on several different stools at once, without falling in between. This book is to help us manage this task. Hence, you will not find detailed information on any of the fields that we need to master – there are other books for that – but you will find an introduction that will help to bring it all together.

The key, then, in my experience, is a concise review. There are three reasons for this. A review, *first*, because there is a need to orient oneself and get an idea of what has, should and could be done. Without this knowledge of the landscape there can be few critical studies questioning conventional truths. Without this ability to find one's own way there may be instead a tendency to follow patronising professors and fashion-able trends. A review, *second*, because we need to know what to look for when, thereafter, probing into the theories on politics and development, the vast amount of empirically oriented studies, and the scattered but vital material that is available only in the field. A review, *third*, that really is concise – because all this work is very time-consuming.

The structure of the book, therefore, is as follows. Part 1 is an introduc-tion to the debate on what the study of politics and development in the Third World should be about. How should one define the problem area? How should the studies be organised in relation to various specialised subjects? What analytical approaches is it possible to discern? What political and other external factors have shaped the studies and the various schools of thought?

This way, we may also formulate questions to structure Part 2 of the book, which is a small-scale survey of the main schools of thought that have framed the study of Third World politics and development over time. We ask how different scholars – during different political and intellectual conjunctures – have delineated the subject and specified, described and explained the problems, and what prescriptions result.

I have striven, on the one hand, to present a critical account, and there are no special attempts to conceal my own views behind purportedly objective formulations. (It is better that the reader be able to ascertain where the author stands – and so can be on guard against possible mistakes and distortions – than that the author employs a purportedly neutral language which makes critical reading more difficult.) Yet I do not, on the other hand, argue on behalf of any particular school. Representatives of the various orientations should be able to recognise the lay of the land as described herein. This is to make it easier for the reader to form a fair and accurate picture of what others have done; thereafter to be able to go ahead on his or her own.

Part 3, then, is on how to proceed after one has settled on a research theme and must decide which orientation, which theories and which analytical approaches are most fruitful. The point of departure must be the issues that one finds to be of particular interest. The next step is to search for those analytical tools and explanations which appear most fruitful, but there is no compulsion to adopt the precepts of any one school hook, line and sinker.

Consequently, Part 3 can only be based on an example of how one can proceed within a particular research theme. The theme chosen as an example is the most central contemporary one: processes of democratisation within the framework of Third World development.

To begin with, I show how one can argue for specifying the problem of democratisation in the context of late development, and how one can take a position on the contributions of the various schools. What are the theories and perspectives on offer? How fruitful are they? Can they be combined? In which areas is more knowledge needed? When trying to answer such questions, it has been necessary, of course, to go beyond the non-partisan review of various schools of thought in Part 2. Here in Part 3, by contrast, I do argue for theses of my own. My initial argument is that there is a need to go beyond the fashionable preoccupation with the middle-class, rational elite and 'good governance', and to focus instead on the problems of democratisation from below.

The next question, then, is what analytical approach to apply – or in this case, how one should actually go about studying democratisation from below. The dominant perspective is of civil society, and of civic community generating social capital. However, I do not find this to be relevant and fruitful. I substantiate my argument in four sections: first, by recalling a vital critique related to the civil society/social capital paradigm's own theoretical and empirical premises; second, by questioning its generalisation to Third World contexts; third (and mainly), by showing how empirical results from my own comparative studies in India, Indonesia and the Philippines of civil society/civic community movements which really give priority to democratisation, speak against the theses. These results suggest instead that it is both more relevant and fruitful to study the *politics* of democratisation. Finally, therefore, I also discuss how this may be conceptualised, and suggest an approach in terms of political space, inclusion and politicisation.

The book has primarily, so far, been used in three intellectual contexts:

- first, as an introduction to the special study of 'politics and development' within politics departments as well as interdisciplinary units of development studies; an introduction which may be accompanied, then, by more extensive materials on special themes (such as democracy, the state, civil society, gender or ethnicity) in different Third World regions. This way the book has been used by graduate as well as undergraduate students with an interest in a critical understanding of various perspectives – for instance, in order to write an essay.
- second, as a regular or self-study introduction to general perspectives before students probe into specialised thematic or area studies courses.

- third, as an overview of the discourse on various perspectives, theories and approaches – and as an introduction to how they may be put to use – for students, journalists and development assistance workers (among others) who are about to carry out inquiries of their own.

Certainly the book consists, for the most part, of critical analyses of different perspectives, and it must be conceded that such texts are often long and difficult. I have tried to write clearly enough, however, that the reader need not know everything about the theories beforehand.

I have also tried to keep the text brief enough so as to leave room for the exploration of other books as well. For after all, as already indicated, we must save enough time to enlarge the picture in just those areas and concrete cases where we are particularly interested.

The references, finally, for reasons of space, have been limited to the works cited, together with certain standard works and (where such are missing) examples of what sort of research is intended. (In the latter case, as a result of my own empirical focus on Asia, studies about that part of the world predominate.) This necessary limitation to standard works used at first hand, however, may also be misleading. Given the increasingly globalised structure of dominance within the field, standard works usually spring out of the dominant English-speaking Western powers. The reader *must* be aware of the fact that many studies – often at least equally good and exciting – are produced in other contexts as well, including, of course, in the Third World.

PART 1

THE STUDY OF THIRD WORLD POLITICS AND DEVELOPMENT

The first part of the book aims to identify what the study of politics and development in the Third World is about – and to simultaneously identify the questions that will structure the review of the main schools of thought in the second part.

In Chapter 1 the debate on the problem area is introduced and the author puts forward his own proposal. In Chapter 2 the organisation of studies of politics and late development in relation to other subjects is discussed and the sub-discipline itself is delimited. Chapter 3 points to various analytical approaches, while Chapter 4 discusses the external factors, politics included, that have shaped the subject and the various schools of thought.

1 The Problem Area

Third World Development

The ultimate reason for this book is what you will not find much about in it – the serious problems of development facing most people in the Third World and also involving the rest of us. Other analysts have already written many good books about those problems. You, being interested in this text, have probably read some of them. Therefore, we shall move ahead instead by focusing on how *politics* affects (and is affected by) development.

Before doing so, however, what do we mean by development and what is special about the problems in the Third World?

In normal usage, the term 'development' is multi-faceted, and usually value-laden too. For scientific purposes, therefore, it is necessary to settle for a more precise definition. On a general level, 'development' refers in this book to a process in which resources are put to better use – in a country, a region, or a sector of society (like industry or agriculture). The term 'better' requires, of course, an explanation of how and for whom a particular way of using resources is more advantageous than another. For a given use of resources might even result in – at one and the same time – the best possible development for one social group and in a negative development for another. The resources in question include natural resources, technology and capital – and human labour, planning and co-operative capacity too. In the social sciences, however, we usually take natural resources and technology as givens and concentrate on what people do.

Studying development problems thus involves identifying and analysing the difficulties people encounter in their efforts to make – on the basis of their varied interests and ideas – the best possible use of the potential of their country, region or sector of society.

To this extent, the problems of development – and the various theories about them – are universal. Yet we focus our attention here on the Third World. At the outset, I would argue that the demarcation of the term is still meaningful. For one thing, the inheritance from colonialism and the national struggle remains significant. For another, development in the Third World – the industrialisation of East Asia included – has been a comparatively late affair. The newcomers may be able to draw on experiences in previously industrialised countries but face rather different conditions, often dominated by the forerunners.[1] Finally, this late development has led to great suffering and adjustment difficulties for extremely large numbers of people, even in cases where the successes have been and are considerable. (Henceforth, 'late development' and 'Third World development' or 'development in the Third World' will therefore be used interchangeably.)

Others question this, talk of diversities and specificities, and recommend beginning at the empirical end rather than with assumptions about a common problem area. It is important, they say, to acquire an unbiased and comprehensive knowledge of individual countries and regions before immersing oneself in political questions, making comparisons and possibly taking up general questions of development too.[2] They give priority, accordingly, to the study of areas with a common culture (southern India or the Arab world, for example), and to institutes such as those specialising in Africa or Asia.

As far as I understand it, there are two fundamental arguments for this standpoint. One is based on the notion that much of the development discussion has to do with models and forms of assistance that confronted each other during the Cold War and the anti-imperialist struggle. Now these models and projects are passé. As a matter of fact, the claim goes, there are not so many overarching alternatives remaining. Cultural and other local differences thus become decisive. The second argument is that, in addition to the invalid political projects, the general-level scientific theories are also unfruitful because developing countries have become so unlike each other, while specific features have assumed such great importance.

I can certainly concur with much of this, especially with the need for thoroughgoing empirical studies. Taken together, however, I think the arguments go too far and put us on the wrong track.

It may be, to begin with, that much of the development debate (and many interdisciplinary development seminars and development studies programmes too) had its roots in the disputes and interests of the Cold War and the anti-colonial struggle. Area studies do not, however, lack skeletons in the closet either. They may be useful for comparative studies of similar cases (to explain differences by identifying missing links), but they originated, primarily, in the interests of superpowers and their allies in gathering the expertise required for influencing former colonies and client states that had become important markets or major recipients of development assistance. So even if such interests often make it easier to procure resources for education and research, this approach, it seems to me, is not exactly innovative, at least not from the standpoint of critical research.[3]

Second, it may be true that many of the development alternatives from the Cold War and the anti-imperialist struggle are now history. They are no longer the current models which need comparing. However, neither history nor the struggle against poverty came to an end with the Cold War. Now there are other models that need to be compared. Neo-liberal structural adjustment, for instance, stood in glaring contrast to the strategy that was applied in the developmental states of East Asia. Out in the field, moreover, new options are emerging, not least among popular organisations. Finally, the study of politics and late development is not just a matter of examining different development policy models; it is also, and in at least as high a degree, a question of analysing how politics and development come together in reality; and though the international balance of power has changed, much of this reality remains the same for most people in the Third World.

Third, granted, developing countries differ increasingly from one another. No longer can we equate the Third World with the Third Estate during the French Revolution, or describe it as a sort of unified proletariat on a world scale. However, structures, institutions and organisations created by colonialism, anti-feudalism and anti-imperialism are still important. Moreover, everyone would seem to agree that internationalisation, and with it various new relations of dependence, is assuming ever greater importance. One need only follow the business and foreign affairs pages in the newspapers to realise what enormous power international financial actors possess. The same may be said of media giants such as CNN and organisations such as the International Monetary Fund and the World Bank.

These common factors, old and new, do not have the same effects, needless to say, in countries that are highly different from each other, such as Tanzania and Taiwan. Internationalisation, for one, interacts with internal political and economic conditions. But we should not forget the fundamental importance of history as well as of new internationalisation just because specific features are decisive when our purpose is to explain the differences. We need instead to analyse these differences and inequalities within the framework of the legacy of the past as an increasingly integrated system.

Fourth, I would argue, not even the politics of development within the various countries has come to vary so much that we are obliged to begin with the specific. There is still a special kind of politics of late development, the political aspect of which calls for closer study.

Let us examine this controversial thesis more closely. For if it does not hold true, then one can question – the earlier arguments notwithstanding – whether it is scientifically fruitful to apply an overarching approach to the study of Third World politics and development.

Third World Politics of Development: The Symbiosis of the Political and Economic Spheres

I shall argue that the particular Third World politics of development – that constitutes the problem area of this book and calls for closer analysis precisely of its political aspects – is characterised by how the political and economic spheres, just as in earlier industrialised countries, are tightly interwoven, but in such a way that the political is particularly important. I shall refer to a symbiosis of the political and economic spheres – having in mind thereby a politically dominated combination of the two – and I shall argue that this can be traced in turn to colonialism, the national revolutions and the comparatively late post-colonial development efforts.

Endogenous Transitions to Capitalism

In feudal societies landlords had to use extra-economic political coercion to force serfs to yield up a portion of what they produced. Peasants had a certain access to production tools and to land, and but for the coercion in question they would have been able to exploit those resources on their own behalves.

In most parts of Europe this changed with the spread of capitalism and the bourgeois revolutions. The old ruling class lost its foothold. At the same time, however, the larger part of the population lost its access to land and the means of production. So even if the feudal lords disappeared, the common people could not survive on their own. Instead they were forced to sell their labour power to the capitalists, who controlled most of the resources. The new ruling class did not need, therefore, to use as much political coercion as its predecessor – its economic power usually sufficed. Politics and economics were still dependent on each other, but in new forms. Politics was now less decisive. It had become possible, for instance, to distinguish between state and civil society.[4]

This took place in a variety of ways, naturally, and the process was an uneven one. Semi-feudal relations lingered, for instance, on large estates in Eastern Europe. In most cases, moreover, mercantilism played an important role.[5] Even in such countries as Great Britain, state regulation and protection were more important than is evident from the dominant description of history drawn from Adam Smith's claims about the ideal free market. If, moreover, we follow the European emigrants to settler colonies such as those in North America, we discover that there it was not anti-feudal bourgeois revolutions, but rather the extermination of the indigenous population – in combination with a libertarian pioneer spirit and later on the abolition of slave labour – that prepared the way for capitalism and the relative separation of state and civil society.

Colonial Expansion of Capitalism

Of particular interest to us, however, is what happened when capitalism started spreading to the Third World, that is, to colonies which could not be conquered as easily as those in North America or Australia. In the Third World, capitalism did not contribute – to any degree worth mentioning – to a relative separation of the political and economic spheres. On the contrary, permanent political coercion was often necessary for subjugating both peoples and existing states and organisations. And this subordination was necessary in turn for creating and maintaining unequal relations of trade, plantation cultivation and raw materials exploitation.

The empire builders could rely to some extent on their own instruments of power and govern directly from the metropolis, for example through governors general. But these power instruments were insufficient. They governed, therefore, by indirect means as well – partly through colonists who established themselves in the new 'provinces' (in Latin America particularly), and partly by propping up local feudal-like lords and letting them do the job (especially in Africa and Asia).

The capitalist empire-builders thus contributed to conserving and *further developing* both the mercantile integration of the political and economic spheres that they brought with them from Europe, and the feudal-like ones which already existed in the colonies. These then reinforced each other, and the irony is that capitalism in the Third World thus shaped not the same but a similar kind of integration of the political and economic spheres which it had undermined in the West. Here, then, is the source of the symbiosis of the political and economic spheres which still characterises the relation between politics and development in the majority of developing countries today.

National Revolution

But that is not all. This symbiosis soon became a fundamental obstacle to development – even, paradoxically enough, for the colonial economy itself. Colonial plantations required, for example, a large measure of political coercion. This inhibited economic dynamism. The soil in which capitalists might grow to economic power and political independence was poor. Sweeping bourgeois revolutions were conspicuous by their absence. Therefore, the Third World counterpart to the bourgeois revolutions of Europe became the national revolutions – which assumed a markedly political character.

Wellnigh all oppositional forces had to orient themselves primarily to the achievement of changes by political means. This was the only way, almost everyone said, to prepare the way for economic and social development. Both bourgeois nationalists and Communists found it untenable to await some sort of natural and progressive capitalist development. They sought, instead, a political 'short cut' to development. Radical political struggle against the imperialists and their henchmen would result in independent nation-states. These would be able in their turn to carry out anti-feudal land reforms and industrial development. Only through such political intervention would the way be opened for a sort of parallel in the Third World to the bourgeois-revolutionary changes and the modernisation processes of the West.

Here, then, we have a further important reason why the political and economic spheres in the Third World continued to grow together in a fashion rendering the former particularly important. Colonial economic dynamism was insufficient. Not only did the colonialists find political coercion necessary for maintaining their exploitative position, but the opposition also had to assign top priority to political work and organising in order to get anywhere.

Nation-State Development Projects

This tendency towards a politically dominated interlacing of the political and economic spheres was further strengthened when the victorious politicians in the Third World assumed control over the old colonial state apparatuses. First in Latin America, where the struggle then continued against American neo-colonialism and feudal-like domestic oligarchies. Then in Asia, and finally in Africa. Radical politicians were able to launch development projects based on the nation-state. It was a question of integrating ethnic and other national minorities, creating a 'real' nation-state and combating all forms of colonialism. Parliamentary and executive organs would be used to get production going, for domestic entrepreneurs were as weak as the big international companies were strong.

In addition to the nationalists, other social engineers were in action as well. Especially following the Second World War, and during the Cold War, 'friendly' governments and aid agencies – in the industrialised countries of both the West and East – were gripped by a similar fascination with the possibilities of achieving rapid development through planned and state-led methods.

The Politics of Stagnation and Rapid Growth

The original nation-state projects in most developing countries are now in crisis. Many political short cuts to a better standard of living have not brought the desired results. Central planning has often proved a failure. The environment has been ruined. More people than anywhere else in the world remain powerless and poor. Women are kept down. Ethnic, religious and other minorities are oppressed. The list of failures is a long one. It is perhaps unsurprising, in view of all this, that for more than a decade now the calls have rung out for deregulation and privatisation – the object being to deepen civil society and to reduce the political sphere.

To begin with, however, it is important to keep a sense of historical proportion here. We should not throw out the baby with the bath water. Just some ten years ago, for instance, we all paid homage to the French Revolution. Commentators noted, certainly, that the revolution derailed and ended in terror. Yet it was the historical significance of this event that was stressed: citizenship; liberty, equality and fraternity; the break-through of the Enlightenment and of rationalism. Some of the better sides, in other words, of a modernism which has now lost its way. So let us not fall victim to the fashionable tendency to ignore (or to emphasise solely what 'went wrong' with) the French Revolution's counterpart in our own time – the modern national revolutions of the Third World.

These revolutions and the movements that achieved them were influ-enced, of course, by modernisation projects in the West as well as in state-socialist countries. These movements took a critical view, moreover, of those they referred to (rightly or wrongly) as traditionalists with roots in obdurate religion, ethnicity or semi-feudal relations. But the really important and historically unique feature of these movements was something else. A good part of them tried, at the same time, to reform their own cultures and religions. They sought to combine positive elements from their own traditions with the valid insights and experi-ences of Western modernism (including bourgeois revolutions and socialist orientations), so that ordinary people could become independ-ent citizens in their own countries; so that they could control and develop their own resources; and so that they could improve their own living conditions. Accordingly, the struggle for democracy and human rights in the Third World is neither new nor an exclusively Western innovation. Quite the contrary.[6]

Of course, the character of these national projects varied. The old Zapatistas (in Mexico), for example, had one line, Nyerere a second, Mao a third, Gandhi a fourth, Nehru a fifth. Granted, it is the history of the nation-state builders which has been written. Regional and local condi-tions have been overlooked. Alternative national identities have been concealed. The perspective of the oppressed has seldom formed the point of departure. And certainly much has gone wrong, as mentioned above, and the outcomes have been far from those intended. However, it is scientifically unfruitful to deny the common effort to reform and synthesise what used to be called the 'traditional' and the 'modern'. Likewise it would be awkward to disregard the historical advances and processes that have been set in motion. Not only such advances as citizenship in independent countries, but also modest and incomplete land reforms – which nevertheless stand out, in comparison with what happened during centuries of colonialism, as rapid and drastic changes for the better.

Moreover, in addition to keeping a sense of historical proportion, we should remember that deregulation and privatisation have not usually

taken place through the increased strength and independence of businessmen and entrepreneurs. On the contrary, the strength of such groups
has depended for the most part on dubious political changes in which
foreign political forces have often taken part. The main result is that
certain politicians, officials and/or their associates have been able to
establish themselves as private or semi-private capitalists – as in many of
the countries where structural adjustment programmes have been carried out, as well as in many of the miracle economies of East and South-
East Asia that now face adjustment.

Finally, most scholars agree that forceful and efficient political regulation lay behind, for many years, the only cases of extensive and rapid
social and economic development to be found in the Third World,
namely those of East and South-East Asia – while the recent crisis in the
area is rather related to the various forms of semi-privatisation and lack
of efficent regulation mentioned in the previous paragraph.

So the crux of the matter is scarcely too much politics, or unwise
political short cuts, or however one chooses to put it. Politics is obviously
needed. The question is rather which political forms, contents and
processes promote what kind of development? Even more importantly:
how, and under what circumstances, do such uncommon politics
emerge? It is clear, in any case, that the symbiosis of the political and
economic spheres is still, for better or for worse, of immense importance
in most developing countries.

Other Themes?

The above delimited characteristics of Third World politics of development in terms of the symbiosis of the political and economic spheres
constitute thus what this author holds to be the most relevant way of
describing the problem area for systematic studies of its political aspects
– that is, the study of politics and late development. Others, of course,
have suggested different themes, including modernisation, dependency,
rent-seeking and transaction costs. In the second part of the book,
therefore, we shall ask precisely what kinds of themes other scholars
have given priority to within their paradigms. Before doing so, however,
it is time to proceed here by asking instead how political science studies
of late development have been organised and should be organised.

Notes

1 On the concept of late development in general, see for a classical study
Gerschenkron, *Economic Backwardness in Historical Perspective.*

2 For a recent example, see Manor, *Rethinking Third World Politics*. (My particular thanks to Inga Brandell, who does not agree with some of my conclusions, for many stimulating discussions on these questions!)

3 As far as analysing the relation between politics and late development is concerned, one might add that problem formulations and the link to ongoing scientific discussions and theories – which often generate exciting and fruitful results – easily receive less emphasis in area studies, especially at institutes without a challenging programme of basic and advanced education.

4 By civil society is usually meant voluntary associations and public (though often privately controlled) communication that are independent of the state.

5 A policy making its appearance in Western Europe in the mid-1500s, whereby the state promoted foreign trade and domestic industry.

6 For a recent stimulating discussion, see Markoff, *Waves of Democracy*.

2   The Subdiscipline

The very political aspects of Third World development have rarely been addressed in their own right. Usually, they have rather been analysed in the margins of three more fashionable frameworks: the study of political modernisation, Third World politics, and the politics of development. There is a need to organise the work in a more fruitful way.

Political Modernisation

Development in general, as we know, is a value-laden concept. Similarly, political development (development of politics, that is) has hitherto been related primarily to the study of equally disputed modernisation. We shall return to the details when discussing the various schools of thought in the second part of the book, but let us sketch some characteristics with relevance to the organisation of the studies.

The point of departure in mainstream studies of political development was non-Marxist analyses of how modern political systems (complex, specialised, legitimate and so on) seemed to work in West-European and North American nation-states.[1] The essential functions that any such system was assumed to handle included political socialisation and recruitment, interest articulation and aggregation, communication, and rule-making, rule application and rule adjudication.[2] In modern societies, the functions were taken care of by institutions and organisations such as interest groups, parties, parliaments and mass media.

In addition there were normative considerations, for instance concerning how a stable and legitimate political system should be designed to prevent the re-emergence of Fascism/Nazism and contain Communism – including by way of representative political democracy.[3]

Finally there were attempts to generalise about the history of the modern political functions and institutions. All countries, analysts of political development said, had faced similar kinds of challenges, such as national integration and participation. The remaining question, therefore, was in what way various actors had tackled them under different conditions.

In the late fifties and early sixties a particularly forceful attempt was made to apply this paradigm to the development of politics in the Third World as well. The studies and the ideals of the West were turned into grand universal theories of political development. These were then applied to the 'non-Western world'. Scholars asked, for instance, how Third World countries dealt with 'universal political functions' such as political socialisation or interest aggregation? Did there develop modern political cultures, as well as institutions like parties, to tackle them? Were the political systems and the politicians able to simultaneously handle challenges such as national integration, social mobilisation, economic development and social welfare which in the West had been spread out over centuries? How would it be possible to build stable and legitimate governments and contain radical nationalists and Communists? Or, to take the approach of dissident scholars, how would it be possible to build stable and legitimate governments to promote a radical nation-state project? Or to build strong political movements to fight 'imperialism, exploitation and dictatorship'?

Theoretically this paradigm capsized.[4] Leading scholars could not even agree on what should be meant by political development. Historians asked to probe into the emergence of modern politics in Europe and North America found little evidence of the general functions and patterns that generalising political scientists talked of.[5] Strict applications in the Third World of political development theories were few, sterile and set aside vital factors which did not fit into the universal categories. Critical studies of Marxist versions of political development theories and political projects pointed to similar problems.[6]

More pragmatic and normative studies of political development, however, survived and got a new lease of life during the eighties and nineties, primarily in the wake of the transition from authoritarian regimes in Southern Europe, Latin America and then Eastern Europe as well. Many of the previous attempts to cover general structural and historical factors were played down and replaced by explicitly normative studies of political institutions and rational action among the elite – in favour of somewhat uncontextualised concepts and values of civil society, human rights, political democracy and good governance.[7]

Third World Politics

The focus upon universalistic grand theories, concepts and norms in the study of political modernisation has continuously been under attack from scholars of 'actual' Third World politics. Their basic argument is that we need to study the institutions, organisations, policies and ideologies as such, take them at face value, contextualise them, and look into their own histories. This, of course, may be done in various ways and to different degrees. Some set aside grand theorising and focus instead on comparative studies of actually existing political institutions, functions and issues.[8] Others apply what they hold to be more appropriate categories such as patrimonialism and patron-clientism.[9] Yet others claim that there is a need to rethink entirely, calling for more explorative, historical and consistent contextual ventures.[10]

Box 2.1   *The political dimension*

We attempt in this book to get a special grip on politics in relation to late development. Hence we may ask ourselves how, in the first place, politics as such can be specified and its most important aspects delineated.

People co-operate in many ways. Let us leave the nuclear family aside (but not kinship bonds and extended families, which often have great political significance in developing countries) and concentrate on the larger society. Let us restrict ourselves, in the process, to questions of economics and of politics. Picture in your mind a public square containing a market and a public gathering area, and a collection of surrounding buildings.

In some of these buildings goods and services are produced and then exchanged in the market. We may term this the economic sphere.

In other buildings different groups of people gather, partly for the sake of their interest in particular questions, partly for discussing if and how, in their view, everyone round the square should co-operate. The different groups then converge in the central meeting area in order to decide what they have in common and how this should be managed. Here is politics!

There is a grey zone of course. This is where political economy is most important: in other words, where politics and economics come together. What happens in production and in the market affects those who collaborate politically. Those who collaborate politically seek to regulate production and to organise the market, perhaps, to further their class interests with the help of both public and private organisations and institutions.

Another way of delineating the political sphere is to specify its scope and to distinguish between its form and its content. We can then locate the political process in a field overlapping both the forms and content of politics. (See Figure 2.1.)

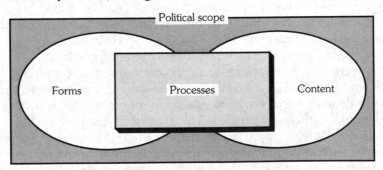

Figure 2.1   *The political scope, forms, content and processes*

To begin with – the *scope of the political sphere*. Which questions, institutions and activities have been politicised or, in other words, have been the object of common societal deliberation? Which are privately conducted and controlled instead? (Which does not mean, of course, that such activities do not also carry political consequences.)

It has become increasingly common, since the beginning of the 1980s, to set the state against civil society. It should be noted, however, that politics and politicisation can mean much more than the state and its expansion. Politicisation can also take place, for example, through movements and organisations in civil society. Politics, therefore, exists both in the state and in parts of civil society. And we should not forget the international level, including various political organisations as well as business corporations.

Then there are the *forms of politics*. These refer to political structures, institutions and organisations. The forms of politics are found on various levels – local, national and international. Such structures and rules include constitutional questions, the *de facto* distribution of power between legislative, executive and judicial branches, the role of the military in society, etc. The forms of government – which may be more or less democratic – also bear mentioning here, as do the informal institutions or rules usually studied in terms of political culture. The forms of politics also include, finally, institutions in the sense of organisations (henceforth I shall only use, in order to avoid misunderstanding, the term 'organisations' or more specific designations). These may be overarching bodies such as states or local governments, or parties and various other organisations and movements active within the political arena (including their leaders and members).

Third, the *content of politics*. In part this means ideas, action programmes and political strategies for furthering development. In part it means the actual decisions taken and their implementation, including within public administration – what is done, that is, by political means.

Let us look, finally, at *the political processes* taking place in the common arena within which political actors operate. The arena and the processes are constituted and limited by the scope, forms and content of politics; that is to say, by the issues that have been politicised, by the political structures, institutions and organisations, and by the predominant ideas and strategies. The political actors then collaborate and compete in their efforts to safeguard various interests and to carry out their plans. And of course their actions have also, in turn, repercussions for the scope, forms and content of politics.

Similarly, it is argued, political scientists in the Third World must be free to build independent and empirically well-rooted studies of their own countries without taking norms and theories based on European or North American experiences as points of departure. Serious scholars from outside should adapt to such standards and, to take a contemporary parallel, not repeat the mistake of the experts of the International Monetary Fund, who use the same tool-box and prescribe the same medicine wherever they find themselves.

Over the years, and in addition to these primarily intellectual arguments, more detailed and contextualised knowledge of specific Third World politics has also been in the interests of international agencies, colonial ex-powers such as Britain, France and the Netherlands, post-war dominants like the USA, their regional allies like Australia, and new formations such as the European Union. With globalisation, similar interests have now also spread to small countries like the Scandinavian ones.

Taken together, these academic and political trends have paved the way for political science inquiries as well as more interdisciplinary area studies of actual politics (including administration and political ideas) in individual Third World countries and regions. Given the relative lack of knowledge, both types of studies are needed, no doubt – but there are important problems as well. The high esteem of universal theories within many political science departments, even in Third World countries, does not encourage the sufficiently serious kind of empirical studies that are needed, including at the local level, in the field and in co-operation with scholars of other persuasions. Separate country and area studies, on the other hand, are often plagued by the even worse disease of non-comparative and non-theoretical empirical explorations. And a basic problem in both institutional frameworks, and in both the North and the South, is that studies of Third World politics often continue to depend on external funding and interests in politically and economically 'relevant' topics, thus making intellectual and concerned ventures somewhat troublesome.[11]

The Politics of Development

Meanwhile, studies of political modernisation as well as of Third World politics have been criticised by scholars arguing that problems of development have neither been the point of departure nor addressed in a fruitful way. On the contrary, they claim, narrow-minded political scientists have deprived themselves of even being able to say anything meaningful about what is probably the world's most serious dilemma: that an absolute majority of its population suffer and cannot even make reasonable use of their own limited resources. Politics, the critics conclude, must rather be studied as part of the general process of development: the study of the politics of development.

To substantiate their thesis, the scholars of the politics of development argue that many circumstances and factors conspire in a process of development. Overarching theories of development – on which factors are most central and how these relate to one another – can certainly be found. Some scholars, for example, stress modernisation, others dependency.[12] Yet, critics concede, we need to restrict our empirical focus as it is not fruitful to study a great many aspects all at the same time. The question is how.

On the one hand it is possible, of course, to focus on some of the most important factors within the bounds of established social science disciplines. Human geographers analyse, for example, how people use natural resources. Sociologists and anthropologists study how norms arise, and what role social differentiation and social movements play. Historians focus on changes over time. Economists look at how people produce goods and services and exchange them in the market. Political scientists concentrate on how people establish institutions to organise society and to acquire influence over developments. Other factors on which to focus include language and religion.

On the other hand, scholars of the politics of development continue, studying development cannot be likened to a smorgasbord to which different experts can each give their contributions. For the character of development, and the fruitfulness of development studies, depends less on the sum of the ingredients than on how these work together. It is a complicated dish with many ingredients which only attains its distinctive character when they have all been cooked together. So even if we need to focus on certain factors (political ones, for example), we must primarily study how these factors relate to others.

Hence, the particular problems of development for which it may at first appear there is room in the traditional disciplines – require a knowledge of adjacent areas. Take the case of human geographers who study the degree to which the natural resources of developing countries can be sustained – such scholars can hardly neglect political and economic interests and organisations. And most development economists realise that, whatever their assumptions about the functioning of perfect markets, they must also study institutional factors.

This quandary, the students of politics and development argue, should be solved, by situating and analysing politics as part of the interdisciplinary problems of development. If we are interested in agrarian development, for instance, we must apply interdisciplinary theories of agrarian problems to identify what essential factors are involved and how they interrelate – and then study the role of politics when all the factors come together. If concentration of land; control of inputs and proper irrigation; fragmentation and monopolisation of markets; class and ethnic organisation; and the subordination of women are among the essential and interacting factors, what is then the importance of politics in this interaction?

These kinds of interdisciplinarily oriented queries have usually proved difficult to pursue within political science departments. Even the somewhat more specific question of how and why politics is used to influence the economy has attracted less interest among established political scientists than among economists. For instance, classical economists such as Adam Smith, Karl Marx and J.M. Keynes focused on the role of politics and organised interests in the economy and vice versa. Then, political economy assumed great importance during the post-war efforts to rebuild Europe and Japan and to generate growth in the former colonies. One classical example in the latter context is Gunnar Myrdal's *Asian Drama*.[13] In more recent years, moreover, theories about rent-seeking politicians and bureaucrats,[14] and about institutional factors, have achieved particular importance.

In glaring contrast, however, many contributions by students of the politics of development, including the role of the state, have required partial disassociation from political science proper.[15] Many scholars have even concluded that, ideally, fruitful studies of the politics of development call for the establishing of a new social science discipline, or at least separate institutes focusing on development. Within such frameworks, and within processes of several interrelating factors including economic, social and cultural, it would then be possible to specialise in the importance of politics. (See Figure 2.2.)

Such projects, however, have not only been up against representatives of established institutes and disciplines, standing guard over their hegemony. One substantial critique of the dissident project is that many of the actually existing development theories, concepts, and norms found their claims to universality on the basis of empirical generalisation from

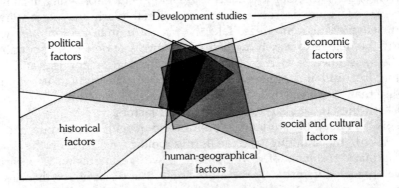

Figure 2.2 *Development studies as a discipline or topic for separate institutes containing various interrelated sub-specialities*

the West just as much as did many theses of political modernisation. Hence, the claim goes, there is a need to turn to more careful empirical explorations, to study the actual processes, including at the grass-roots level, with more open concepts, and to pay more attention, for instance, to historical and cultural aspects.[16]

While this critique, however, can be dealt with within the framework of studies of the politics of development, another objection is more troublesome for students who want to focus on the very political factors. The argument implied in this more serious objection is that most theories of development, within which we are supposed to set our studies of the role of politics, give little room for qualified in depth study of the particular dynamics and importance of politics – including administration and forms of government, institutions and organisations, ideologies and discourses, policies and strategies. The most frequently given examples are the 'old' socio-economically oriented theories of modernisation and dependency,[17] but one may just as well refer to the currently more fashionable attempts at building an alternative theory for 'another development', within which politics is not only opposed to civil society but often even seen as 'part of the problem'.[18]

Politics and Late Development

The major problems with the frameworks delineated so far are thus:

- that studies of *political development* lack sufficient empirical foundation in the Third World, tend to uncritically apply Western norms, and tend also to focus on the level of the 'national' elite;
- that attempts at providing this missing empirical foundation through explorations and descriptions of *Third World politics* run the risk of being particularistic;
- that both these frameworks have politics rather than problems of development as their point of departure;
- that interdisciplinary analyses of the *politics of development*, first (just like studies of political development), often apply Eurocentric grand theories and, even more serious, lack a theoretical format giving due space to the importance of politics.

Many of these problems may be tackled, I would argue, by going beyond the old frameworks to identify and combine, instead, their advantages. Students of politics who share a serious (but not necessarily primary) interest in problems of development should thus be able to carve out a new subdiscipline within political science which, for short, may be labelled 'politics and development'. A subdiscipline which may be likened to that of development economics within the larger subject of economics. A subdiscipline, though, which should define its questions in the framework of how politics relates to other factors in processes of development, but then concentrate on empirically well-grounded studies of the relevant aspects of politics itself (rather than on their interrelation with all the other factors), and only thereafter turn to universal comparisons.

Starting off with the Politics of Development

Initially, when studying politics *and* development, we draw, thus, on the advantages of the studies of the politics *of* development. The importance to any inquiry of formulating the problem is well understood. The point of departure of our subdiscipline (just as in the first chapter of this book) is not politics but problems of development. What are the difficulties people encounter in their efforts to make (on the basis of their interests and ideas) the best possible use of their potential? As this question involves many different factors, it must be specified in co-operation with scholars from many disciplines, in relation to relevant development theories, and from knowledge of people's actual problems. As this co-operation in turn requires that students of various development-oriented subdisciplines can meet, seminars and centres for development studies are necessary. (See Figure 2.3.)

Within this framework, however, our next task is to identify our problem area: the politics of development (see pp. 9–14). What are the political aspects of development? As our general development question is what difficulties people face in their efforts to make the best possible use of their potential, our politics-of-development question is what role politics plays in this, and what role it might play.

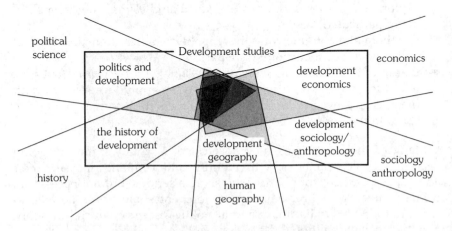

Figure 2.3 *Various development-oriented subdisciplines co-operating within the general field of development studies*

Relating to and Focusing upon Third World Politics

This question about the role of politics in processes of development is what students of the politics *of* development would probe into. For us, however, it is enough to have identified the major relations between politics and development and the key problems involved. Thereafter we like to proceed by focusing on the relevant aspects of politics itself. *This* is our homework, within political science. For instance, if we know of the general importance of the state in the process of agrarian development, we may focus on the dynamics of the state; or if we see that democratisation might enable many more peasants to make better use of their resources, we may concentrate on the problems of such democratisation. The point is simply that once we are reasonably well informed about how politics relates to the various aspects of development, then we can focus on the relevant political ingredients.

At this point we turn instead to the advantages of the study of Third World politics. That is, to the attempts at overcoming invalid old theories and insufficient empirical bases with solid field studies, descriptions and sometimes even explorations. However, there is an in-built tendency in this venture towards particularism. So how can we plan and carry out well-grounded empirical queries in theoretical and comparative perspective? This should be possible if we employ our politics-of-development questions to identify *both* the relevant questions to focus upon within Third World politics *and* the appropriate theories and categories within general political science. (In addition to this we may thus, within political science, go beyond 'comparative politics' – the established subdiscipline to which students of Third World problems have usually been referred – and also involve relevant parts of the study of public administration, political ideas and international relations.)

Thus if we were to summarise the new subdiscipline, so far and in one sentence only, we would do so by referring to the specific study of the political institutions, structures, agents and processes that affect (and are affected by) Third World problems of development. (See Figure 2.4.)

Four examples of questions that might be raised in the study of politics and development follow:

- In studies of rapid economic development in newly industrialising countries, the role of a comparatively autonomous state has been given special importance. Within this area of the politics of development we may now ask questions, for instance, about the characteristics of this kind of autonomous state and how it has come about in the first place.
- In discussions of problems of local development, the negative role of centralised and compartmentalised governance as well as increasingly fragmented socio-economic interests has been emphasised.

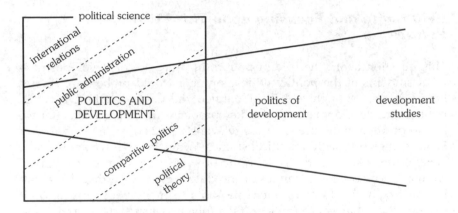

Figure 2.4 *Situating the study of politics and development*

Within this field of the politics of development we may then ask, for instance, when, how and what kind of decentralisation may affect these problems.

- Many NGOs and new popular movements try to promote develop- ment. When, then, do they find out what kind of democratisation would help? What problems do they face when trying to favour such democratisation? What is the importance of such efforts at democrat- isation at local as well as national levels?

- Structural adjustment in itself may be defined as a particular kind of politics of development, including the privatisation of public resources and deregulation. Hence we may ask, for example, how this affects state governance, the functioning of democracy or the problems of corruption.

Broadening and Turning the Study of Political Development Upside-Down

The major drawback of mainstream studies of political development, as previously mentioned, is the lack of empirical foundation in the Third World, the bias in favour of models of democracy based on empirical generalisations from the West, and the focus upon the elite level. Despite this, however, I find nothing wrong with efforts at generalisation or even grand universal theories. On the contrary, this 'technical' advantage of studies of political development (and especially of their more exciting critics, the comparative historians) may help us compensate for the inevitable tendency towards fragmentation in Third World studies when building the solid empirical base that is missing.

In other words, what we should do – as soon as there are reasonably solid empirical foundations for various aspects of politics and development in the Third World – is to broaden the study of political development and turn its empirical and theoretical basis upside-down! First, that is, we should widen the framework by starting off not with the narrow issues of the development of politics, but with more relevant questions on the role of politics when people try to improve their lives and make use of their resources. Second, we should no longer start with empirical generalisations based on European and North American norms and experiences, but rather with our empirical results on Third World politics and development. Finally, only then should we turn to the West to look for experiences which may enlighten our understanding of what has happened in the Third World, but also to offer fresh perspectives on the West itself. Actually, much of the approach and methods to do this has already been developed by comparative historians. (We shall return to them in Chapter 6.)

Two examples of how one might broaden and turn the study of political development upside-down follow:

- Much of the discussion of Third World economic development has drawn on empirical generalisations from the West and on its theoretical doctrines of free markets. Less biased empirical studies of the rapid growth in East and South-East Asia, however, show that state interventions (including the previous strengthening of the home markets) was decisive. The idea is that when taking *those* results as points of departure for comparisons with earlier industrialised countries, we may go beyond idealised versions of the independent rise of private capital and turn instead, for instance, to mercantilism, some aspects of the rather late industrialisation in the Northern and Eastern parts of Europe, and, of course, to Japan. This way our understanding of Third World development (and, as a side-effect, of the West too) may improve greatly – some efforts have already been made.[19]
- Similarly, much of the discussion of democratisation in the framework of Third World development falls back on idealised versions of the historical experiences of the West, including the importance of civil society. When results from less biased empirical studies of actual Third World processes of democratisation come forward, it should be equally fruitful, I would argue, to take *those* results as points of departure for comparisons with earlier cases.

Difficult but Necessary

Of course, this way of solving the quandary by building a new subdiscipline within political science – and then meeting other scholars within the framework of area or development studies rather than settling there – is far from simple. Those carrying on advanced studies make their way more easily by broadening their competence within the established subdisciplines of political science rather than by supplementing their competence with knowledge of the politics of development and by carrying out 'thick' empirical investigations in the field. Yet this demanding road is unavoidable if one wishes neither to forego the study of development problems nor to abandon the pursuit of scientific rigour.

To succeed, therefore, efforts in this direction must be given institutional support. First, I would suggest, by favouring interdisciplinary co-operation and studies within interdisciplinary centres or institutes where relevant problems of Third World politics of development can continuously be identified, before focusing on their very political aspects within one's own department. Second, within the politics departments, by giving introductory courses on the general themes, theories and approaches of politics and late development *before* teaching Third World politics. Otherwise we may be unable to involve relevant expertise beyond comparative politics; or we may be liable to favouring the particularistic, non-theoretical and non-comparative aspects of area studies.

In other words, we must sit reasonably stably on three different stools at once: on one to define our questions within the framework of the politics of development; on another to engross ourselves in the importance of Third World politics; on a third to make comparisons with other cases. But that is not enough – all three stools must also stand on solid empirical ground.

Actually, good studies of politics and development require the devotion of an uncommon amount of time, energy and empathy to the acquisition of solid empirical knowledge. Partly, of course, this reflects the fact that it takes extra time to acclimatise oneself to cultures and conditions other than one's own, not only when coming from the North but also from comparatively privileged circumstances in the Third World itself. What is more, a solid empirical foundation has become even more important than before. As already emphasised, colonialism and the struggle against it – which most developing countries earlier had in common, and which could be studied in a relatively uniform way – is now history. The various developing countries, and their difficulties, have become increasingly disparate in character. The earlier overarching theories have proved insufficient, and complicated local circumstances often play a decisive role.

Once our questions have been identified within the realm of the politics of development, and once our studies have been specified and designed within the discourse of politics and late development, there is, therefore, a special need for institutional support of solid empirical studies, often including field studies. This calls for extra time and funding to acquire some knowledge of new methods and sometimes of

languages too – to collect material and information in external libraries and through fieldwork, to co-operate with other scholars and (for students as well as senior researchers) to get supplementary guidance from experts on the ground. Of course, we should not waste time and money – but this is exactly what we would do were we trying to initiate studies of Third World politics and development without such institutional support.

Other Views?

Naturally, this way of organising the study of Third World politics and development is only the way this author would have it. Over time and in various contexts, scholars have put forward different opinions, including on whether we should focus on the study of political development, on Third World politics, on the politics of development, or on trying to combine them. In the second part of the book, therefore, we shall ask how these matters have been perceived within the major schools of thought. But before doing so, let us proceed by discussing briefly what kinds of approaches one may discern and apply.

Notes

1 Of course, there were also similar but much less influential discussions of ideal socialist governance and of actual state-socialist rule.

2 Almond, 'Introduction: A Functional Approach to Comparative Politics'.

3 See, for example, Dahl, *A Preface to Democratic Theory*; Kornhauser, *The Politics of Mass Society*; and Schumpeter, *Capitalism, Socialism and Democracy.*

4 For a recent critique, see Cammack, *Capitalism and Democracy in the Third World.*

5 See at first hand Tilly, *The Formation of the National States in Western Europe.*

6 See, for example, Törnquist, *What's Wrong with Marxism? Vols 1 and 2.*

7 We shall, of course, return to these studies in Part 2 of the book. For a summary of, in my view, the most fruitful of the grand projects, see O'Donnell and Schmitter, *Transitions from Authoritarian Rule.* For a recent manifestation, see the World Bank, *World Development Report 1997.*

8 For a textbook example, see Cammack et al., *Third World Politics.*

9 For a textbook example, see Clapham, *Third World Politics.*

10 See, for example, Manor, *Rethinking Third World Politics.*

11 For an example, see the recent interesting discussion on US area studies related to Asia, in *Bulletin of Concerned Asian Scholars*, Vol. 29, Nos 1 and 2.

12 For a comprehensive review, see Martinussen, *Society, State & Market.*

13 Myrdal, *Asian Drama.*

14 I shall use the umbrella term 'theories of rent-seeking behaviour' in reference to the work by scholars, to whom we shall return in Part 2 of the book, such as Bhagwati et al., who emphasise 'directly unproductive profit-seeking'; public choice theorists like Buchanan; and Mancur Olson, with his analysis of the behaviour of organised special interests.

15 This, as far as I understand, is not only a Scandinavian experience.

16 See, for example, Schuurman, *Beyond the Impasse*; Sachs, *The Development Dictionary*; Carmen, *Autonomous Development*; and parts of Hettne, *Development Theory and the Three Worlds.*

17 Cf., for example, Manor, *Rethinking Third World Politics.*

18 Cf. Part 3 of the book for a critical analysis of this tendency.

19 Cf., for example, the comparisons with the Japanese experience (primarily outlined in Johnson, *MITI and the Japanese Miracle*; in White, *Developmental States in East Asia*; in Wade, *Governing the Market*; and in Johnson, 'Political Institutions and Economic Performance'). Cf. also Gunnarsson, 'Mercantilism Old and New'.

3 Analytical Approaches

In our efforts to identify what the study of Third World politics and development is and should be about, we have discussed the problem area and the organisation of the inquiry. Now we must also ask how the very analyses may be designed.

Several analytical approaches are possible. At this stage I shall not argue in favour of any one in particular. That might imply using the book to put forward a thesis to the effect that approaches associated with one particular orientation are better than others, before having presented the different schools in a fair, accurate and critically independent way. Only when we have acquired as correct a view as possible of the different orientations, and the approaches related to them, shall we proceed in Part 3 to discuss how to evaluate what others have done and how to go ahead with ideas of our own.

In other words, in this brief chapter we should get an understanding of what analytical approaches are possible in principle. Thereby we may also work out analytical tools that will help us to identify and discuss in Part 2 of the book which approaches are actually applied within the different schools of thought.

- *To begin with, we must pay attention to how researchers use historical perspectives.*

Some researchers content themselves with sketching a historical background, whereupon they proceed to emphasise contemporary factors. Others analyse politics and development by reference, for instance, to the colonial heritage or to pre-colonial institutions. Some do this by stressing continuity, others by emphasising the ways in which old institutions or ideas function under new conditions.

- *Above all, however, we must pose two additional questions: (1) What kinds of factors do researchers emphasise when analysing politics and development? (2) On what level of society do they localise these factors?*

(1) Do the researchers analyse politics and development by primary reference to: (a) the acting subjects; (b) structures and institutions (which create the basis for what actors can do, as well as the limits thereof); or (c) the interaction between the actors and those conditions?

An example of such interaction would be when actors are influenced by the rules of the game and the relations of power, while at the same time interpreting and trying to change them. Hence, I do *not* mean how structures/institutions affect actors or how actors affect structures/ institutions (whereby the focus is still on structures/institutions on the one hand and actors on the other). Rather, I mean the very interaction itself.

(2) Do the researchers localise these actors, structures/institutions and interactive patterns mainly in (a) society; (b) the state; or (c) the linkage between society and the state (for instance, electoral and party systems, corporative arrangements, etc.)?

By the linkage between society and the state, then, I do *not* mean some sort of boundary area or overlap between society and the state (in which case one would still be referring to society and the state, respectively), but rather the linkage or connection itself.

Box 3.1   *The concept of institution*

While discussing analytical approaches we should again stress an important conceptual matter – namely, the meaning assigned to the term 'institution'. This term is often thought to refer both to the rules of the game (which indicate what actors can and should do) and to organised frameworks of rules (such as a state or a local government, or for that matter a university department). The latter sense includes institutions which are themselves capable of acting. In order to avoid misunderstanding, therefore, I shall henceforth use 'institution' solely in the former sense (the rules of the game), and shall otherwise use the term 'organisation', or other more specific designations like 'state' or 'party'.[1]

Let us sketch those dimensions and questions in the form of a matrix which classifies analytical approaches according to which factors the scholars hold most important, and where they localise said factors. The picture we get is more complex, of course, than if we had only asked the common questions about state versus society and actors versus structure. But then there would be no space for the increasing number of (in my view) fruitful attempts to also look at the linkages and interrelations.

In square one – actors in society – we find scholars who view the behaviour of individuals and groups in society as decisive in the analysis of politics and development. Studies inspired by so-called behaviourism belong here.

In square two – the interplay between actors and structures/ institutions in society – we find analysts studying class consciousness, the culture of civic co-operation ('social capital'), and social organisation and mobilisation.

In square three – structures/institutions in society – we find the greater number of Marxist analyses of social and economic structures.

What are the central factors?

Where are the factors localised?	actors	interplay between actors and structures/ institutions	structures/ institutions
in society	1	2	3
in the linkage between society and the state	4	5	6
in the state	7	8	9

Figure 3.1 *Analytical approaches*

Such structures are assumed to be decisive for the relation between politics and development. This square also contains economists, sociologists and others who, in a similar fashion, stress institutional factors in society as a whole.

In square four – actors in the linkage between society and the state – fall those scholars who consider it most fruitful to focus on the role such actors as politicians and parties play in the connection between society and the state.

In square five – the interaction between actors and structures/institutions in the linkage between society and the state are found, for instance, those researchers who focus, simultaneously, on parties' and popular movements' interpretion of, and influence upon, the structures and institutions that condition their actions, and what role this plays in the connection between society and the state.

In square six – structures/institutions in the linkage between society and the state – we place researchers who analyse the significance of, for instance, corporative institutions in the connection between society and the state.

In square seven – actors in the state sphere – fall researchers who take the view that politics and development are best studied by taking a close look at the doings of state and local government officials (including so-called rent-seeking bureaucrats), who are assumed to behave in a rational and self-interested manner.

In square eight – the interaction between actors and structures/institutions in the state sphere – are found, for instance, those who investigate how so-called hardliners and softliners within the state are affected by, interpret and try to change forms of government and relations of power.

Square nine – structures/institutions within the state sphere – contains, for instance, those stressing the importance of grasping the capacity of state institutions for governance and administration.

In lieu of a conclusion, let us underline that many researchers combine, of course, analytical approaches (one after the other, however, rather than all at once). For example, economists focusing on so-called transaction costs[2] examine institutions in both society and the state. In the same way, there are Marxists who place as great an emphasis on how public firms in the state sphere are controlled as on how private firms out in society behave. Yet, the analytical tools should help us in making a general analysis in the second part of the book of what kind of approaches are associated with the different schools of thought. Thereby, moreover, the actual character of the different approaches that until now have only been hinted at will all become clearer.

Notes

1 For a more detailed discussion of the concept of institutions and of institutionalist perspectives, see Chapter 10.

2 Costs for creating contacts between economic actors, for reaching agreements, and for ensuring that contracts entered into are kept.

4 Political and Scientific Conjunctures

Before turning to a review of the various schools of thought, however, it is important to sketch, in an integrated fashion, the context which left its imprint on the study of politics and late development, especially with regard to normative ingredients and policy prescriptions. For social scientific theories and analyses are not simply the result of an internal process of renewal within each respective field. This applies in the highest degree, moreover, to inquiries into Third World politics and development.

The Colonial and Anti-Colonial Inheritance

Most studies of politics and development prior to the Second World War were influenced by the needs of the mother countries (and of neo-colonial powers such as the USA) for expertise about old and new colonies. Investigations into 'inferior but exotic cultures' – of a sort acceptable in polite society – fell into this category as well. The object was the maintenance of supremacy and the furtherance of the economic interests of the citizens of the metropolis. Such studies rarely played, therefore, any significant role after decolonisation or during the fight against neo-colonialism.

On the other hand, a good many of the forceful arguments worked out in dissident circles – in connection with the agendas of the victorious nationalists – achieved a lasting importance. These included studies and theories on imperialism, on the importance of effective political mobilisation and organisation, and on the need for land reform and state development planning. One reason for this continued relevance was that the movements which had taken state power, and which were able to push through their plans from above, often sought to achieve land reform and state planning. Another factor was that more radical organisations who instead became part of the opposition against the new regimes frequently pushed for similar but (as they saw it) more consistent solutions; not least in Latin America, where powerful movements took aim at North American neo-colonialism and the domestic oligarchies allied with it. In addition to this, of course, the struggle for freedom continued in Vietnam, the Portuguese colonies and in South Africa.

Great Power Interests, Area Studies and Modernisation Theory

At the same time, the anti-imperialist struggle and the national revolutions in the Third World led to febrile activity on the other side, in the leading industrialised countries. The former metropolitan countries had striven to uphold their dominion but failed. First in Latin America and the Philippines – where the USA took over – and then, after the Second World War, elsewhere as well. The initiative had passed to the USA and the Soviet Union. These two superpowers then embarked on the Cold War – a world-spanning competition over political and economic interests.

Both sides needed expertise quickly about a vast number of countries and areas of strategic and economic importance. When it came to knowledge of the colonies, however, newcomers such as the USA, the Soviet Union and Australia lacked the traditions of old-timers such as Britain, France and the Netherlands. Institutions for area studies were therefore established. At such institutions, students, researchers and experts could learn languages and study cultures, and also immerse themselves in such matters as politics and economics.

In addition, competing models of development and forms of assistance to the newly independent countries grew in importance. Special development studies programmes were therefore set up – some within the traditional disciplines, others related to area studies institutes, and still others as institutes in their own right.

Most scholars assumed that Third World countries were on their way towards an ideal-type European development model. They then proceeded, on the basis of this assumption, to study the problems and opportunities arising during the journey. This so-called modernisation perspective predominated in the West and in the developing countries allied with it. A Marxist-oriented variant was applied in the East and in the more radical developing countries. The modernisation perspective is therefore – in its most important variants – the obvious place to begin when we review the major schools of thought.

Interest in Development Problems, Thematic Studies and Dependency Theory

It took a longer time for these tendencies to make their breakthrough within development policies and research in less dominating countries. In countries, that is to say, which lacked colonies and which had not yet developed significant interests in the independent developing countries. On the contrary, during the sixties and seventies there was room here for a different political reaction to the changes in the Third World and the interventions of the great powers.

This alternative political line aimed at studying and assisting the liberation movements and the new nation-state projects 'on their own terms'. This did not necessarily entail a naive and uncritical approach, even if that sometimes was found. The object was simply to ensure that such studies and assistance programmes were based on the interests and problems of the developing countries, rather than those of the established great powers.

In the Scandinavian countries, for instance, this orientation even acquired a certain official backing for ten years or so. It also formed an important point of departure for development studies programmes; the problems of the developing countries were placed at the centre, and thematic rather than area studies were encouraged. Similar tendencies were also significant, however, in connection with reorganised development agencies, voluntary organisations and research institutions in other countries.

In this context, revised and partly Marxist-influenced formulations of the modernisation perspective assumed great importance – for example the works of Gunnar Myrdal. Soon enough, however, theories of international dependency spread widely and formed a school of their own. This occurred in connection with the rise of radical new political movements and development efforts, particularly in Latin America, parts of Africa and to some degree East and South-East Asia.

The so-called dependency school, accordingly, forms the second point of departure in our review of the most important scientific ideas about politics and development. These scholars took the view that imperialism prevented the emergence of an ideal-type European development model in the Third World. They then proceeded, in accordance with this framework, to study how this took place more exactly. Despite the political radicalism common in dependency circles, economic and sociological perspectives predominated. The lack of fresh political studies was probably exacerbated by a frequently uncritical interpretation of the injunction to support the Third World on its own terms and to avoid interference in the internal affairs of the new countries. Gradually, however, the new nation-state projects were subjected to radical critiques voiced by dissidents in these countries themselves. Refined analyses emerged thereby of the politics of development in general, and of the social and economic bases of the state in particular.

On the Terms of the World Market – Area Studies and Neo-Classical Theory

Soon, however, the tide shifted. The time of the national revolutions was over. Many of the new nation-state projects ran aground. In the large

Western countries and in the powerful international organisations, neo-liberal explanations and prescriptions became popular. We shall look mainly at neo-classical theories about rent-seeking politicians and bureaucrats, and at so-called structural adjustment programmes.

Remarkably enough, political studies now got a lift as well. On the one hand, certainly, the praises of the free market were sung. But, on the other, first economists and then a series of political scientists blamed the developing countries' failures on excessive political intervention in general, and attempts at radical political short cuts in particular. They also recommended external political intervention – in countries where, as these scholars put it, 'parasitical' politicians and bureaucrats prevented a 'sound market-oriented development'. They called for political inter-vention on the part of the aid-giving countries and, if possible, political liberalisation, including human rights and a certain degree of demo-cratisation.

The strategic thesis was that the self-interest of politicians and bureau-crats, together with the role of political institutions and forms of govern-ment, were of wholly decisive importance. This argument legitimised, in turn, an almost hegemonic ambition among political scientists, at times as narrow-minded as that exhibited by economists with their claims about the fundamental role of capital and the market.

Hence, a new generation of studies suddenly emerged – on corruption, inefficient political institutions, elections, and what might be called crafted instant democracy. At worst, the old insights of both modernisa-tion and dependency researchers about the many complicated conditions necessary for solid democratisation were disregarded.[1]

At the same time, the demand increased for more country- and area-focused studies, roughly as in the USA during the fifties and sixties. Important groups and institutions with an interest in the developing world are now also found in small countries like those of Scandinavia. It has been considered important for a while, for example, to acquire 'relevant knowledge' about the economically dynamic countries of East and South-East Asia. At the same time, conditional assistance and political intervention become more common, especially where – as in Africa – economic developments have been disappointing.

In Search of New Models – Institutionalist and Post-Marxist Perspectives

Since the close of the 1980s, however, the picture has changed once more. The Cold War is over. Neo-liberal prescriptions have seldom led to the promised results. Increasing numbers of scholars and experts have realised that the most impressive economic record in the Third World – that of East Asia – has at the same time contained a heavy element of political intervention. Others have become increasingly sceptical of 'conventional' development as well as of politics as such, deconstructing instead the dominating views and focusing on various, often 'non-political', alternatives.

No matter how important the critique, however, it is reasonable here to focus on politics. Among those scholars doing so, the grand substantive theories claiming general validity have tended to be replaced by broad analytical frameworks, within which researchers can formulate and test hypotheses; hypotheses that have often been disassociated and carried along from earlier schools of thought, but also some new ones.

One such framework focuses on institutions and organisations within both state and civil society. Aid agencies sponsor the growth of civil societies and search for the roots of legitimate, appropriate and efficient forms of government – while puzzling over how such 'good governance' can be encouraged and over how civil societies could generate equally 'good democracies'. James Buchanan's neo-liberalism is passé, while Samuel Huntington's work on modern political institutions and organisations is experiencing something of a renaissance.[2] For the moment, however, though fashion is changing rapidly, it is probably Huntington's contemporary and less conservative counterparts who enjoy the greatest prominence – for instance Adam Przeworski, who combines institutionalism and game theory;[3] Douglass North, who stresses the importance of stable and predictable rules of the game;[4] Robert Putnam, who explores the critical role of civic communities in civil society;[5] Robert Wade, who analyses the central role/part played by state governance in East Asia;[6] and Peter Evans, who talks of 'embedded' states and likes to combine hard institutions and soft social capital.[7]

Another analytical framework taking shape is the one I have termed post-Marxist. This does not primarily refer to the many post-modern critics of development. Rather, this is a book on *politics* and development and I am mainly referring to those studying actual politics, not just criticising the ideas involved and 'giving up' on politics. Of course, some of the scholars focusing on politics are also applying post-modern perspectives in a fruitful way,[8] but there is, primarily, a widespread dissatisfaction with both neo-liberal and East Asian prescriptions. Critical assessments of the old Left, and the emergence of new movements with their own agendas, show that neither history nor the renewal of radical perspectives has ceased. Square-shaped Marxist theory does not suffice either, of course, but increasing numbers of scholars are also dissatisfied with narrow studies of markets, political institutions and forms of government. It is obviously necessary to analyse not just the state but also what happens out in society. And when the object is to understand the conflicts and processes involved, both revisionist institutionalists and rethinking Marxists are often agreed that *certain* Marxian elements are fruitful, *and* can be combined with insights offered by the above-mentioned institutionalists.[9]

Notes

1 For one stimulating analysis of the latter point in defence of modernisation, cf. Leftwich, 'On Primacy of Politics in Development' and 'Two Cheers for Democracy?'.

2 Huntington, 'Political Development and Political Decay' and *Political Order in Changing Societies*. Cf. also Huntington, *The Third Wave*.

3 See especially Przeworski, *Democracy and the Market*.

4 See in particular North, *Institutions, Institutional Change and Economic Performance*.

5 Putnam, *Making Democracy Work*.

6 Wade, *Governing the Market*.

7 Evans, *Embedded Autonomy*; and Evans, 'Introduction: Development Strategies across the Public-Private Divide' and 'Government Action, Social Capital and Development'.

8 Cf. Blom Hansen, *The Saffron Wave*; and Heryanto, 'Discourse and State-Terrorism'.

9 See, to mention just three examples, Martinussen, *The Theoretical Heritage from Marx and Weber in Development Studies*; Mouzelis, *Post-Marxist Alternatives*; and some of the articles in Migdal, Kohli and Shue, *State Power and Social Forces*.

PART 2

THE DISCUSSION ON THIRD WORLD POLITICS AND DEVELOPMENT

Among the descriptions and explanations of the role of politics in the process of development which have formed the basis for various schools, we can only devote our attention here to the most important ones. What I hope to achieve is an overview without missing essential similarities and differences.

At this point we will use the tools honed in the first part of the book. The point of departure, therefore, is *not* the themes typical of comparative politics (military coups, the consolidation of democracy, etc.) but the role of politics in processes of development – whereafter we focus on the very dynamics of the political aspects. Moreover, while the following questions from Part 1 may not always be put in strict order, each school of thought will be distinguished and analysed according to them:

- *How do the researchers specify the problem area?* How do the scholars relate to the various ways of characterising politics and development in the Third World that were discussed in Chapter 1? Which questions should receive priority?
- *How do the researchers in question delineate the study of politics and development?* How do the scholars relate to orientations such as those discussed in Chapter 2, including the study of political development, Third World politics and the politics of development? What subject(s) forms the basis and which scientific orientations are involved?
- *How do the researchers describe and explain the problems?* Where in the matrix from chapter 3 (Figure 3.1) would it be possible to situate the paradigmatic texts? Do their authors focus on actors, structures/ institutions or the interplay thereof? Are these factors found in society, the state sphere, or the linkage between society and the state? How are historical perspectives employed?
- *What political development policies have shaped various scholarly orientations, descriptions and explanations, and what policies do they give rise to?* What political and scientific conjunctures sketched in Chapter 4 have

framed perspectives and analyses? How, according to the scholars, can and should development be promoted by political means? Which political-economic measures are recommended?

To begin with, we can distinguish between schools based on overarching theories of modernisation and of dependency, including attempts at further developing them. To these we can add the neo-classical theories, as well as the two less homogeneous frameworks with the greatest significance today. In all, we will look at seven schools (where possible, in their order of emergence).

(1) Our starting point is the modernisation school, including its Marxist-oriented variant. (2) Thereafter follow the most important attempts made to revise this perspective (such as by those who have studied patron–client relations). We also discuss prominent prescriptions offered within this tradition – for instance Samuel Huntington's 'politics of order', and the 'non-capitalist development' analysed by the Marxists of the former Eastern bloc.

(3) We then move back a bit in time again, change over to the opposite viewpoint, and discuss the dependency school. (4) Here as well follow the most important attempts made to refine perspectives and prescriptions (primarily by those who have studied the social and economic bases of the state, and its relative autonomy).

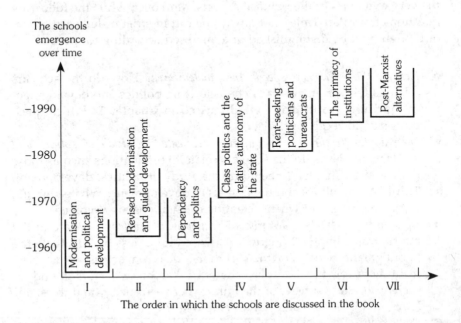

Figure P2.1 *Seven schools of thought about politics and development in the Third World*

(5) Then follow the neo-classical theories of politics in terms of rent-seeking activities, with neo-liberal structural adjustment programmes as the medicine prescribed for the ailment's cure.

Finally, we look at the two more eclectic analytical frameworks with the greatest significance today: (6) One is the institutionalist perspective, which focuses on the rules of the game in state and civil society. Within this framework, for instance, many scholars stress 'good governance', some with inspiration from the developmental states of East Asia, while others talk of 'social capital' and the ability to co-operate in society. (7) Another approach is offered by those tentatively labelled post-Marxists, who seek to combine the analysis of material factors, institutions and social movements. Elements from Marx's and Weber's theories and methods are often brought together; while some add, for instance, post-structuralist analyses of hegemony and the significance of ideas and identities, or stress the importance of popular organisations.

I should already point out here that the various schools and their theories do not always exclude each other. Sometimes this is because they look at different parts of the Third World; sometimes it reflects a focus on different problems. When one has made the acquaintance of the various schools and has chosen a research theme, therefore, it is not always necessary to sign up for one or another strict school of thought. Instead, one can often combine different theories within a looser analytical framework. We shall return to these questions in the third part of the book.

5 (I) Modernisation and Political Development

If one were to seek within a single sentence to capture the essence of the modernisation perspective, one could say that researchers in this tradition first assumed that the developing countries were and should be on the way towards an ideal-type European development model, and then investigated the degree to which, and the problematic manner in which, this took place.

The Political Sociology and Economy of Modernisation

How did the modernisation theorists initially approach the study of politics and development? How did they delineate the subject?

Most political scientists occupied themselves, at the beginning of the 1950s, with political theory and with comparatively static analyses of political institutions (such as constitutions). They were consequently ill-equipped to discuss dynamic changes, including politics and development. The most important source of alternative approaches was instead systematic, empirical and sometimes interdisciplinary studies of social behaviour. In the absence of new thinking within the field of political science, researchers interested in making a new start borrowed the analytical concepts developed by sociologists and to some extent economists and economic historians as well.

As far as the study of politics and development is concerned, three sources of inspiration should be stressed.

Some researchers proceeded, to begin with, on the basis of one of Max Weber's several lines of inquiry, that on the importance of values and attitudes[1] (including his claim that not just favourable structural conditions but also Protestantism paved the way for capitalist development in Western Europe). These scholars distinguished traditional from modern or development-promoting attitudes and values. According to their approach, 'traditional man' is 'anxious, suspicious, lacking in ambition, oriented towards immediate needs, fatalistic, conservative, and clings to well-established procedures even when they are no longer appropriate'. 'Modern man', on the other hand, is 'adaptable, independent, efficient, oriented to long-term planning, sees the world as amenable to change and, above all, is confident of the ability to bring change about' by way of politics.[2]

Second, the work of many scholars in the field proceeded from how leading sociologists had interpreted and developed Weber. One of these sociologists, Talcott Parsons,[3] took the view that increased structural complexity (including social differentiation) was tantamount to increased efficiency. The structures and institutions varied, but every social system must maintain certain functions in order to promote development. People must follow certain patterns of behaviour. Parsons identified five dichotomies between traditional and modern behaviour:

1. between emotional and emotionally neutral social relations;
2. between a collective orientation and a focus on the self – for instance, among old-style merchants and modern entrepreneurs respectively;
3. between particularist and universalist criteria – among public servants, for example;
4. between an assessment of persons' achievements with an eye to their social background and on the basis of what they have actually done; and
5. between functionally diffuse and functionally specific relations (as between employers and employees).

Consequently, political scientists wondered now how politics was affected by such patterns and what positive or negative role political functions could play in different structural and institutional frameworks.

Third, the stages of development identified by economists had great importance here, as did the driving forces of economic history. The theories of Karl Marx concerning the transition from feudalism to capitalism and then to socialism belonged in this category; so did the claim of Lenin and others that imperialism spread capitalist development to certain parts of the Third World but held it back in others;[4] and so did the anti-colonial Marxist thesis that capitalism, in order to maintain its hegemony, not only spread capitalist relations but also developed traditional feudal-like relations further. The recipe, therefore, was modern political organisation and state intervention on the basis of class interest – to promote modernisation through land reform and industrialisation. Similarly, we should also recall Walt Rostow's 'non-Communist' alternative, with its various steps from tradition through take-off to a mature mass-consumption economy.[5] It is difficult, in his traditional stage, to expand production on account of the lack of scientific and technological thinking. Agriculture is dominant, as are hierarchical social structures (which do not allow social mobility), family and clan relations, and 'long-term fatalism'. In the second stage, however, the conditions for take-off are created, as the tools of modern science reach industry and agriculture in Europe and are thereafter spread to the rest of the world. During the third and critical stage, companies generate extensive profits, reinvest a large proportion of them, demand more inputs, and employ more workers. A period of 'sustained growth' follows in the fourth stage with the spread of modern technology, after which society reaches the fifth stage – that of so-called mass consumption. According to this 'non-Communist manifesto', then, development problems are internal in character, and they can only be solved through external stimulation, entrepreneurship, and modern science. Consequently, political scientists tried now to formulate a parallel of sorts in the political field to all these social and economic stages identified by Marxists as well as non-Marxists. What kind of politics went together with the stages and the driving forces?

From Tradition to Modernity

How, then, did the scholars with a special interest in politics and development specify the problem area? What, characterised, in their view, politics in relation to Third World development? What called for closer study?

On a general level, the major theme of the leading non-Marxists was that the developing countries found themselves on an inherited and undeveloped traditional level. This reflected their own backwardness, rather than such things as colonialism. Political and other forms of development in these countries required modernisation of a similar kind to that, according to these scholars, today's developed countries had undergone. The developing countries did not, however, need to reinvent the wheel, but could in most cases take a short cut by copying the advances pioneered by the developed countries.

Political modernisation, according to these researchers, was an effect of social, economic and cultural modernisation. In principle, the political systems could thereby develop as well – so as to resemble in important respects the Western democracies of the developed world.[6] The problem was how this would be possible, given the many constraints. The developing countries had to handle so many aspects of modernisation at the same time, including the building of nation-states, economic growth, welfare, and extended political representation. Moreover, how would it be possible to contain radical nationalists and Communists, and to build a reasonably stable and democratic polity? Actually, on the latter point the non-Marxist analysts did not only draw on modernisation perspectives but also on the post-war theories in the West of how to prevent the re-emergence of Fascism/Nazism and resist Communism by way of representative and rather elitist democracy.[7] We shall soon return to the details of this.

In principle, classical Marxists cherished similar notions. The undeveloped and traditional must be transcended. Imperialism would probably, despite everything, contribute to a comparatively progressive capitalist

course of development in the former colonies. This included industrialisation and bourgeois democratic changes. Only thereafter could there be
talk of socialism. The classical Marxists were soon opposed, however, by
a new generation which had been influenced by the anti-colonial struggle and the Russian Revolution. They claimed that 'backwardness' was
mainly the result of imperialism and colonialism. Drastic political measures were therefore necessary in order to change the prevailing state of
affairs. Only in this way could the conditions be created that would
enable the developing countries to achieve an economic, social and
political modernisation reminiscent of that in Europe. At the same time,
it was both possible and appropriate to introduce socialist policies,
including state direction.

Broad Society-Oriented Analyses

Modernisation theorists thus stressed the relation between politics
and society. But how, more exactly, did they describe and explain
problems of politics and development? In accordance with our matrix in
Chapter 3, did they give analytical priority to the actors and the
structures/institutions themselves, or rather the interaction between
them? Did they examine said elements in the state sphere, in society, or
in the linkage between them? What historical perspectives did they
use?

The non-Marxist modernisationists were the most numerous. Those
inspired by perspectives drawn from political sociology asked how
actors – private individuals, groups and organisations – thought and
behaved. Those influenced by economic theory devoted special attention
to entrepreneurs and innovative scientists. And many of them wondered
how all this affected politics and development.

Over the years, thus, studies of political modernisation or 'political
development' emerged. In accordance with the theories of social and
economic systems, any political system was assumed to handle functions
such as the socialisation and recruitment of people into politics, the
articulation and aggregation of interests, and the making, application
and adjudication of rules. A political system contained, thus, in principle,
both inputs in the form of demands and support, and outputs in the
form of authoritative measures or policies.

Similarly, in correspondence with the modernisation of the social and
economic systems, political development was associated with a more
complex, specialised and legitimate system to handle the ever-present
political functions with broader, secular, universalistic administration,
political representation, parliaments, elections, parties, interest groups,
mass media etc. Finally, there should also be a 'civic' political culture, 'for
maintaining a stable and effective democratic process'.[8] A 'civic' political
culture is one where 'attitudes favourable to participation within the

political system play a major role . . . but so do such non-political attitudes as trust in other people and social participation in general.' Hence, 'political activity, involvement and rationality exist but are balanced by passivity, traditionality, and commitment to parochial values'.[9]

According to the leading non-Marxist scholars, this was far from the state of affairs in the developing countries. How, then, these scholars asked themselves, did specific systems survive? How, on the one hand, did the formulation and organisation of sundry demands and interests take place, and how, on the other, did the legislative and executive organs function? Did modern political cultures and institutions (such as parties) emerge? Were the system and the politicians able to handle simultaneous challenges such as national integration, social mobilisation, economic development and social welfare – which in the West had been spread out over centuries – and to simultaneously contain radical nationalists and Communists? What capacity did the political system have to contribute both to its own and society's development by extracting material and human resources, regulating the behaviour of individuals and groups, and distributing resources and opportunities?[10]

For the non-Marxists, then, it was most important to study how actors behaved and systems functioned. It was, furthermore, their behaviour and manner of functioning out in society, rather than in the state sphere (although also in some measure in the linkage between society and the state), that explained the mutual relation of politics and development. And even if these scholars analysed contemporary phenomena in the main, they made general historical references to what in their view were the pre-colonial roots of backwardness and tradition.

The Marxist modernisationists differed on three points. First, they frequently had more to say about the central role of politics during imperialism, during the struggle against it, and in the course of the efforts made to achieve rapid development. Second, they related the larger part of politics and its manner of functioning to the economic structure, and the interests of classes rooted therein, rather than to attitudes and human behaviour. Structures and institutions were assumed to determine what people and organisations could do, as well as how systems in general and politics in particular functioned. By contrast to the non-Marxists, finally, the Marxists explained these structures and institutions mainly by reference to the role of imperialism and colonialism in sustaining them.

A majority of modernisation researchers were ultimately agreed, however, that the developing countries had to follow a sort of idealised Western (or Soviet) model of modernisation. Accordingly, the progress of the developing countries could be described and explained in comparison with these models.

All of these researchers stressed, moreover, the importance of empirical data. Ironically, however, few of them actually immersed themselves in specific social processes and historical events. And the whole lot of them based their choice of analytical instruments on such classifications and definitions as, at best, had shown themselves fruitful for the study of politics and society in Europe and North America. Hence, they were rarely able to capture the reality of the Third World.[11]

The Western Modernisation Project versus the Radical Nation-State Project

In what sense, then, did these researchers – and the politicians and others who read them – argue that politics could be used to promote development?

Two political modernisation projects crystallised. One based on the non-Marxist theories, with the backing of the West and its allies in the developing world. Another on the basis of the Marxist-oriented analyses, with the support of the East and of left-wing nationalists in the Third World (and their friends elsewhere).

We may call the first the Western modernisation project. The idea was to concentrate initially on promoting social, economic and cultural modernisation or development. Simultaneously political development would become possible or even inevitable. The latter included, of course, Western democratic forms of government.

The foremost obstacles were of a domestic nature, and consisted of traditional values, institutions and organisations. These were best counteracted by encouraging the same values and actors (such as entrepreneurs) who were said to have lain behind the modernisation of the West. But it was not necessary to do everything all over again. Many of the advances which had been made in the West already – including attitudes and institutions favourable to development – could be imported and copied (via trade and investment primarily, but also through aid).

According to Almond and Powell, great demands were therefore placed on the political systems of the developing countries.[12] To recall a previous point: not only did the political elite have to build states (in order to create an efficient bureaucracy) and nations (to transfer people's loyalties from such units as tribes and villages to the central political system), they also had to handle rapidly growing demands for political participation and welfare provision – which might be used by radicals of sorts.

The second project may be designated the radical nation-state project. Certainly, it proceeded from the view that social, economic and cultural modernisation were needed to prepare the way for political development. But it also argued that tradition and backwardness could not be eliminated unless imperialism and neo-colonialism were combated, and replaced with genuine national and economic independence.

The object was indeed to promote those social forces which were believed to have lain behind Western modernisation, including dynamic capitalists, farmers and workers. Therefore, said the radicals, it was crucial to favour such entrepreneurs as promoted the development of the national economy. Therefore, radical land reform had to be carried out; dynamic effects would result if the under-utilised capacity for development possessed by the mass of producers was released. Therefore, the people's standard of living had to be improved so that they could become less dependent – economically, politically and culturally – on their traditional rulers, and so that they could support and participate in rapid changes in the economy and elsewhere. All this required, furthermore, political organisation and forceful state intervention. For the other side was as strong, economically and militarily speaking, as national capitalists, peasants and workers were weak.

Trade, investment and development aid were naturally welcome, to the extent that they did not undermine the policies indicated. In practice, however, the effect of imposing this condition was that developing states following this strategy had to rely on the East and the non-aligned countries.

Summary

1. Modernisation researchers proceeded according to the assumption that developing countries were on their way towards an ideal-type European model of development. They then studied the degree to which, and the problematic manner in which, this happened.

2. Behaviourism formed the point of departure, in the form of systematic, empirical and often interdisciplinary studies of social behaviour. Modernisation researchers were inspired by sociologists and economists who distinguished the modern from the traditional, and who identified different stages of development.

3. As a result of social, economic and cultural modernisation, the political system would develop as well. Third World countries were backward. It was a question of approaching modernity roughly as the developed countries had done.

4. There were both non-Marxist and Marxist variants of this view. Both non-Marxists and classical Marxists were agreed that imperialism and capitalism undermined the development-blocking feudal-like features found in the developing countries. Anti-colonial Marxists, by contrast, argued that much of the Third World's backwardness

was supported and exacerbated by imperialism. Political intervention was therefore required – just as in old Russia.

5.	The non-Marxists mainly studied how actors out in society behaved,
how social and political systems functioned, and, to some extent,
how the political system linked society and the state together. They
explained the relation between politics and development by these
methods. The primary question was whether and how the political
system and leaders would be able to build modern institutions and a
legitimate polity despite the inevitable rapid modernisation. The
Marxists had more to say on the importance of politics. At the same
time, however, they explained political patterns in terms of class
interests and the economic structure.

6.	All were agreed, however, that the developing countries had to
repeat the model of modernisation developed either in the West or
the East. The theories and analytical tools employed, moreover, were
based on studies of Europe and North America.

7.	Among non-Marxists, a Western modernisation model crystallised
that gave priority to social and economic change – which simultaneously would lead to political development as well and contain
radical nationalists and Communists. Among Marxists, a radical
nation-state project took shape that stressed the importance of state
direction – with the support of the East and of left-wing nationalists
in the Third World (and their friends elsewhere).

Notes

1 In sharp contrast to Weber himself, then, these researchers did not combine
such factors with structurally rooted conditions. In Weber's own words: 'Not
ideas, but material and ideal interests, directly govern men's conduct. Yet
frequently the "world images" that have been created by "ideas" have, like
switchmen determined the tracks along which action has been pushed by the
dynamic of interest.' Quoted in Rudebeck, 'Traditional/Modern in Modernised
Modernisation Thinking', p. 136.

2 I am drawing on the fine summary in Randall and Theobald, *Political Change
and Underdevelopment*, p. 18.

3 Parsons, *Structure and Process in Modern Societies*.

4 Lenin, *Imperialism*.

5 Rostow, *The Stages of Economic Growth*.

6 Among the classical theorists here was Lipset. See, for example, his 'Some
Social Requisites of Democracy'.

7 See, for example, Dahl, *A Preface to Democratic Theory*; Kornhauser, *The
Politics of Mass Society*; and Schumpeter, *Capitalism, Socialism and Democracy*.

8 Almond and Verba, *The Civic Culture*, p. 493.

9 Ibid., p. 32.

10 Among the leading scholars here were Almond and Coleman (see, for example, their anthology *The Politics of the Developing Areas*); Powell, (see Almond and Powell, *Comparative Politics*), who built largely on the work of Talcott Parsons and David Easton, the political scientist and systems theoretician; and Pye (see his *Aspects of Political Development*).

11 For examples which are both early and plain, see Almond and Coleman, *The Politics of the Developing Areas*. Cf. also, for a recent critique, Cammack, *Capitalism and Democracy in the Third World*.

12 Almond and Powell, *Comparative Politics*.

6 (II) Revised Modernisation and Guided Development

The modernisation theses soon proved inadequate from both an analytical and a political point of view. Revisions were inescapable. The main interest was still with problems of efficient, legitimate and stable politics in transitions from traditional to modern politics. A shift took place, however, from broad, functional and systems-oriented perspectives and explanations, to more detailed and contextualised analyses of organised interests, political institutions and the importance of political interventions and leadership.[1] This occurred in a variety of ways; we shall examine the most important here.

First, there were those scholars who did not find the very general toolbox on modernisation very helpful when trying to explain how actual institutions and processes in different cases were changing over time. There were two major tendencies. On the one hand, students of modernisation in Europe and North America began focusing on conflicts (for example, between organised interests) instead of cultural patterns and functional balance. Let us call these researchers *comparative historians*. On the other hand, many students of actual Third World institutions stressed the fact that the traditional and the modern were hard to keep apart – hence labelling them, for instance, patron–client relations. Let us call these scholars *clientelists*.

Second, there were researchers who emphasised the importance – above and beyond the modernisation taking place out in society – of the state, of political institutions, and of political leadership. This group consisted in part of non-Marxist researchers, whom we may term *interventionists*[2], and in part of Marxist-inspired scholars, to whom we may refer as *statists*. The two latter groups, moreover, produced distinct yet quite similar recommendations: the so-called politics of order from the West, and non-capitalist development from the East.

New Points of Departure in Conditions of Incomplete Modernisation

To begin with, thus, many scholars questioned the theories and concepts related to the study of political development, drawn as they were from attempts at generalising the functioning of political systems in the industrialised world. Some began enquiring into the actual historical transitions – and found them to be much more specific than the universal and often normative theses focusing upon functional harmony.[3] This was the start of several exciting studies of *comparative history,* primarily stressing conflicts between actors with different interests and ideas in historically unique contexts. Initially there were few paradigmatic studies of problems related to late development; possibly with the exception of Barrington Moore's book on the social origins of dictatorship and democracy, which also involved some Third World cases.[4] Later, however, similar perspectives made their way into fruitful studies of the actual political transformations in various Third World countries. And in the process, several scholars improved upon their analyses of organised interests by instead aligning themselves, first, to those studying class politics within the framework of the revised dependency perspectives (to which we shall return in Chapter 8), and then to the contemporary frameworks as well (Chapters 10 and 11).

Others disputed the fruitfulness of the modernisation theses more on the basis of empirical observations in the Third World. The *clientelists* demonstrated that such analytical tools disregarded a large part of the Third World's complex reality, and misinterpreted the remainder as either primarily modern or traditional. This was the start of empirically more well-grounded but less development-oriented studies of Third World politics (cf. Chapter 2).

According to critics such as Lloyd and Suzanne Rudolf, there was no such thing as the distinctively modern or traditional.[5] The application of 'modern' Western democracy in the Indian framework, for example, could exacerbate ethnicity and old caste loyalties, while these latter phenomena could channel a degree of popular participation and sustain a 'modern' democratic political system of sorts. Accordingly, these critics continued, it was important to avoid grandiose systematic analyses and misplaced analytical tool-kits from the West. It was necessary, rather, to carry out in-depth studies – if necessary with a political-anthropological approach – of actually existing institutions.

In addition, many students of political modernisation argued that there had been a tendency within modernisation theory to take it for granted that social and cultural modernisation would necessarily be associated with political development as well. Even scholars of political development had underestimated the problems. Here we come to the *interventionists.*

According to the most eloquent scholar, Samuel Huntington, stable Western democracy was not emerging in accordance with earlier expectations.[6] True, as we know, many of his colleagues had already pointed to the difficulties involved in the transition to more modern, legitimate and stable political systems. But Huntington almost turned things upside-down. Modernisation seemed rather to create political unrest, Communist movements, and sundry totalitarian forms of government. It was necessary therefore to complement society-oriented explanations of politics with studies of political institutions, organisations and their leaders.

These latter played an independent and decisive role, clearly, in whether or not the political system developed. Economic and social development would not materialise to any substantial extent, moreover, without a stable and well-developed political system.

Even economists such as Gunnar Myrdal stressed – from his standpoint as a politically less conservative economist – the part played by institutions and organisations. In particular, he blamed a good part of the problems of development on a 'soft', inefficient state.[7]

Our third group, the *statists*, took an alternative approach. They agreed, certainly, that the process of social and economic modernisation was incomplete and insufficient. But they interpreted this as meaning, first and foremost, that nationally oriented business and the middle class were not powerful enough to carry out the bourgeois national revolutions which scholars and activists had expected – not even with the support of broad popular movements and Communist parties. Instead, the statists continued, there were signs of progressive change within the so-called superstructure of society – the state. In many countries, they added, 'progressive' politicians, state officials and even officers tried to change from above social and economic structures that blocked development. As examples, the statists adduced Nehru's India, Nasser's Egypt, Sukarno's Indonesia (until 1962), and several of the new African countries. More attention should be paid, they argued, to the role and possibilities of the state.

Conflicts, Clientelism, Inefficient Institutions and State Room for Manoeuvre

How was the demarcation of the problem area affected and changed? Which questions were placed at the centre?

Let us begin with the *comparative historians*. Their basic argument was that the general theses of modernisation, based on the assumption of the harmonious development of political functions and structures, had to be replaced by enquiries into the specific historical transitions rooted in conflicts between various organised actors with different interests and ideas. The European experience will not repeat itself, the proponents argued, but the general themes related to historical change may well be focused upon in comparative perspective, such as the linkages between political leaders, organisations and social classes, or the increase of state power, or the political expropriation and redistribution of resources; and ideally one should continuously relate one's study to the international constraints in terms of dominance and dependency. Hence, as already indicated, many comparative historians soon chose rather to frame their research within the revised dependency perspectives (to be reviewed in Chapter 8), and later on within the contemporary ones as well.

Second, the *clientelists*. As mentioned above, they criticised universal desk-theorising and the rigid dichotomy between the modern and the traditional. Hence, they made their way out into the empirical world with the aim of studying 'traditional' institutions; institutions which, certainly, had survived, but yet, had changed as well – in accordance with the degree of modernisation that had been achieved. Within this category of traditional institutions, the clientelists included ethnicity, patron–client relations, and so-called patrimonial administrations. These stood in opposition to Weber's rational-legal bureaucracy, characterised as the latter was by impersonal rules, clearly defined areas of competence, rationally ordered relations between superiors and subordinates, free and contractual employment, promotion according to competence, regularised and adequate training, and compensation in the form of fixed monetary wages.

Many scholars in the field, including those focusing on public administration, are now agreed that the relation between politics and development is characterised by the use of clientelism and patrimonialism by dominant groups to capture for themselves a large part of society's resources, and to subjugate and exclude the masses.

But what do these concepts mean? 'Patron–client relations' are based on mutual personal exchange of goods or services between unequal actors. The term originates in politically oriented anthropology. Local patron–client relations arise, for instance, when powerless peasants (clients) need to relate to the world outside their families, fields and hamlets. For this they require material support and protection from large landowners and other influential persons (patrons). Reciprocation comes in the form of loyalty and various services.

Patron–client relations in a wider political context also take the form of an exchange: politicians and officials offer favourable treatment to businessmen and large landowners on the one hand, and significant voting groups on the other. They receive economic and political support in return. Political clientelism, primarily, is associated with bosses on different levels with their own capacity to deliver patronage in return for services and votes. This game is played two ways. First, through 'political machines' with no more ideological substance than a determination to distribute political benefits in proportion to the investment of their sponsors. Second, through a patrimonial administration in which officials who are related to their superiors (or otherwise please them) may use their positions as they like.

Christopher Clapham has produced an accessible textbook along these lines. He locates the phenomena in question, moreover, within (formally) modern institutions and state apparatuses. He terms the resulting symbiosis neo-patrimonialism.[8]

The *interventionists*, on the other hand, concentrated on the state. What characterised politics in the context of Third World development, they averred, was the lack of stable and efficient political institutions and organisations; institutions and organisations which could incorporate, reconcile and handle the varying pressures and demands generated by social and economic modernisation.

In Huntington's view, the most important difference between countries was not their form of government (more or less democratic, for instance) but the ability to govern. Political stability and order were the primary things. He considered one or a few strong, flexible and modern political parties especially important here. But how could these be created? Entrepreneurs were usually as weak as peasants were many and conservative landowners strong. The interventionists concentrated their attention, accordingly, on the new middle class of bureaucrats and professionals. In the final instance, analysts such as Huntington placed their hopes in so-called progressive officers and modern military organisations.

The *statists*, finally, offered a more Marxist-inspired analysis of modernisation. They argued that capitalist development was 'uneven'. A strong bourgeoisie – one able to pursue a stable and effective policy in its own interest – was conspicuous by its absence. So if capitalism and the capitalists were weak, the Third World state may have the chance to become more independent and significant. In reality, state actors such as politicians, state officials and officers enjoyed considerable room for manoeuvre. It was *this* which characterised politics in the context of Third World development. It was thus important to study if, when and how such key groups chose to found their policies on the interests of the common people, and to take up the fight for land reform, industrialisation and national independence *vis-à-vis* 'neo-colonialism'.

Organised Interests, Historical Continuity and Political Leadership

The *comparative historians'* approach, as already hinted at, was to focus on conflicts between organised interests in the relations between politics, state and society – in the framework of unique historical transitions and international constraints. The methods included, primarily, the contrasting of contexts, in order to generate fruitful descriptions and hypotheses of specific issues, as well as the critical discussion of them by comparing similar cases or different cases, thus explaining differences by locating missing links or explaining similarities by identifying common denominators respectively.[9] Soon enough, however, many of these ideas were further developed in connection with more specific theses, such as clientelism, to which we shall return below, or class politics, as in Chapter 8, or the contemporary frameworks to be reviewed in Chapters 10 and 11.

Rather, it was the clientelists' critical approach and more nuanced description of complex conditions, on the one hand, and the interventionists' and statists' interest in political institutions, organisations and leadership, on the other, that really constitituted a revised modern-isation school. The very explanations they proposed, however, were less innovative and striking. Let us recall, again, the matrix on different analytical approaches in Chapter 3. The original modernisation theorists had stressed actors (and to some extent structures) in society in general and the political system in particular; the revisionists, by contrast, focused more on actors and institutions within the state, or in the linkage between state and society. Ultimately, however, the revisionists retained the old causal perspectives within the modernisation perspective; the interventionists and statists even enhanced its normative orientation.

The *clientelists*, to begin with, often explained their central claim – that patronage and patrimonialism survived in connection with modern struc-tures – in terms of the continuity of institutions. The role played by such institutions in a wider (and contemporary) social and economic context was played down. The conclusions of the clientelists, however, still rested on the thesis of incomplete modernisation. The lingering elements of traditional society would be undermined, they seemed to think, by stronger market forces, state administrations of an increasingly legal-rational type, and more enlightened, conscious and free citizens in nation-states of diminishing heterogeneity. Like the original modernisation theorists, moreover, the clientelists gave priority to domestic factors.

In addition, the *interventionists'* thesis about the lack of political order was also explained in terms of domestic historical inertia. Colonialism and imperialism played but a small role here. The focus was on how the social and economic modernisation of society undermined – or at any rate could not always be handled by – traditional political institutions and organisations. Some scholars took the view that certain modern parties and military organisations ought to be encouraged. (Specialists in political clientelism and patrimonialism, however, met with no great difficulty in finding destructive features in these organisations too.)

Political rules and the behaviour and ideology of actors also interested the Marxist-oriented *statists*. In the end, however, they explained the freedom of action enjoyed by the state and by political actors in terms of structural conditions. The economic and social structure, they averred, was enormously complicated. In many developing countries, no one mode of production was dominant, and capitalism and the bourgeoisie were but weakly developed.

The Politics of Order versus Non-Capitalist Development

The *comparative historians'* analyses did not furnish the basis for a coherent development project. The *clientelists* basically issued general recommendations for the promotion of modern state administration, better functioning markets, and genuine rights and freedoms. The *interventionists* and *statists*, however, worked out two distinct projects: one based on the interests of the Western powers and affirming the centrality of firm and efficient political institutions and organisations; another based on the interests of the Eastern states and stressing the room for radical political changes.

The first project, that of the *interventionists*, may be termed the politics of order. The basic idea here was that social and economic modernisation was not only insufficient for furthering, but also much more difficult to combine with, political development and Western-style democracy than expected. On the contrary, efforts in this direction risked creating political unrest and instability, and enhancing the prospects of radical nationalists, Communists and others. In the end, the fundamental project of social and economic modernisation – with Western Europe and the USA as the model – would be threatened as well. The time, we may recall, is now the early sixties and onwards.

It was necessary, therefore, to concentrate on stable political institutionalisation and organisation. This meant an efficient state apparatus and a dominant party (plus a few smaller ones on the side, ideally). These institutions would handle the various interests and demands, and limit the risks of uncontrolled popular participation. (Purely instrumentally, in fact, the then North Vietnamese Communist Party was regarded with a certain envy, especially in comparison with the Americans' allied regime in Saigon.) Where better options were lacking, moreover, resources could be channelled to other organisations considered to be modern (including the military). The historical task of such organisations was to open the door to the middle class, while keeping the political participation of the masses within reasonable limits. Among the contemporary catchwords (not least in the Latin-American context) was middle-class *coups d'état*.

It is hardly an exaggeration to say that arguments of this type served to legitimise much of the long-standing US support to so-called authoritarian but non-Communist (and thus, presumably, 'non-totalitarian') regimes in developing countries. In Indonesia, to take but one paradigmatic example, the US had already lost much of its interest in democratically oriented 'modernisers' in the late fifties. Nationalists and Communists had proved much more capable of winning even democratic elections. Support was shifted instead to outright technocrats, on the one hand, and friendly officers, on the other – who, in 1965, formed the infamous New Order regime.

Finally, the *statists'* project was usually termed non-capitalist or socialist-oriented development. Its premise was that social and economic development had taken so uneven a form that neither the bourgeoisie nor the workers could direct society along its favoured course. Neither a clearly capitalist nor a plainly socialist course was possible, in other words. Instead, the adherents argued, there was room for something in between – non-capitalist development – under the leadership of progressive officials, politicians and officers. Such forces had – in addition to good ideas – the opportunity to use the state in the fight against neo-colonialism and despotism, and for land reform, the nationalisation of foreign companies and rapid industrialisation. Support from the Eastern bloc was important for enabling such radical leaders to stand up to the West, to gain the support of the masses, and to avoid exploiting the peasantry in order to promote rapid industrialisation. In time, the proponents thought, a powerful labour and peasant movement would emerge, and changes in a socialist direction would become possible.[10]

The so-called national-democratic states which, according to the theorists, followed this path included most of the developing countries with which the Soviet Union kept close relations. Examples include Nasser's Egypt, Sukarno's Indonesia (until 1962), Ben Bella's and Boumedienne's Algeria, Nehru's and Indira Gandhi's India (albeit with some reservations), the former Portuguese colonies in Africa and, finally, Ethiopia and Afghanistan prior to their collapse.

Summary

1. A certain shift took place from broad, functional systems-oriented social and economic perspectives to more detailed and contextualised analyses of organised interests, political institutions, and the importance of political interventions and leadership.

2. A first group of modernisation revisionists, the *comparative historians*, refuted generalisations of the functioning of political systems in the West, including ideas of relative balance and harmony. Fruitful explanations called instead for the focusing upon conflicts between actors with different interests and ideas in historically unique contexts, constrained by international dependency relations. Soon enough, thus, many of the comparative historians improved upon their ideas and carried out their studies within other frameworks, such as those on class politics (Chapter 8) and the contemporary ones on institutions and post-Marxism (Chapters 10 and 11).

3. The second group, whom we have called *clientelists*, criticised the universal usage of analytical frameworks based on the experiences of the West and the rigid dichotomy between traditional and modern. They called instead for detailed studies of the institutions and organisations that had survived and yet changed in step with modernisation. These included ethnicity, patron–client relations, and non-modern or patrimonial administrations.

4. Politics in the context of Third World development was characterised, according to these scholars, by the fact that dominant groups

used clientelism and patrimonialism to capture the fruits of development for themselves, and to subjugate and exclude the masses. The general prescription for this ailment included modern state administration, better functioning markets, and civic rights and freedoms.

5. A third group of modernisation revisionists, whom we have denoted *interventionists*, criticised the thesis that economic, social and cultural modernisation would promote political development as well. Even scholars of political development had underestimated the problems. The result was often exactly the reverse. Politics and development in the Third World was characterised by the lack of stable and efficient political institutions and organisations; institutions and organisations which could incorporate, reconcile and handle the varying pressures and demands generated by social and economic modernisation.

6. The form of government (democracy or the lack of it, for example) was therefore less important than the capacity of government. It was necessary to invest in stable institutionalisation and organisation – the politics of order. Where better options were unavailable, military organisations might have to be backed. The object was to admit the middle class while keeping the political participation of the masses within 'reasonable' limits.

7. We come, lastly, to the Marxist-inspired revisionists, whom we have termed *statists*. They too considered the social and economic modernisation that had taken place to be disappointing. The pattern of development was so uneven, they claimed, that neither the bourgeoisie nor the workers could drive society forward. Not even when the 'progressive' bourgeoisie received the support of the workers and peasants did very much progress occur.

8. In this situation, they continued, the state and its politicians, administrators and officers enjoyed unusually wide room for manoeuvre. With the help of the Eastern bloc they could change society from above in a direction that might be termed non-capitalist, if not exactly socialist. This would attract the support of the peasants and create a working class which, in the fullness of time, could push through socialist solutions.

Notes

1 Hence, as far as I can see, Cammack – in his recent analysis (*Capitalism and Democracy in the Third World*) of the studies of political development – is right in emphasising the continuous focus upon problems of combining transitions from tradition to modernity with the emergence of stable Western democracies. In this sense Huntington, among others, to whom we shall soon return, may have had little new to say. The other 'revisions' just indicated in the main text, however, still motivate a separate discussion.

2 Since the first Swedish edition of this book, I have changed the former label 'institutionalists' to the present 'interventionists'. This is to underline the difference, with the more recent framework (to which we shall return in Chapter 10) stressing the primacy of institutions.

3 For the early attempts within the framework of the original studies of political development, see for example Binder et al., *Crises and Sequences in Political Development.* (According to Cammack, *Capitalism and Democracy,* p. 147, publication was delayed – research started much earlier.) For the more critical enquires see, for example, Tilly, *The Formation of the States in Western Europe.*

4 Moore, *Social Origins of Dictatorship and Democracy.*

5 Rudolph and Rudolph, *The Modernity of Tradition.*

6 Huntington, *'Political Development Political Decay'* and *Political Order in Changing Societies.*

7 Myrdal, *Asian Drama.*

8 Clapham, *Third World Politics.* Clapham describes the historical and socio-economic context as well.

9 Cf. Skocpol and Somers, 'The Uses of Comparative History in Macrosocial Inquiry'.

10 For a review and discussion of 'non-capitalism', see Palmberg, *Problems of Socialist Orientation in Africa.*

7 (III) Dependency and Politics

If one sought, in the same way as with the modernisation school, to summarise the essence of the dependency perspective in a single sentence, one could say that dependency researchers presumed – in sharp contrast to their modernisation-oriented colleagues – that imperialism prevented the emergence in developing countries of an ideal-type European or self-centred development model, and then proceeded to study how in particular this prevention took place.

The Political Effects of Underdevelopment

One way of sounding out the dependency school is to focus on its four main sources of inspiration.[1] The first consisted of theories rooted in the work of the United Nations Economic Commission for Latin America,[2] which argued that free international trade was not always advantageous for developing countries. A second source was Paul Baran's powerful analysis of the obstacles to development created by colonialism in South Asia.[3] A third was Lenin's theory of imperialism; most influential here was the supplementary argument that, in unevenly developed countries like Russia and many Third World states, it was the proletariat – not the weak bourgeoisie – which could and must accomplish the bourgeois revolution (after which radicals would be able to place socialism itself on the agenda). A fourth source of inspiration, finally, was the bold and rapid revolution in Cuba.

Another – perhaps overly pedagogical – way of characterising the dependency school is as a scientific and political reaction from a Third World standpoint against the modernisation perspective. After all, the only really important thing that the modernisation and dependency schools shared was an idealised picture of Western development. Four points of conflict were particularly important here.

First, modernisation theorists related the problems of Third World countries to internal historical factors. Modernisation Marxists, for their part, usually contented themselves with the addendum that the colonisers had conserved the feudal-like structures which they had encountered in the developing countries. The dependency school, however, turned all this upside-down, putting the blame on external capitalism – whether in the form of colonialism yesterday or imperialism today.

Second, modernisation researchers (including the Marxists among them) claimed that the problems of developing countries reflected a shortage of capitalism; it was therefore necessary, they claimed, to spread dynamic modernisation from the industrialised to the developing countries and from the city to the countryside. Dependency theorists, on the other hand, argued that the problem was too much capitalism (of a parasitic variety, at least), not too little. The industrialised countries and the cities had developed by *under*developing Third World countries and the countryside. The ideal Western model of productive capitalism was therefore unthinkable in the Third World.

Third, modernisation Marxists said it was important not to press socialist demands prematurely, and that the need of the hour was rather to join with the so-called progressive bourgeoisie and their allied politicians and officials in bringing about changes of a bourgeois-nationalist character. The dependency theorists retorted, however, that capitalism and the bourgeoisie had subjugated the Third World already. The oppressed, therefore, must fight for socialism directly.

Fourth, devotees of the revised modernisation school immersed themselves in such matters as clientelism, unstable political institutions and state room for manoeuvre. Dependency researchers, on the other hand, argued that studying such problems was virtually meaningless – unless they were explained as part of a broader context marked by international dependency and by social and economic conflict.

For dependency scholars, then, studying politics in the context of Third World development was not central in itself. They asked, certainly, how politics and development went together. They focused, moreover, not just on economic dependency, but on political dependency too. They clearly held definite notions, finally, about political matters, including about what ought to be done. However, they regarded the policies open to the developing countries as so circumscribed by social and economic structures in general, and by international dependency in particular, that very little could in fact be accomplished. Accordingly, more specific studies of how problems of development related to the forms, contents and processes of politics seemed rather marginal.

The really important thing – the thing that united the developing countries and that ought to be the central subject of study – was the relations of international economic dependency, both historical and contemporary. These also formed the natural point of departure for analysing social, cultural and political dependency – which in turn affected the relationship between politics and development.

Dependency meant, among other things, that national political sovereignty was undermined already. Improvements in political institutions and organisations seemed virtually meaningless. The Third World state was basically an instrument for international capital and its domestic underlings. Democratic forms of government were improbable. Rulers lacked a basis of popular support and thus needed to resort to authoritarian methods to maintain their position. The traditional working class was comparatively privileged and in any case too small to provide the driving force for an alternative project. On the other hand, the truly poor and marginalised (who were exploited by capitalism indirectly) could play an important role.

International Economic Determinism

As indicated above, dependency theorists explained almost all of this in deterministic terms – by reference, that is, to the economic structure. (Cf. the matrix on different analytical approaches in Chapter 3.)

For one thing, they pointed to a series of unequal relations – on the local, national and international levels – between the metropolitan countries and their satellites. Each metropolis dominated and monopolised its satellites, expropriated a large part of their economic surpluses through the market, and used most of the resulting resources unproductively.[4]

For another, dependency theorists formulated a theory of unequal exchange. They claimed that countries and regions producing comparable products did not receive comparable payment – on account of differing wage costs in particular.[5]

Third, dependency scholars contrasted an ideal self-centred core economy with an outward-oriented peripheral economy. The self-centred model was based on the coexistence of two mutually supportive branches of industry – one producing means of production, the other producing goods for mass consumption.[6] The outward-oriented model, on the other hand, was dependent on the export of raw materials to the industrial countries and the import of means of production from them. Dynamic connections between industry and agriculture were absent. The economy as a whole consisted, moreover, of several interwoven modes of production – capitalist and non-capitalist.[7]

At the same time, then, that the dependency school cast light on some extremely important connections, it brought the state of research back to a condition that had characterised the original modernisation school – the universal application of a rigid macro-theory to widely varying developing countries. The dichotomy between development in the West and underdevelopment in the South soon proved, moreover, as stiff and unwieldy as that between the modern and the traditional.

Anti-Imperialism and Self-Centred Development

What were the implications of the dependency perspective in terms of a political development project?

An ideal pattern of self-centred development required, in principle, that the developing countries resist imperialism and cast off the destructive relations of dependency. Dependency scholars claimed they were able to show that, during certain periods when imperialist penetration was less intensive in particular countries or regions, there were signs of a more fruitful and independent pattern of political and economic development.

This did not have to mean isolation – 'only' less unequal relations with the developed world. Some researchers emphasised the need for particular caution when dealing with the West in general and the USA in particular. Others said the state-socialist countries of the time were not much better. Nearly all were agreed, however, that co-operation between developing countries – through the Non-Aligned Movement, for instance – had to be strengthened. (Above and beyond their advocacy of self-centred development, of course, most dependency researchers recommended a socialist-oriented policy.)

This was by no means impossible, in the view of the dependency school's adherents, in reasonably independent developing countries. But, said many, where the imperialists and their henchmen were dominant, revolutionary changes (by violent and undemocratic means) could not be avoided.

As mentioned above, the dependency theorists rejected earlier left-nationalist and Communist projects. After all, the starting point of such projects had been that, before solutions of a socialist nature could be attempted, it was necessary to carry out (with or without Communists in leadership positions) national, bourgeois and anti-feudal revolutions. Dependency theorists, by contrast, took the view that Third World countries were already thoroughly penetrated by capitalism (of a parasitic type).[8] Even if, moreover, the popular majority had not been transformed into traditional wage-labourers, and had 'only' been marginalised instead, all of its elements had an interest in revolutionary socialist policies. It would therefore, the proponents argued, be best if the old movements were bypassed – as happened in Cuba, and as Che Guevara then attempted elsewhere.

With the passage of time, however, the significance of these important theoretical and political differences gradually diminished. The Vietnamese were victorious, and China and the Soviet Union quarrelled. The Vietnamese were so successful in their conventional yet revolutionary line that all groups on the left paid them homage, and contented themselves thereafter with interpreting the basic Marxist-Leninist texts to their own advantage. In many quarters, furthermore – as in many Western solidarity movements – a sort of unholy alliance emerged between those anti-imperialists who decorated their walls with posters of Che Guevara and those reserving their highest esteem for Chairman Mao. Both camps called, after all, for a sterner revolutionary struggle than that recommended by Moscow. And despite the fact that the Maoists were conservative – in the sense of continuing to urge the primacy of the so-called anti-feudal struggle – they now did all that they could to counteract leftist movements which were more or less friendly to Moscow. (Actually, the Philippines – the Latin America of Asia – is one of the few cases where revolutionaries inspired by Maoism, on the one hand, and the Latin American dependency school, on the other, not only carried out a common divorce from the Moscow-oriented Communists but also formed the two most important poles within the radical left.)

Summary

1. Dependency theorists assumed that imperialism prevented the emergence of an ideal-type European or self-centred model of development. They then proceeded to study how this prevention came about.

2. The root of the evil was not internal but external conditions, and not too little capitalism but rather too much (at least of a parasitic sort). It was therefore meaningless to focus on internal factors such as clientelism without seeing them as part of a larger context. And it was absurd to fight against traditional feudal-like structures when it was capitalism that dominated, and socialism that should be put on the agenda.

3. The explanations offered were economic and determinist in character. The development of the industrialised countries and of the metropolitan zones of the developing countries took place at the price of the underdevelopment of the Third World and of the countryside. The room for policy-making was severely circumscribed by unequal relations of dependency. National sovereignty was undermined. The state was an instrument of international capital and its domestic underlings. Democratic forms of government were unlikely. The popular majority remained marginalised and poor.

4. Ideal self-centred development required that developing countries cast off the destructive relations of dependency. In countries where the imperialists and their henchmen were in firm control, revolutionary changes were needed.

Notes

1 For a review and analysis of the dependency school, see Blomström and Hettne, *Development Theory in Transition*.

2 United Nations Economic Commission for Latin America, ECLA, including economists such as Raoul Prebisch and Celso Furtado.

3 Baran, *The Political Economy of Growth*.

4 The outstanding figure in English was Andre Gunder Frank. See, for example, 'The Development of Underdevelopment'; *Capitalism and Underdevelopment in Latin America*; *Latin America: Underdevelopment or Revolution*; *Lumpenbourgeoisie – Lumpendevelopment*; and 'Dependence is Dead, Long Live Dependence and the Class Struggle'.

5 The outstanding scholar here was Emmanuel, *Unequal Exchange*.

6 The means-of-production branch of industry produces machinery for the consumer-goods branch of industry, which manufactures goods demanded by wage-earners in both sectors.

7 Samir Amin was the foremost researcher here. His field of study was Africa; in English, see at first hand *Accumulation on a World Scale*; *Unequal Development*; and *Imperialism and Unequal Development*.

8 Thus they also rejected the thesis (in the theory of non-capitalist development – see Chapter 6) that a wide space for political manoeuvre had arisen on account of a weakly developed capitalism.

8 (IV) Class Politics and the Relative Autonomy of the State

A criticism often brought against the basis of the dependency school was that its macro-perspective made it difficult to distinguish nuances. Classical dependency theory took little account, for instance, of differences in the policies and actual paths of development followed by different countries and regions. Many of those who were inspired by the dependency approach, therefore, found it important, on the one hand, to learn from the comparative historians' more contextualised studies (which we pointed to in Chapter 6) and, on the other hand, to revise the original dependency argument and to improve on two of its weak points. The first was the claim that virtually all development in the Third World was blocked. The second was the view that Third World class antagonisms and political patterns were determined by ubiquitous capitalist relations of production.[1] We shall consider each question in turn.

The Actual Pattern of Development

To begin with, thus, the basic premise of the dependency school – that capitalist expansion in the Third World generated underdevelopment and made ideal self-centred development impossible – came in for hard self-criticism. It became increasingly evident that a series of outward-oriented Third World economies were developing very rapidly. We shall distinguish four critical tendencies among scholars in this area.

It bears mentioning, first, that some researchers abandoned the dependency school altogether, and essentially returned to classical developmental optimism. Scholars like Bill Warren, for instance, pointed to the rapid economic growth taking place in East Asia and declared that, with colonialism at an end, and with several developing countries in a stronger position, international capitalism was no longer parasitic but rather progressive – roughly as Marx once had argued.[2]

Among those modifying and refining the original dependency thesis, however, one group studied the world system. Immanuel Wallerstein took the view that a world capitalist system had emerged as early as the 1500s. He analysed the upswings and downturns of this system over time. Each country's prospects for development were determined by these cyclical variations, he averred, as well as by its place in the system. To a certain extent, then, the position of individual countries in the system could be changed. The developing countries were not eternally doomed. Wallerstein also distinguished a middle level of sorts – the so-called semi-periphery.[3]

Another and broader approach was taken by those who studied the actual development which – dependency notwithstanding – was taking place in a number of countries. At an early stage, for example, Henrique Cardoso (later on the President of Brazil) took part in a pioneering Latin American study[4] which related various paths of development to different classes and interests. Similar analyses were done of other countries, for instance of Kenya.[5] Increasing numbers of scholars took the position that a domestic bourgeoisie was investing in dynamic sectors and gaining in economic and political strength. On the whole, moreover, the dependency school had never won much support among radical scholars in a country like India, with its sizeable domestic market and powerful private companies.[6] Actually, even the successful outward-oriented East Asian economies had initially been based on the expansion of the domestic markets; a fact, of course, which many avoided for ideological reasons.

In the rapidly developing economies of East and South-East Asia, however, it was particularly hard to detect any up-and-coming domestic private capitalists who could be described as the driving force. The state, rather, was the decisive factor – but not the strong suit of the dependency theorists. They continued along the international path instead. They explained the new economic miracles as quite simply the result of a new international division of labour which had arisen alongside the old one. In former times, the main task of the developing countries had been to produce raw materials, while developed countries had largely manu-factured industrial products. Now, the claim went, the ever-more advanced and powerful capitalism at the core had made it possible for expansive transnational corporations to locate some of their industrial production in developing countries with a favourable business climate (including low wages).[7]

All those dependency revisionists, certainly, considered also the political consequences of their amended economic analyses.[8] Yet, although the new knowledge gained about actual economic developments was important, the researchers in question remained for the most part on a similarly economistic playing field to the original dependency theorists. The framework of analysis and the object of study were largely the same. The task was to inspect the economic analysis critically and to improve it. Innovative studies of the political sphere and its impact were mainly conspicuous by their absence. The result – which in itself is not to be despised – was if anything a sort of deepened determinism regarding the political economy of the developing countries.[9] (Cf. the matrix on different analytical approaches in Chapter 3.)

Classes and Interests

In a similar way, the argument of the dependency school that problems of development arose from universal capitalist relations of production came under critical scrutiny. According to the dependency theorists, a destructive pattern of capitalist exploitation had left its mark on the social and economic antagonisms and classes of the Third World as a whole (minus some explicitly socialist countries). International capital, therefore, led the Third World state by the nose. Hence, the majority of the people had a common interest in placing socialism on the agenda.

Soon enough, however, the actual pattern of development indicated that things were less simple. In dealing with that question too, many of the revisionist researchers at first set political questions aside. In this case, however, they did so in favour of a fundamental *socio*-economic analysis. This was important, for the focus on socio-economic conflicts and interests afforded new opportunities for transcending the economism which had been so prominent earlier. Thus, in the end, it even became possible to discuss the specific actions of the state and of other political actors in greater detail. We shall return to this. Let us first turn, however, to the socio-economic studies themselves. It is true that some of the scholars (mentioned in the former section) who investigated the actual pattern of economic development noted that the conflicts in question were complicated, and that both the interests of classes and the relations of strength between them had changed. Others, however, dug deeper. Let us follow them.

The time was now the early seventies. The interest in rigorous Marxist analysis, and in Leninist and Maoist strategies too, was at a high point. Many of the prescriptions may now be passé, but there is good reason to make use of the critical-theoretical insights that emerged then.

Regardless of whether one based one's arguments on the classics or on in-depth empirical studies, it was clear that the original dependency theorists were on less than firm ground when talking about capitalism and classes. While Marx started out from production in general – and its technical level and social organisation in particular – the pioneers of dependency theory, like A.G. Frank, focused their greatest attention on trade and capital accumulation.

None of the critics denied, certainly, that trade and capital accumulation had already been found throughout the world for several centuries. Nor did any contest the view that the developed capitalist countries dominated the Third World and expropriated its resources and surplus production. But this did not necessarily mean, these critics averred, that the mode of production operating in the developing countries was itself capitalist in character. For the capitalist mode of production was characterised not just by capitalists but also by 'free' wage-workers, who did not have to be forced to work by explicitly coercive means.

This capitalism existed in Third World countries only in part. Several different modes of production coexisted with each other. The variations were especially marked with respect to the social organisation of production, including the control of the means of production. 'Free' wage-workers were certainly to be found, primarily in modern industries. Most prominent, however, were the vast numbers of socially and politically subordinated workers, oppressed peasants of various sorts, diverse craftsmen and traders, domestic servants, and so on. The dominant classes varied as well. Semi-feudal landlords retained considerable importance, for example. The antagonisms were many and the interests various.[10]

These insights had the effect of shifting interest from general-level economic models, focusing mainly on external factors, to detailed analyses of internal class relations. Intricate debates over modes of production were conducted far and near.[11] How did the actual subordination and exploitation function, and how would an ideal class analysis look?[12]

Moreover, as mentioned above, those deepened socio-economic analyses even generated new and fruitful perspectives on politics and the state (which cannot be said of the criticisms offered of the dependency school's claims about economic development).

To begin with, the interest in a better analysis of production relations entailed recognising the need to take ideological and political factors into account in some manner. For the production relations requiring closer study were not purely capitalistic arrangements. Of particular importance here was the involvement of a large measure of extra-economic coercion in the subordination of labour.

Second, the increased interest in social conflicts and conditions (over and above the economic factors that had been omnipresent earlier) meant that researchers were better able to draw conclusions about how different *actors* used politics and the state in order to promote their interests.[13]

Third, the deepened class analyses had great importance when it came to discussing and evaluating political strategies.[14] Assume, for example, that new findings indicated that very few authentically capitalist conflicts could be found. A reasonable conclusion might in that case have been to reject a large part of the criticism launched by dependency scholars of the old Left's argument that, before socialism could be placed on the agenda, it was necessary to fight against quasi-feudal production relations. In other words, ultra-leftists like Che Guevara might have been fashionable but there was something to the old argument that people would not stand up for socialism just because some brave guerrillas took the lead.

Two different ways of specifying and explaining the relation between politics and development emerged in accordance with these criticisms. Most of the researchers were drawing on the contextualised approaches of the comparative historians (see Chapter 6),[15] but within the first path they focused on state power and class and within the other on the relative autonomy of the state. We shall examine each tendency in turn.

Class Politics

Researchers applying the first perspective analysed how different classes and factions used the state to further their interests. They tried in this way to explain the forms, content and processes of politics in general, and the political economy in particular. An early example in this direction is the Latin American study done by Cardoso and Faletto. These authors distinguished three paths to so-called dependent industrialisation. A 'liberal' one in Argentina, where foreign capital dominated. A 'nationalist-populist' one in Brazil, where a range of social forces collaborated through the state. And a third in Chile and Mexico, where a 'developmental state' sought to handle foreign dominance and the lack of a strong domestic capitalist class by promoting industrial development, and by building an alliance between the middle class and the previously mobilised masses.[16]

Another illustration may be found in John Martinussen's comparison of how different dominant classes in India and in Pakistan sought to safeguard their interests through the state. Martinussen found, among other things, that the survival of parliamentary democracy in India reflected a comparatively strong 'national bourgeoisie', which often sought to assert its interest through relatively stable representative organs.[17]

Many scholars returned, moreover, to Marx's analysis of 'Bonapartism' in France, and Engels's examination of Bismarck's rule in Germany.[18] These researchers sought to test (but often contented themselves with applying) the thesis that, when the emerging bourgeoisie and working class are still relatively weak, an authoritarian state results.

Guillermo O'Donnell, for example, spoke of three Latin American phases: an 'oligarchic' state dominated by the elite that was based on the export sectors; a 'populist' period during which the new bourgeoisie relied on import substitution, domestic demand, and a tactical alliance with the urban masses; and a 'bureaucratic-authoritarian' stage, in which import substitution was dropped and military and civilian technocrats invited in foreign capital, and representatives for various associations among the ruling groups joined in a kind of authoritarian elite corporatism.[19] Similar analyses were also done of other regions – for instance, East and South-East Asia[20] and parts of Africa.[21]

It bears mentioning, finally, that researchers such as Claude Meillassoux and Issa Shivji argued that, where the private bourgeoisie was unusually weak and the state relatively strong, it was the emergence and character of a strong state bureaucracy that ought to be discussed. On the one hand, this bureaucracy was based on the petty bourgeoisie and acted in its interests. On the other hand, it also appropriated state organs and resources.[22]

Much earlier, Mao himself, certainly, had spoken of 'bureaucratic capitalists' who combined a strong base within the economy with control of the state apparatus. But the more researchers and activists were forced to take the control of state resources (rather than private capital) into account, the more conventional class analysis had to be stretched.[23] (As for how today's scholars have tackled the matter, we shall return to this question later on.)

To sum up, the approaches described were based on a deepened analysis of socio-economic structures and of the interests, conflicts and alliances of classes. Political power rested ultimately on the power of classes in production. State and political institutions – not least the parties and interest organisations which bound state and society together – were indeed important. They were not, however, important in themselves, but rather because classes could take advantage of state organs, political parties, trade unions and influential politicians. (Cf. the matrix on different analytical approaches in Chapter 3.)

The Relative Autonomy of the State

The second perspective focused instead on what happened on the political level (with its forms, content and processes), given the complex class structure and its historical roots. This meant both in the state and in the linkage between state and society.

An innovative analyst of Marx and Antonio Gramsci[24] during this period, Nicos Poulantzas, emphasised that, while the economic and political spheres had been interwoven under feudalism, the political sphere was relatively autonomous under capitalism. It was only in the final instance, and in the long term, that the state served the interests of the ruling class.[25]

Scholars such as Hamza Alavi extended this approach to the developing countries.[26] Even a brief analysis of South Asia made it clear, for example, that it was far from always the case that political institutions, organisations, bureaucrats and politicians served the economically dominant classes. Despite the fundamental similarity of socio-economic conditions in many Third World countries, the forms, content and processes of politics varied.

In other words, conditions in the political sphere could not just be seen as the result of external dependence and of class. The relative autonomy enjoyed by the post-colonial state was clearly unusually great. This made it necessary to study the significance of political institutions, organisations, bureaucrats and politicians in their own right – not least in order to understand the relation between politics and development.

But how, more exactly, could the relative autonomy of the political sphere be identified and explained where the Third World was concerned? It was hardly the case, after all, that the developing countries were characterised by the sort of highly developed capitalism that, in Poulantzas's view, endowed the political sphere with extensive autonomy. It seemed, rather, that the converse condition obtained in the Third World – that politicians and the state were strong where capitalism was weak.

Many of the researchers who emphasised class interests and class struggle tried again to solve this mystery with the aid of arguments supplied by Marx and others about Bonapartism in France and Bismarck's iron hand in Germany. According to this approach, the importance of politicians, and their freedom of action as well, arose from a stalemate in the class struggle. The old European landlords were on their way out. Neither the capitalists nor the workers were strong enough to seize the dominant role. The scholars in question took the view that a similar equilibrium obtained between classes in developing countries. This explained why politicians could act so freely.

It still remained, however, to specify how contemporary conditions in the Third World corresponded to those in Europe a century before. In addition, of course, the autonomy of the political sphere needed to be delimited and defined.

In order to solve this problem, these researchers turned again to the complicated class structure prevailing in the developing countries. It was this, they argued, that explained why no group was strong enough to rule the roost. The field was relatively free, rather, for politicians and bureaucrats able to establish a reasonably stable and legitimate regime. For example, rather radical development strategies were by no means impossible, as long as the long-term interest of the dominant groups in the maintenance of private ownership was guaranteed.

But freedom is one thing and capacity another. Otherwise put, how could one explain the fact that politicians and bureaucrats were not only free to act but were also capable of acting forcefully? Well, the claim went, the colonial and neo-colonial background was decisive here. In the Third World the state was actually 'overdeveloped', seen in relation to the socio-economic structure of the countries themselves. In developing countries, politics and the state reflected more than just the domestic social and economic structure. Had this not been so, politicians and bureaucrats would not have been so important or so capable of effective action. Developing countries had also inherited advanced and extensive colonial and neo-colonial institutions and organisations. These were created by previous rulers who *did* have a strong class base (and one ultimately rooted in the industrialised countries). Now, therefore, politicians and bureaucrats in the Third World could build further on these impressive institutions and organisations, including the public bureaucracy, the police and the military.

One could say, in sum, that the peculiar importance of politics and the state in developing countries was explained by the inability of any one contemporary class to push through its own particular agenda, and by the capacity of politicians and bureaucrats to use the institutions and organisations (both in the state and in the linkage between society and state) that powerful colonisers had built up. (Cf. the matrix on different analytical approaches in Chapter 3.)

This mixture of explanations – based variously on class, institution and organisation – was not a bad one. Yet it remained, of course, to work out and to explain how all this changed over time. When the relative autonomy of the Third World state had diminished, one could certainly point out that the position of domestic and foreign capitalists had been strengthened instead. Alternatively, as in India for example, different classes and factions had succeeded in penetrating the state in order to promote their own particular interests. Yet how could it be that it was often precisely bureaucrats and politicians – in parts of East and South-East Asia for example who had succeeded in gathering greater power both for the state and for themselves? This is, thus, another question we shall have reason to discuss further on – when we consider how contemporary scholars have approached similar issues.

Political Marxism

Many researchers concluded their analyses, certainly, with recommendations about how development could be promoted by political means. However, the further development of the dependency perspective along lines of class and relative autonomy implied no new common and coherent development project.

Many nourished a healthy scepticism, for example, towards the slogans of dependency theory that no development worthy of the name was possible in the Third World without revolutionary socialist changes. It was necessary to refine insights, theories and methodologies. On the other hand, some of these scholars doubtless also believed that radical political organisations would be able to use the deepened class analyses and the insights about the relative autonomy of the state in order to promote alternative development. In the end, therefore, one could probably conclude that over-simplified voluntaristic prescriptions gave way to hopes among some researchers that good Marxist analysis and realistic political engineering could alter the state of things.

Summary

1. As extremely rapid growth came to be noted in a number of outward-oriented developing countries, a central argument of the

dependency school – that capitalist expansion in the Third World generated underdevelopment and made 'real' development impossible – came under sharper criticism. Some researchers claimed, for instance, that the domestic bourgeoisie had grown in strength, while others discussed a new international division of labour.

2. A second thesis of the dependency school – that it was a parasitic but nevertheless *capitalist* exploitation that determined social and economic conflicts and classes in the Third World – also came under critical scrutiny. For it became clear that the state did not always do capital's bidding, and that 'the people' did not always share the same interests. Many scholars shifted from general-level economic models and external factors to detailed analyses of internal class relations.

3. The deepened socio-economic analyses generated new and fruitful perspectives on politics and the state. Production relations were not of a purely capitalist type. It was also necessary to devote great efforts to the study of politics and ideology. In doing so, many scholars were drawing on the contextualised approaches of the comparative historians (see Chapter 6).

4. Some researchers analysed how different classes and factions used politics and the state to promote their own interests.

5. Others focused on the political level (both the state sphere proper and the linkage between state and society). The Third World state exhibited, they claimed, an unusually high degree of autonomy. The complex class structure meant that no class could drive its own project through. At the same time, politicians and bureaucrats could use the 'overdeveloped' state institutions and organisations left behind by powerful colonisers.

6. The simplistic prescriptions of the original dependency school were replaced by a striving for refined insights, theories and methodologies. The hope was that these could contribute – with an improved political Marxism – to changing the state of things.

Notes

1 The critical reader may wish to know that the author was a founding member of the Swedish-based research group Akut which – from the early 1970s to the mid-1980s – was among the expressions of this effort to develop the dependency perspective. Thereafter, however, the individual researchers – in what now is only a network – sought other paths as well.

2 Warren, *Imperialism, Pioneer of Capitalism.* (Warren's original article was published in *New Left Review,* no. 81, 1973.)

3 Wallerstein, *The Capitalist World Economy.*

4 See especially Cardoso and Faletto, *Dependency and Development in Latin America.* (Revised version of the Spanish original published 1971.)

5 Leys, 'Capitalist Accumulation, Class Formation and Dependency'.

6 Among the best analyses of contemporary Indian capitalist development may be mentioned Bagchi, *Private Investment in India 1900–1939.*

7 In English, see especially Fröbel, Heinrichs and Kreye, *The New International Division of Labour.*

8 Some researchers were also inspired by so-called theories of regulation, which focused on how production and work processes had changed in countries such as the USA. (The state also played an important role here.) For an application to questions of Third World development, see Ominami, *Le tiers monde dans la crise.*

9 For a good example from the period, see Marcussen and Torp, *Internationalisation of Capital.*

10 Among the ground-breaking studies was Laclau, 'Feudalism and Capitalism in Latin America'.

11 The Indian debate was probably the most comprehensive. For a good overview and critical examination, see Thorner, 'Semi-feudalism or Capitalism'.

12 For a solid work in this tradition from the period, see Djurfeldt and Lindberg, *Behind Poverty.* (See also their later work, which they authored together with Athreya, *Barriers Broken.*

13 For the most clear-cut example from the period that I am aware of, see Martinussen, *Staten i Perifere og Post-koloniale samfund.*

14 For an example from the period, see Törnquist, *Dilemmas of Third World Communism.*

15 A study often referred to was Moore, *Social Origins of Dictatorship and Democracy.*

16 Cardoso and Faletto, *Dependency and Development in Latin America.*

17 Martinussen, *Staten i Perifere og Post-koloniale samfund.*

18 Marx, *The Eighteenth Brumaire of Louis Bonaparte,* Engels, *The Origin of the Family, Private Property and the State.*

19 O'Donnell, *Modernisation and Bureaucratic-Authoritarianism.*

20 See, for example, Higgot and Robison, *Southeast Asia.*

21 For a critical discussion, see Beckman, 'Whose State?'.

22 Meillassoux, 'A Class Analysis of the Bureaucratic Process in Mali'; and Shivji, *Class Struggles in Tanzania.*

23 For a critique, see Törnquist, *Dilemmas of Third World Communism* and *Whats Wrong with Marxism.*

24 Pioneering Communist theorist and leader during the twenties and thirties in Italy.

25 See, in English, in the first place, Poulantzas, *Political Power and Social Classes.*

26 Alavi, 'The State in Post-Colonial Societies'.

9 (V) Rent-Seeking Politicians and Bureaucrats

No Short Cuts to Progress

It was now the late 1970s and early 1980s. Rapid economic and social development was indeed evident in certain places, and particularly in East and South-East Asia. Yet attention was focused at first on regions where the problems were extensive and earlier expectations had come to naught.

The failure of the political development projects could often be traced to the drastic recommendations of the dependency school or to the ideas of modernisation revisionists about stronger political institutions and state intervention. Increasing numbers of researchers, therefore, came to agree that the problem lay in the deficiencies of the political system and in the underdevelopment of civil society. There was a markedly increased interest in the role of the state, the forms of governance, and the character of civil society.

It was a question, then, of understanding what was wrong with the state and with civil society. Most of the old theories were also thought to be part of the problem. Those who tried to solve this by further developed concepts such as class politics and the relative autonomy of the state, however, were not welcome in polite society during the eighties. Civil society and the state should not, it was thought, be discussed in such a manner. Sharp tools were generally lacking, moreover, for analysing in depth the political aspects of development. The field was therefore left free for new ideas (or resuscitated old ideas, more exactly).

Neo-Classical Premises

It was natural for many economists to base their investigations on neo-classical models and assumptions regarding the manner in which an ideal capitalist market economy functioned. This included a limited role for the state.

To begin with, these economists laid their models and assumptions over the observed economic reality like a template. In this way, they were able to discern which policies followed 'the only way' and which diverged from it. The conclusion, unsurprisingly, was that state intervention had been excessive.

Then, of course, these interventions had to be described and explained. It should in principle be possible, these theorists averred, to study the political system in the same manner as the economic. One way of doing this was to apply the concept of a political market. Once again, in other words, these theorists pulled out their models and assumptions concerning the capitalist market economy. This time, a slightly modified economic template was laid over the political reality. Which arrangements accorded with the ideal, and which departed from it, were evident thereby.

The idea, then, was that politicians, bureaucrats and voters could be studied in more or less the same way as rational and self-interested businessmen and consumers in the market. This was a kind of neo-classical answer to the Marxist thesis that political behaviour was determined by the interests and struggles of classes. (Interests and struggles which were dictated by people's place in the economic and social structure rather than the neo-classical assumption of self-interest.)

Too Much Politics

These premises defined a large part of the problem. For if one places the image of an idealised capitalist market economy over both economic and political reality, the problem appears necessarily to be one of excessive political intervention.

Already by definition, then, the risk was obvious that politics and the state served to hinder rather than to promote production and the market. It was a question, in fact, not of developmental but rather of predatory states.

Politicians and bureaucrats were assumed, just like businessmen, to be rational actors who attended to their economic self-interest. Organised groups in society (trade unions for example) were said to represent the special interests of their members. In the long run, certainly, such groups had an interest in promoting economic development. Doing otherwise, after all, would mean sawing off the branch on which they themselves were sitting. The promotion of development, then, was in the common interest. In the short run, however, a great many problems presented themselves. The political sphere seemed not to function like an ideal capitalist market in which each entrepreneur had to produce more and more efficiently in order to survive. It appeared to be completely rational, rather, for political actors to use their influence and position to redistribute resources in their favour – instead of trying to make the pie bigger.

The problem got still worse, these theorists claimed, when large groups of voters found that they would lose out if they did not vote for politicians who promised benefits of various kinds, or if they did not join powerful organisations which defended special interests rather than the common interest. In the end even businessmen had to concentrate their efforts on cultivating good contacts with powerful politicians and bureaucrats.

In this way a destructive logic was created. A great deal of time and money was spent on unproductive activities that actually amounted to no more than costly redistribution. Those charged with the institutionalisation and regulation of politics and the state discovered that rewards were to be had – in the form of greater voting support and more money – by increasing red tape, duplication and redistribution. Entrepreneurs too needed to invest in protection and reduced competition in order to make money. Growth thus came to a halt.

At the same time, of course, the indispensable constitutional state – with its business legislation and its civil rights and freedoms – was undermined. Those dominating the system monopolised the political institutions and organisations, and gained special treatment thereby. According to this perspective, then, intervention in the capitalist market undermined not just the economy but democracy as well. The converse also applied: a capitalist market economy was a precondition for democracy. Some scholars even considered it a part of democracy.

If this state of affairs could be changed, then, it would no longer be necessary to spend energy and money on unproductive activities. Dynamic effects would also result, for businessmen would need to invest in production, and people would have to work harder. Further benefits included better law and order, enhanced rights and freedoms, and Western-style democracy.

Economistic Explanatory Models

At first some political scientists were probably pleased. For now even the economists were saying that the source of all problems was to be sought on the political level. Yet it soon proved the case that, notwithstanding some digressions into political philosophy, the economists explained political problems in their own way and using their own economic terms.

The most important factors, accordingly, were thought to be located on the political level – particularly in the state sphere, but also to some extent in the linkage between society and the state. The focus, moreover, was on individual actors like politicians and bureaucrats, not on structures or institutions or the interaction between structures and actors. (Cf. the matrix on different analytical approaches in Chapter 3.)

Three explanatory models predominated. The first was the so-called public choice school, with Nobel Prize winner James Buchanan at the head. According to this view, the causes of the destructive state interference in the market were to be sought in the political and bureaucratic actions of self-interested actors, whose behaviour was perfectly rational (in a short-term sense).[1]

The second model was that presented by Mancur Olson. Olson argued that strong interest organisations had a tendency to hitch a free ride off the efforts of others, and to favour the short-term interests of their members over the common interest.[2]

J.N. Bhagwati and R.A. Srinivasan formulated a third approach.[3] They argued that great social and economic waste resulted when certain actors attempted – by political and bureaucratic means – to create and maintain monopolies, and to collect rents therefrom. So-called directly unproductive profit- or rent-seeking activities[4] were an obstacle to development-promoting investment. Examples included offering bribes or lobbying for protective tariffs.

What these three approaches had in common, however, that they explained the negative impact of politics on development with the argument that the political system made rent-seeking behaviour possible. In an ideal capitalist market, individual utility maximisation led to new production. Politics and the state, by contrast, enabled self-interested and rational individuals and interest groups to bring about a redistribution of the economic surplus in their favour. This generated economic and social waste.[5]

Disarm the State and the Special Interests

The conclusions were given. There were no political short cuts to progress. The market and the individual had to be liberated. The state and the special interests had to be disarmed.

This meant, to begin with, the privatisation of state activities, the deregulation of markets, the elimination of various licence systems and trade barriers (regarding imports and foreign investments, for example), and the radical reduction of state benefits. Politicians would have less to distribute, and individuals and special interests would have less to fight over.

Second, the remaining political sector was assigned the performance of one critical task – the creation of efficient institutions and organisations for upholding the constitutional order. This meant maintaining law and order, safeguarding private ownership, and enacting good business legislation. Many of the activities remaining within the state sector were to be decentralised. Freedom of information was necessary as well – to counteract monopoly and to facilitate market exchange.

Third, it was necessary to deepen and to strengthen civil society *vis-à-vis* the state. The private sphere had to be widened. This meant encouraging a variety of organisations – including business associations, churches, Rotary Clubs, and Amnesty International. Many neo-classical theorists brought in the nuclear family as well. Trade unions, however, did not qualify (they were special interests, and at worst politicised). Civil rights and freedoms had to be protected – against the state – and Western-style political democracy needed to be established.

Fourth, it was necessary to adapt the methods of international cooperation and assistance to the need for these structural changes. Aid had often been a source of extra rent for politicians and bureaucrats. This had enabled them to avoid essential changes. Donors should therefore encourage a free capitalist market economy, adjustment to the realities of international competition, and strong state institutions and organisations for guaranteeing public order and stable business conditions. Civil rights and freedoms should be promoted, and where possible democratic elections too. Indeed, donors ought to make their assistance conditional on a wholehearted adoption of such policies by recipient states.

This approach not only furnished the framework for the well-known structural adjustment programmes, it also lay behind much of the stress put by leading Western states and organisations on human rights, so-called NGOs (voluntary non-governmental organisations), and the transition from authoritarian to more democratic forms of government ('in ordered forms', as the point is commonly expressed).

Summary

1. On the basis of neo-classical models and assumptions, adherents of this school argued that politics and the state hindered rather than promoted development.

2. Individual utility-maximising behaviour led, in an ideal capitalist market, to new production. Politics and the state, by contrast, enabled self-interested and rational individuals to redistribute resources in their favour, generating social and economic waste in the process.

3. There were no political short cuts to development. The individual and the market had to be liberated. The state and the special interests had to be disarmed. Constitutionalism and freedom of information had to be protected. Civil society (not including the special interests) had to be strengthened. Aid had to be structured so as to promote structural adjustment and civil rights and freedoms.

Notes

1 See, for example, Buchanan, Tollison and Tullock, *Towards a Theory of the Rent-seeking Society*; and Buchanan, *Liberty, Market, and State*.
2 Olson, *The Rise and Decline of Nations*.

3 See, for example, Bhagwati, *Essays in Development Economics*; Bhagwati, 'Directly Unproductive Profit-Seeking (DUP) Activities'; and Bhagwati and Srinivasan, 'Revenue Seeking'.

4 Directly unproductive profit seeking (DUP), and rent seeking, respectively.

5 For two overviews favourable to this school, see Srinivasan, 'Neoclassical Political Economy, the State and Economic Development'; and Findlay, 'Is the New Political Economy Relevant to Developing Countries?'.

10 (VI) The Primacy of Institutions

From Earlier to Renewed Discussion

We are now approaching the contemporary discussion. The original modernisation and dependency paradigms can therefore be regarded as matters of history in the main. Yet many researchers still carry the old orientations with them like a kind of ballast – for the most part in the positive balancing sense, but also to some extent like skeletons in the closet.

Exciting research is still produced, moreover, within the framework of the revisionist schools. As we shall see, many of today's democracy studies, for example, have their roots in revised modernisation perspectives. The arguments about rent-seeking politicians and bureaucrats, moreover, still play an important role, and so do those of class politics.

It bears stressing, finally, that the paradigms of today are not based on grand substantive theories claiming general validity. Rather, they are broad analytical frameworks that permit us to borrow valuable insights and hypotheses from earlier schools. Two tendencies, in my view, are most important here. One is the renewed study of institutional factors. The second is the attempt to develop a post-Marxist alternative. Let us begin with the institutionalist perspective.

The Individual and the Market are not Everything

As mentioned above, the neo-classical diagnosis of the 1980s held that development problems arose from too much state and politics and too little civil society.

Many political scientists gave a respectful reception to this view. The neo-classicists of the eighties had outmanoeuvred the Marxists of the seventies. After some time, however, mainstream political scientists found this to be a pyrrhic victory. They were now confronted with even more economistic explanations. The scope, forms, content and processes of politics were not recognised as possessing virtually any explanatory value of their own.

Rather, many economists were also critical of the fact that everything that did not form part of a pure market was viewed as something that the cat had dragged in.[1] In 1993, in fact, one of the leading critics,

Douglass North, even received the Nobel Prize in economics. Certainly, one of his arguments is that some specific institutions inhibit development and lead to large transaction costs. Granted, it is possible to read this as a contribution in line with the neo-liberal thesis of political predation. North himself, however, took the view that institutions were neither foreign and external nor necessarily disturbing to the functioning of markets. They formed, rather, an integral part of the development of markets.[2]

Hence, a series of both political scientists and economists reached much the same conclusion: the study of self-interested individual behaviour in political and economic markets does not suffice – not when the purpose is to analyse the relation between politics and economics on the one hand, and problems of development on the other. Rather, they claimed, we should devote our primary efforts to studying institutions.

What, then, did they mean by institutions?[3] Some definitions are so wide as to render the concept virtually synonymous with manners and customs (informal institutions). Others, by contrast, require organisational arrangements – a state-enforced system of rules, for example. At the same time, many scholars conceive of parties or state organs in institutional terms. In the latter sense I have chosen, as earlier mentioned, to speak of 'organisations' rather than 'institutions'. Accordingly, one may conclude that most definitions 'have in common the general idea of an institution as the locus of a regularised or crystallised principle of conduct, action or behaviour that governs a crucial area of social life and that endures over time'.[4] For example, North emphasises 'rules, enforcement characteristics of rules, and norms of behaviour that structure repeated human interaction';[5] this includes rights and duties in economic transactions and in political work. In other words, institutions are the more or less formalised rules of the game in a society.

Let us look more closely, then, at some of the major institutionalist approaches to problems of development. First those that focus on economic factors, then those that place politics at the centre or that specialise in politically relevant institutions in civil society.

Transaction Costs and State Direction

Institutionalist economists who study development usually focus on what Douglass North calls transaction costs.[6] Costs arising, that is, in connection with the exchange of goods and services; costs for establishing contacts between economic actors (with the help of information), for reaching agreements, and for ensuring that contracts entered into are kept. The more complex the transactions, the higher the costs and the greater the need for appropriate institutional arrangements. It is in

connection with the formalisation and development of such arrangements that the state enters the picture. The study of transaction costs is
thus a key to understanding the relation between politics and development. A characteristic feature of Third World economies is that transaction costs are high. In certain places, however, progress has been
achieved – above all, many still say, despite the current crisis, in parts of
Asia.

Actually, the greatest strength of the institutionalist economists –
alongside their ability to explain why shock therapy has not in itself
sufficed to solve the problems of Eastern Europe – can be seen in their
way of analysing the advances observed, at least till recently, in East and
parts of South-East Asia.

In the matter of East and South-East Asia's original so-called developmental states, broad social-structural analysis, including that of Marxist origin, did not shown itself to be so fruitful. Generally speaking it was
not, in these countries,[7] strong private capitalists and other forces in the
market-place and civil society who were responsible for getting development going. Rather, it was politicians, bureaucrats and the state. Nor
have neo-classics – who have lavished all their care and attention on how
markets should function, rather than on how they actually work and
develop – been very much help. According to the neo-classics, transaction cost are externalities. Hence, the almost sole contribution of
political institutions to economic progress is to safeguard private ownership and otherwise to keep clear of the market. And of course this fits
very badly with the fact that, in East and parts of South-East Asia, state
organisation and regulation was exceedingly prominent, and to some
extent still is, despite being undermined by privatisation. Partially, this
was finally acknowledged even by the World Bank in its 1993 report on
the 'East Asian Miracle', in spite of many political compromises.[8]

It is the institutionally oriented economists, rather, who have produced
the most exciting and promising analyses of how and why state organisation and regulation prepared the way for the economic miracles. The
measures in question have involved more than just stable legislation for
the conduct of business. One major pillar of the original model (of
Taiwan and South Korea) was state-led land reforms making it possible
for large groups of people to increase production and make it more
efficient, thus forming the basis for dynamic domestic markets. Two
other and more generally applicable pillars were, on the one hand, at
least initially, comparatively weak private capitalists, and, on the other,
powerful politicians, officers and technocrats who, again initially, did not
have to take orders from either unions, big landlords or big business. At
best, for instance, they were rather against old destructive monopolies
and promoted productive investment. And as state leaders they called
for national unity, usually against Communism. Finally we should not
(as many analysts tend to) forget the equally important fourth pillar in

the form of the repression and subordination of people in general and the work-force in particular.

The idea of a developmental state is an old one; it was a central concept in the thinking of, for instance, Friedrich List (who loomed so large in the debates over Germany's late modernisation) and Karl Marx. The contemporary concept was established in the early 1980s by Chalmers Johnson in his studies of Japan in particular.[9] Adrian Leftwich has recently proposed the following general definition of developmental states: 'states whose politics have concentrated sufficient power, autonomy and capacity at the centre to shape, pursue and encourage the achievement of explicit developmental objectives, whether by establishing and promoting the conditions and direction of economic growth, or by organising it directly, or a varying combination of both.'[10] In other words, institutionalists can show that the type of interventions that were so important for the creation of rapid growth in East Asia call to mind those used in earlier developmental states, such as Germany and other late industrialisers. Nor was it the case, in these earlier instances, that a pure and free market created development on its own.[11] In fact, many of the measures taken in East Asia today can even be said to resemble old European mercantilism.[12]

These scholars are not, naturally, agreed about everything.[13] True, nearly all of them claim that a fundamental condition of development in East Asia has been that the state – its leading economic decision-makers and bureaucrats especially – has been far more autonomous *and* energetic in relation to various economic and political interest groups than in, for instance, Latin America.[14] In the latter region, powerful landowners and private businessmen with special interests have often prevented effective efforts towards development. In South-East Asia much the same holds true of the Philippines. And though there was not the same concentration of land in countries like Indonesia and Thailand, land reforms were aborted there as well.

There is considerable disagreement, however, on the degree and type of state autonomy. It is quite obvious at present that much of the original autonomy has been undermined by the processes of privatisation and internationalisation. But were the state technocrats wholly independent earlier, or were they involved – together with the bureaucrats – in a densely institutionalised co-operation with the managers of state and private enterprise?[15] Moreover, how rational and uncorrupt are the administrators really? There are great differences, for example, between South Korea and Indonesia?[16]

Moreover, what factors besides state autonomy as such were the most significant? Some researchers stress the importance of selective and often authoritarian state intervention in the economy aimed at promoting productive investment in certain key sectors and ensuring that these become competitive.[17] Others argue that state intervention takes place in most developing countries, and that the truly distinctive feature of the

East Asian model was its combination of an efficient and autonomous state able to reduce transaction costs, with a free and dynamic business sector.[18] The various developmental states vary in this respect too, of course; South Korea comes nearer the first model, Taiwan nearer the second.

In any event, the conventional Marxist theory of state autonomy – that the state's room for manoeuvre is greatest when the most important classes balance each other – clearly does not suffice. The classes were weak and the state strong from the start. Moreover, Weber's contra-position of a development-inhibiting patrimonial administration with a development-fostering rational-legal bureaucracy does not fit the case well either. Rather, we usually find a kind of mix that may promote development anyway.[19]

Opinions vary yet more on the most important question of all: how can we explain how these success stories came about and then changed? We shall soon return to this in a section on the explanatory approaches within the institutional framework – but also in the next chapter when discussing post-Marxist alternatives. Actually, analyses of social forces and their struggle over resources have become increasingly important. The original regulations have been undermined during the last decade by more or less private vested interests, both national and foreign, while the middle and working classes have also grown.

Political Institutions and Organisations

For their part, the majority of political scientists grasped the opportunity to refocus interest on what they considered the core area of their subject – political institutions and organisations. The 'specifically political' was stressed, after decades during which the primary focus was on personal actors and (within development studies not least) so-called external explanations focusing on social behaviour, class interest and individual economic self-interest.

Bringing the State Back In

To begin with, it was claimed, many organisations (also often called institutions) function as significant actors with interests of their own. These include bureaucratic apparatuses, military organisations, and ultimately the state as a whole. Theda Skocpol, among others, is working in the tradition of comparative historians like Barrington Moore.[20] These scholars took the view that the state comprises a collection of admin-istrative, policing and military organisations which are more or less co-ordinated by an executive authority. As such, the state develops its own imperatives and functions. It tries to maintain political stability, for instance, and to deal with other states successfully. To obtain resources for such purposes, moreover, the state must among other things compete with the dominant classes. For this purpose it may be necessary to acquire the support of the masses. Hence, scholars should bring the state back into their analyses.[21]

In the debate over the relationship between politics and development, precisely such external threats to the state have been adduced to explain, partly, the emergence of development-fostering states. Threats and competition have facilitated the use of national feelings to mobilise the whole population in self-sacrificing development efforts. Examples include South Korea *vis-à-vis* North Korea, Taiwan *vis-à-vis* China and Suharto's so-called New Order regime in Indonesia *vis-à-vis* the domestic Communists in the mid-sixties.

The Renaissance of Political Development Studies

From the eighties onwards there has also been a revival of important traits in the discourse about political development. This, primarily, was in the wake of the transitions from authoritarian regimes in Southern Europe, Latin America and, finally, in Eastern Europe as well.

As indicated earlier in the book, much of the previous attempts at covering general structural and historical factors was played down. Most of the old ballast in terms of modernisation theory was thrown overboard. Two characteristics remained – and became even more explicit than in the original political development thinking as structural explanations based on modernisation (or dependency) were done away with. First, normative studies of liberalisation, the rule of law, human rights, Western democracy, and good governance. Second, explanations in terms of political behaviour and leadership within given institutional frameworks. In other words, the claim goes, political institutions form a pattern which influences human behaviour. Among the institutions in question are constitutions, forms of government, co-operative arrangements, rules and ordinances, and the organisation and *modus operandi* of the state administration. Moreover, many add, administration and governance are also affected by the strength and structure of civil society. Let us first discuss the explicitly political institutions and then turn to the importance of civil society.

Democracy and Governance

In relation to the state, to begin with, three main themes crystallised: studies of democratisation, the links between democracy and development, and the problems of governance.[22]

Most new queries into *democratisation* are normative – not only by being in favour of democracy, as most students are, but also by taking

Western democracy as an unproblematic point of departure. Definitions of democratisation and democracy focus on their current Western forms, and on how they can be promoted, rather than acknowledging that different claims and forms have evolved in various contexts, and over the years and even centuries. Most studies, moreover, focus on the elite level, thus showing less interest in popular demands, resistance and organisation. (We shall return to those problems in the remaining chapters of the book.)

Within this framework, researchers first tend to emphasise the transition from authoritarian rule to basic Western forms of democracy, then its consolidation.

Two, or some would say three, schools of thought dominate the literature on the transition to democracy. The first is an updated version of the revised modernisation perspective. The general perspective is Lipset's thesis that socio-economic modernisation generates democracy.[23] In addition to the economic determinants, however, a long list of intermediate variables are now taken into consideration – political culture, regime legitimacy and effectiveness, historical development, class structure and the degree of inequality (especially the rise of the middle classes), national cleavages, state structure, centralisation, political and constitutional structure, development performance, international factors and, most importantly, political leadership. The basic works include the three volumes on *Democracy in Developing Countries*, edited by Larry Diamond, Juan J. Linz and Seymour M. Lipset, as well as Samuel Huntington's *The Third Wave*.[24]

The second perspective looks into democratisation as part of the incomplete processes of liberalisation during periods of economic and ideological crisis and institutional disintegration. A common structural pre-condition is that most of the bourgeoisie has turned against authoritarianism, but the basic argument is that crisis and decay give more freedom to the leading parties and leaders involved – and render their rational action most important. Hence, the focus is upon the conflicts and compromises and pacts between 'hard-liners' and 'soft-liners' within the elite over constitutions, electoral rules, the control of the army etc. One argument is that the chances for a Western democracy to emerge are best if there are compromises among the elite without too much influence and pressure from radical forces from below. The standard works have primarily grown out of the research programme on *Transitions from Authoritarian Rule in Southern Europe and Latin America*, co-ordinated by Guillermo O'Donnell and Philippe Schmitter.[25]

More recently, Michael Bratton and Nicolas van de Walle have added a comparative study of regime transitions in Africa. One of their conclusions is that the African heritage of

neopatrimonial rule . . . distinguishes Africa from the world regions where authoritarianism took on more bureaucratic forms. . . . Mass political protest (is more important than) incumbent state elites. Moreover, the impetus for political liberalisation does not originate in splits between moderates and hard-liners among the rulers but from conflicts over access to spoils between insiders and outsiders to the state patronage-system. . . . And because the stakes . . . are the state and its enormous resources, struggles are . . . leading to zero-sum outcomes rather than compromises and pacts.[26]

A refined version of the original perspective is represented by Adam Przeworski's analyses of actors' rational actions within given institutional conditions. Theoretically, thus, the specific contexts are less important and various formalised games among the elite may be applied almost universally.[27]

The yardstick in the mainstream studies of the consolidation of democracy, just like in the studies looking into the transition from authoritarian rule, is the current forms of Western democracy. There are two ways of looking at this. One defines consolidation in positive terms. The actors must adhere to the system of political democracy and subordinate their actions to the institutions of political democracy. The institutions, in turn, must reinforce this process and must promote free elections.[28] Another delineates consolidation of democracy negatively by pointing to what has to be excluded, including reserved domains of authoritarian rule, tutelary powers by still dominating lords, and fraudulent elections.[29]

A related orientation within institutional studies of politics is the renewed interest in what form of government best promotes development. This debate relates to the controversies during the Cold War and whether there is a need for authoritarian rule in order to accumulate and direct resources to promote rapid development. With the victory of the West in Europe in 1989, the focus of attention has shifted to the Third World in general and to East and South-East Asia in particular. Much of the debate is a normative one about Western liberties and democracy as against, as they use to be called, autocratic Muslims and the authoritarian rulers of the East.[30] There are also interesting empirically oriented studies, however, on the relations between various forms of government and development – on the central as well as the local level. Research into decentralisation, in fact, has caught much attention.[31]

It bears noting, furthermore, that many researchers find questions on the form of rule to be less important than those on the actual ability of a government to govern. In this respect the issue among students of political institutions is not so much *whether* state intervention promotes development, as *how* direction and administration are carried out. The result is studies of the degree to which administrations are autonomous, corrupt, legal-rational, and so on. Much of the discussion on problems of development in Africa (but also in parts of Asia), for instance, has been about patrimonialism and clientelism.[32] Atul Kohli, moreover, has used governance capacity and the degree of effective institutionalisation to explain whether or not different states in the Indian subcontinent succeed in their development policies.[33] Some of this is reminiscent of Huntington's old thesis about the need for more efficient political institutions. But while Huntington employed modernisation theory to explain how socio-economic development undermined 'traditional' institutions and called for more 'modern' ones, Kohli and others refer to the transition of the very institutions, and to the ways in which democracy has spread to the local level. In the case of India most institutions deteriorated, and the Congress Party was undermined by local leaders and groupings, during and after the populist and centralised government of Indira Gandhi – with the main exception being West Bengal, where the Communists held sway.

Many researchers, furthermore, discuss how state direction and administration *should* be organised – so-called good governance. The object is to improve public sector management, ensure political and financial accountability, and promote transparency and the rule of law. In addition, many argue that the forms of administration and of governance should be legitimate.[34]

We shall return to this shortly, when discussing explicit prescriptions among scholars giving priority to institutions. It should be emphasised at the outset, however, that by abandoning many of the old structural explanations based on modernisation theory, students of governance often set aside continued analysis of the conditions under which their good principles may have the chance to emerge and be applied.[35] For while institutionalist economists have taken a broader approach (compared with their neo-classical colleagues, with their focus on the market only), many political scientists have narrowed their sights instead to the 'core' of politics.

Civil Society and Social Capital

In a certain measure, perhaps, this is balanced by a renewed interest among some political scientists in how administration and governance are affected by civil society. Democratisation in Eastern Europe and parts of Latin America, they contend, was primarily about the resurrection of civil society. Moreover, others add, democracy is not only about elections – which might turn into the rule of the mob – but also about various rights and liberties as well as constitutional arrangements. After all, they conclude, that is why we talk of *liberal* democracy.[36]

Those liberal foundations of Western democracy, to a large extent, are reflected in the notion of civil society. Civil society, usually, is defined as a sphere of what may be called 'self-constitution and self-mobilisation', aside from the family and independent of the state. It consists essentially of voluntary organisations and public (though privately controlled) communication. It is institutionalised through various rights *vis-à-vis* the state (but also upheld by the state); and it has emerged through the rise of relatively independent socio-economic relations, as against the family, the feudal lord, and the absolutist state. Hence, corporate activity in the market is also included in classical analyses of civil society, but not the intimate sphere, the family. For liberal theorists like Tocqueville, civil society is rather civilised social interaction between the 'mob' and the state. In the contemporary and often more radical social movement discourse, on the other hand, civil society is also (or should be) independent of the market. Like the state, the capitalist economy is seen as a threat to autonomous social relations and co-operation. And in this case, identity-based social movements – including those related to ethnicity, religion, sexual orientation or alternative life-styles, and at times the family as well – may also be part of an attempt to strengthen the autonomy of civil society. To 'new' movement analysts, 'even' people traditionally included in the 'mob' or the 'mass' may associate and act as rationally as well-behaved burghers.[37]

The common thesis on civil society and democracy, therefore, is that the former is a pre-condition for the latter; that civil society is a guarantee against 'totalitarian democracy' and dictatorship; that the stronger (or more vibrant) the civil society, the better the democracy; and that just as civil society is threatened by 'too much' politics and an extended state, so is democracy. To favour democracy one should instead strengthen civil society as against the state and politics, including, some say, by supporting the growth of a capitalist market economy, or, others say, by simultaneously promoting the autonomy of civil society (including identity-related movements) against the market.

The slightly extended proposition about social capital is that civil society is not enough – but that it takes a civic community. This is more than a debate between libertarians, emphasising markets and rights, and communitarians, stressing deep-rooted communal relations. Many of the current ideas on civic virtues are based on Robert Putnam's enticing book *Making Democracy Work*.[38] Putnam studies similar institutional reforms of local government in different parts of Italy, finds markedly better democratic performances in the north than in the south, and argues that this is due to more social capital in the former than in the latter. Social capital is primarily defined as interpersonal trust that makes it easier for people to do things together, neutralise free riders, and, for instance, agree on sanctions against non-performing governments. Trust in turn, according to Putnam, varies mainly with the vibrancy of associational life, including comparatively unhierarchical choirs, football associations and bird-watching societies. And this rich associational life in the north, he concludes, is due to its roots in the late medieval city-state culture – in contrast to autocratic feudalism in the south. Consequently, if there is hardship, social disintegration, inefficient government performance and lack of democracy, one should support the creation of networks and co-operative community development schemes.[39]

Much of this, of course, is open to criticism. To begin with, the paradigm is explicitly normative. Most studies are not about the 'actual existing' civil society but about normative assumptions of good and bad, and about generalising Western experiences – or *one* way of interpreting Western experiences. Moreover, the paradigm sets aside relations of power in civil society and assumes citizens to be equal. Rather, it is the density and structure of associations and public discourse that are relatively independent of the state (and, at times, of the market as well) that matter. And though that is important, the processes behind all this are not focused upon by the paradigm.

Further comments, however, will have to wait. Some of the critique is related to the post-Marxist framework, to be reviewed in the next chapter. Additional points will be brought up in Part 3 of the book, where studies of democratisation and democracy are discussed more closely, as an illustration of how one may go ahead from general schools and frameworks to an enquiry of one's own.

Institutional and Historical Explanations

As already indicated, many of the explanations used by the institutionalists are reminiscent of those applied by the non-Marxist modernisation revisionists considered earlier. In terms of the matrix on different analytical approaches in Chapter 3, however, the relation between politics and development is now described and explained more unambiguously as political (and especially state) institutions and organisations. For one thing, many of these state-related institutions (in the sense of organisations) function as independent and significant actors; for another, institutions set limits and function as customs or norms for other actors (including individual persons). To some degree this is complemented, moreover, by the institutions linking the state and society – as well as by the institutionalised historical culture of liberalism and co-operation prevailing in civil society. In studying culture, finally, some researchers have also departed from purely institutional explanations and taken a greater interest in the interplay between actors and institutions. The same goes for analysts who elucidate the institutional rules of the game while applying rationalist theory in order to explain the behaviour of individual actors definitively.[40]

In a way, these approaches recall the Marxist thesis that classes comprise actors in their own right and determine people's behaviour at the same time (since people belong to classes.) So the next question is how classes or institutions should be delineated and explained. Marxists point to how production takes place – and run into difficulties thereby.

But what do institutionalists do? That is not always clear, and the problems are considerable.

To begin with, the concept of institutions is sometimes (though not always, of course) unclear and nearly all-embracing. Needless to say, a theory is not so adequate if its central explanatory variable may include next to everything possible.

Certainly, moreover, when the purpose is to explain these (not always clearly delineated) institutions, authorities such as Douglass North claim that institutions point to the way in which societies develop and constitute the key to an understanding of historical change.[41] A term used in this context is 'path dependence', whereby it is meant that, when two countries have (for example) similar constitutions and economic resources, the result will not be equally happy for them both, because they have different historical starting points. The term is mostly used, however, to refer to the historical continuity with earlier-established institutions.[42] North adds, accordingly, that while institutions have certainly governed human behaviour, the latter has altered institutions. Ultimately, then, it is 'the learning process of human beings [which] shapes the way institutions evolve'. 'It is culture that provides the key to path dependence.'[43]

On a general level, therefore, many institutionalists may find little with which to differ in the causal explanation proffered by modernisation theorists in terms of human behaviour and culture. The institutionalists, however, abandon orthodox modernisation theories, and discuss the matter historically, without always preaching the superiority of Western culture. Moreover, scholars who take an interest in 'learning processes' and culture often go a step further, by focusing on the interplay between actors and institutions. For instance, one may thus combine the analysis of institutional rules of the game with that of actors' rational behaviour.

Crafting Democracy and Good Government

No simple recommendations or unambiguous political-economic development projects follow automatically from institutionalist analyses. On the contrary, it has been a fundamental point of departure for many institutionalists that one cannot simply top off economic shock therapy with new rules of the game. It takes a long time to establish norms and behaviours that issue in strong and flexible institutions.

Yet it is important, all agree, to try to identify and to foster development-promoting forms of government, institutions and organisations (by means of which transaction costs in particular can be reduced). We may identify three general recipes: one on promoting what may be called instant democracy, another on favouring 'good governance', a third on combining support for 'social capital' and 'good governance' in favour of 'good government'.

The first prescription is simply to promote economic and political liberalisation, or the deepening of civil society, to thus undermine authoritarian regimes and strengthen business and the middle classes. Meanwhile one should craft compromises and pacts among the elite in order to pave the way for an orderly transition to limited forms of Western democracy – with elections in the forefront – and the rule of law. An extreme case in point was the United Nations-brokered elections in Cambodia in May 1993.

This, for many years, has been the general idea of most scholars of democratisation and governments and agencies in the West. Later on, more interest has been devoted to the consolidation of democracy by transforming 'electoral democracy' into 'real' Western 'liberal democracy'. This, according to Huntington, is when you have 'restrictions on the power of the executive; independent judiciaries to uphold the rule of law; protection of individual rights and liberties of expression, association and belief, and participation; consideration for the rights of the minorities; limits on the ability of the party in power to bias the electoral process; effective guarantees against arbitrary arrest and police brutality; no censorship; and minimal government control of the media.'[44] Some, of course, would hesitate in also supporting Huntington's argument that this means turning against non-Western cultures (such as those influenced by Islam), but most are in favour of spreading and crafting Western forms of liberalism.

Others are less interested in forms of government than in governability and 'good governance'. In the late eighties and early nineties, as neoliberal oriented structural adjustment policies did not produce the expected results, especially in Africa, the World Bank said that much of the failure was due to a 'crisis of governance'. Hence, there was a need for 'sound development management'. The key dimensions were: capacity and efficiency in public sector management; accountability; the legal framework; information; and transparency. The problems were primarily associated with, to use the World Bank terminology, an inability to separate private and public and to establish a predictable legal and political framework for development, excessive regulations, misallocation of resources, and non-transparency in decision-making.[45] This, of course, was a rather technocratic view. Simultaneously, however, the development assistance committee of the OECD[46] took a more political stand. Governance criteria, it was argued, should be taken into account in foreign aid policies and World Bank definitions should be linked with participatory development, human rights, elements of democracy and, generally speaking, legitimate government.[47]

As already indicated, however, much of the interest in good principles of governance and administration is isolated from broader investigations (including by the now-abandoned modernisation theorists) of how and when efficient and relatively incorrupt administrations can emerge and foster development. Similarly, the historical explanations offered for the growth of a strong civil society are debatable. Such explanations scarcely lead, in any case, to clear-cut options for action. Hence, some experts have been trying for years to export good rules of the game almost as boldly as IMF economists sell 'universal' market solutions.

As of recently, however, the World Bank has made a serious attempt in its 1997 World Development Report, *The State in a Changing World*, to analyse and put forward ideas about how to promote both good govern-ance in the managerial sense and 'good government'.[48] On a general level, actually, the report indicates that the times have changed not only within academic circles but also in Western policy-making institutions like the Bank, if not always in practice then in principle. Now it is no longer a matter of only 'getting the prices right' but also the institutions.

The background of the report includes, first, the recognition of the partially positive impact of state regulations in the previously mentioned World Bank study of the rapid economic growth in East and South-East Asia.[49] (Ironically, however, the current crisis in the area has hardly confirmed the latter report's preference for the less regulated South-East Asian 'models' of Thailand and Indonesia as compared with the East Asian ones – and the Bank's chief himself has actually admitted that it had 'got it wrong'.[50]) Second, the report reflects the growing insights about the problem of shock therapy and the need for proper institutions in the former state-socialist countries and the structurally adjusted countries in Africa, not to mention the outright collapses in cases such as Afghanistan and Somalia. Third, of course, the report is drawing on the previously mentioned discourse and actions in favour of 'good govern-ance'. Fourth, however, now also to this is added the importance of the civil society and of people's ability to trust each other and to co-operate.

What, then, are the main points of the new report? The bottom line, it is asserted, is that neither state managed development nor its total absence has been successful. Using the same terms as many NGOs when characterising their interventions in civil society, the World Bank would like the state to be a 'facilitator', 'catalyst' and 'partner'. As in earlier writings of 'good governance', efficiency is rendered fundamental, but now the Bank launches a two-stage rocket.

The first stage is 'matching to capabilities': to focus on what is imperative, to carry it out well and to cut down on the rest, including on 'extensive' interventions and social services; to focus, that is, on law and order, macro-economic stability, a reasonable infra-structure (including basic health), to help the most vulnerable (for example, at times of natural disasters), and to protect the environment. Hence, much of the first step resembles the previous structural adjustment measures and, it is argued, still applies in major parts of the Third World, including in most of Africa, several countries in Latin America, the Middle East,

South Asia and parts of the former Soviet Union. At present the Bank would probably add much of South-East Asia as well. The second and more innovative stage is to 'reinvigorate', thereafter, state institutions and to fight corrupt practices. On the one hand the major steps are to improve the rules of the game, to favour checks and balances, and to favour competition (for instance with regard to services that used to be provided by the state, such as health and education). On the other hand, 'voice', 'partnership' and 'participation' should be stimulated. Democracy, the claim goes, may be fine – but participation and social capital (with non-governmental organisations as vital agents) are more important.

> This does not mean that Western-style democracy is the only solution. Experience from parts of East Asia suggests that where there is wide-spread trust in public institutions, effective ground-level deliberation, and respect for the rule of law, the conditions for responsive state interventions can be met.[51]

Hence one cannot help recalling previous recommendations on the basis of the East Asian experiences for how to establish state efficiency, as summarised by Robert Wade:[51]

- Establish a 'pilot agency' or 'economic general staff' within the central bureaucracy whose policy heartland is the industrial and trade profile of the economy and its future growth path.
- Develop effective institutions of political authority before the system is democratised.
- Develop corporatist institutions as or before the system is democratised.

An attempt has now been made, moreover, by Peter Evans, and hinted at by the Bank, to bring the two perspectives together.[53] Ideally, it is argued, one should combine East Asia's (at least till recently) efficient state institutions *and* social capital in civil society. Thus the outcome may be 'good government'.

How shall this be accomplished? Compared with previous documents, the World Bank now proceeds from mainly putting forward aims to also considering means. The major problem, it is argued, is all the vested interests in the current state of affairs. 'Policy-makers in favour of change', however, have a chance in times of crisis, when there are strong external threats, and before an incoming government has established itself. In such situations one should learn from Machiavelli and should use proper strategy and tactics, identify winners and losers, and intro-duce reforms in such a sequence that at each stage one is able to get a majority of winners on the 'right' side – and can compensate powerful losers.

How shall we characterise – from a critical point of view – those policy recommendations? It is true, of course, that the report still includes elements of previous structural adjustment policies. In that respect the actual policies applied by the International Monetary Fund and the World Bank in the face of the current crisis in Asia are a step backwards. But to only point to the obvious compromise between this and new efforts at also getting the institutions right would be shallow. Rather, I suggest, a critical reading should benefit from the following more analytical points.

To begin with the report revives important elements of the political development thinking of the sixties – with its Western-based global theses about politics matching different stages of socio-economic development, universal political functions, 'modern' institutions, and few conflicts and contradictions (just 'dysfunctions'). In similar ways the Bank analyses the relations between politics and economics, and between state and civil society.

Similarly, the preoccupation with efficient political institutions resembles Samuel Huntington's old theses to some extent, though the present politics of order (with Iraq as the main exception) is less based on sending in the marines.

A new feature, however, is the attempt at combining strong efficient state institutions and social capital in civil society. This may sound fair enough, but the new proposition is also associated with a dubious stand on democracy. While echoing fashionable NGO criticism of so-called electoral democracy, co-operation, partnership and consultation are given priority to, and even the actual democratisation of the state and politics is set aside.

Finally, and equally importantly, the report is still very limited when it comes to identifying what interests and what social, economic and political forces might enforce 'good government'. Even yesterday's political development theorists' preoccupation with socio-economic modernisation as a framework for change in their functional political systems is abandoned. There is little sign of the comparative sociological historians' (not to talk of the Marxists') conflicting interests and groups. In state as well as civil society, people are rather assumed to be reasonably equal and able to co-operate – aside from certain vested interests that enlightened policy-makers may fight at times of crisis, with the assistance of the Bank.

To sum up, then, the major new World Bank policy document draws on major theses within the institutional school of thought and is an important step beyond the neo-classical structural adjustment schemes. Yet it does not identify the driving social, economic and political forces. Moreover, the report restricts democratisation to the introduction of elections, moving on instead to the opening up of efficient state institutions in consultation with co-operating people in civil society; people who are assumed to be reasonably equal and to share similar ideas and interests.

Summary

1. The study of self-interested behaviour in political and economic markets, many political scientists and economists have said, is insufficient. Institutions – the rules of the game – should be scrutinised instead.

2. Institutionalist economists often focus on transaction costs – that is, costs for creating contacts between economic actors, for reaching agreements, and for ensuring that contracts entered into are kept. These costs are high in most developing countries. In parts of East Asia, however, it was, many scholars agreed till recently, possible to bring these costs down by means of a comparatively autonomous and effective 'developmental state'.

3. Political scientists stress the importance of political and especially state institutions and organisations in their own right, as against those who explain political outcomes and processes in terms of social behaviour, class interest or individual economic self-interest. For one thing, the state functions as an actor with its own interests, and sometimes its actions promote development. For another, there has been a revival of important traits in the discourse about political development in the wake of the transitions from authoritarian regimes. Many of the previous attempts at covering general structural and historical factors were played down. Two characteristics remained: (a) normative studies of liberalisations, the rule of law, human rights, Western democracy, and good governance; (b) explanations in terms of political behaviour and leadership within given institutional frameworks.

4. Political ideas and institutions form a pattern influencing human behaviour. Among the institutions are constitutions, forms of government, co-operative arrangements, rules and ordinances, and the organisations and *modus operandi* of the state administrations. Many add that administration and governance are also affected by the strength and structure of civil society.

5. Institutions in turn are primarily explained by reference to earlier institutions, which influenced human behaviour, which led in turn to institutional changes. Some scholars take a further step by immersing themselves in the interplay between actors and institutionalised rules.

6. Many institutionalists take a critical view of simple prescriptions. It takes a long time to establish norms and behaviours that issue in strong and flexible institutions. Yet these scholars certainly consider it important to try to identify, and to contribute to the emergence of,

development-fostering institutions and organisations. Some give priority to certain principles of 'good governance' (but sometimes forget the pre-conditions which must obtain for such good governance ever to emerge); at the same time, they wish to strengthen civil society (but are not altogether clear about which measures might actually do this).

7. The World Bank has made an attempt in its 1997 World Development Report on the state to analyse and put forward ideas on how to promote 'good government'. It is no longer a matter of only 'putting the prices right' but also the institutions. Yet the report does not identify the driving social, economic and political forces. Moreover, it tends to restrict democratisation to the introduction of elections. The opening up of efficient state institutions in consultation with co-operating people in civil society is rendered more important.

Notes

1 See, for example, Toye, *Dilemmas of Development*.

2 North, *Economic Performance Through Time*.

3 For a basic review of the neo-institutionalist perspective, see March and Olsen, 'The New Institutionalism', pp. 734–49; a more developed account by the same authors is found in *Rediscovering Institutions*.

4 Martinussen, 'General Introduction to the Theme in the Context of Development Studies', p. 7ff.

5 North, 'Institutions and Economic Growth', p. 1321.

6 It bears mentioning, perhaps, that even if many institutional economists study what we have termed transaction costs here, they do not always employ the concept.

7 In this and the following discussion we set aside the city-states of Hong Kong and Singapore.

8 World Bank, *The East Asian Miracle*. See also the fascinating analysis of the conflicts and compromises during the very production of the report in Wade, 'Japan, the World Bank, and the Art of Paradigm Maintenance'.

9 Johnson, *MITI and the Japanese Miracle*. Cf. also White, 'Developmental States and Socialist Industrialisation in the Third World'; and *Developmental States in East Asia*. (Cf. also Amsden, *Asia's Next Giant*.)

10 Leftwich, 'Bringing Politics Back In', p. 401.

11 See Gunnarsson, 'Development Theory and Third World Industrialisation'; and 'Mercantilism Old and New'.

12 Whether or not they can be explained in the same way is, of course, another question.

13 For some brief overviews, see Lauridsen, 'The Debate on the Developmental State'; *Institutions and Industrial Development*; and Adrian Leftwich 'Bringing Politics Back In'.

14 Cf. Evans, 'Class, State, and Dependence in East Asia'.

15 For one interesting article with an institutional perspective, see Evans, 'Predatory, Developmental, and Other Apparatuses: A Comparative Political

Economy Perspective on the Third World State'. (For a more comprehensive analysis, see Evans, *Embedded Autonomy.*)

16 Cf., for example, Leftwich, 'Bringing Politics Back In'.

17 See especially Wade, *Governing the Market.*

18 See, for example, Gunnarsson, 'Dirigisme or Free-Trade Regime?'.

19 Cf. Leftwich, 'Bringing Politics Back In'.

20 Moore, *Social Origins of Dictatorship and Democracy.*

21 See above all the school-forming anthology Evans et al., *Bringing the State Back In.*

22 For two good general examples, see Hadenius, *Democracy and Development*; and *Democracy's Victory and Crisis.*

23 Lipset, *Political Man.*

24 Diamond et al., *Democracy in Developing Countries, Vols 2, 3 and 4*; and Huntington, *The Third Wave.* For an attempt at further developing the perspective, see Diamond, 'Economic Development and Democracy Reconsidered'. Cf. also Linz and Stepan, *Problems of Democratic Transition and Consolidation.*

25 For a summary and further references, see O'Donnell and Schmitter, *Transitions from Authoritarian Rule.* For a partly relevant review article, see Shin, 'On the Third Wave of Democratisation'.

26 Bratton and van de Walle, *Democratic Experiments in Africa.*

27 See at first hand Przeworski, *Democracy and the Market.* Cf. also Przeworski and Limongi, 'Modernisation: Theories and Facts'; and Karl and Schmitter, 'Modes of Transition in Latin America, Southern and Eastern Europe'.

28 Cf. O'Donnell, 'Transitions, Continuities, and Paradoxes'.

29 Valenzuela, 'Democratic Consolidation in Post-Transitional Settings'.

30 Huntington, *The Clash of Civilizations?*

31 For example, Sirowy and Inkeles, 'The Effects of Democracy on Economic Growth and Inequality'; Sørensen, *Democracy, Dictatorship and Development*; and *Democracy and Democratization*; Turner and Hulme, *Governance, Administration and Development*; and Crook and Manor, 'Democratic Decentralisation and Institutional Performance'.

32 See, for example, Sandbrook, *The Politics of Africa's Economic Stagnation*; and *The Politics of Africa's Economic Recovery*; cf. also Jackson and Rosberg, *Personal Rule in Black Africa.*

33 Kohli, *The State and Poverty in India*; and *Democracy and Discontent.*

34 See, for example, World Bank, *Governance and Development*; *World Development Report 1997*; and Hydén and Bratton, *Governance and the Politics in Africa.*

35 Cf. Leftwich, 'Bringing Politics Back In' (p. 421, among other places); and 'Governance, Democracy, and Development'.

36 See, for example, Huntington, 'After Twenty Years'; and Bell et al., *Towards Illiberal Democracy in Pacific Asia.* Cf. also the references in the following footnote on civil society.

37 On civil society, see at first hand Cohen and Arato, *Civil Society and Political Theory*; and Keane, *Civil Society and the State.* Cf., for example, also Karlsson, *The State of State*; and Hadenius and Uggla, *Making Civil Society Work.*

38 Putnam, *Making Democracy Work.*

39 For attempts at applying Putnam's theory in a Third World context, see Agora Project, *Democracy and Social Capital in Segmented Societies*; and Evans, 'Government Action, Social Capital and Development'.

40 See, for example, Przeworski, *Democracy and the Market.*

41 North, *Institutions, Institutional Change and Economic Performance*.

42 See, for example, Putnam, *Making Democracy Work*, p. 179ff.

43 North, *Economic Performance Through Time*, p. 3 and p. 14ff. respectively.

44 Huntington, 'After Twenty Years', p. 7.

45 See World Bank, *Governance and Development*; and *Governance: The World Bank's Experience*.

46 Organisation for Economic Co-operation and Development.

47 OECD, *DAC Orientations on Participatory Development and Good Governance*. Cf. also Hydén, 'Governance and the Study of Politics'; and Hydén, *Assisting the Growth of Civil Society*.

48 World Bank, *World Development Report 1997*.

49 World Bank, *The East Asian Miracle*.

50 *Jakarta Post*, 5 February 1998.

51 World Bank, *World Development Report 1997*, p. 116.

52 The quotations are from Wade, *Governing the Market*, Ch. 11: 'Lessons from East Asia' and include 'prescriptions' 7, 8 and 9, pp. 370–77.

53 Evans, 'Government Action, Social Capital and Development'. (The 'distinguished panel of external experts' from which the team that put together the Bank's report 'received useful advice', includes Peter Evans, Atul Kohli, Seymour Martin Lipset and Douglass North.)

11 (VII) Post-Marxist Alternatives

The Need for Revised Marxism and Institutionalism

I have chosen to describe the second tendency in contemporary debate as post-Marxist, although it also contains post-institutionalist elements and although, unfortunately, the notion is sometimes associated with post-modernism. To be quite clear: under our post-Marxist heading are found revisionist Marxists who not only refine but also go beyond deterministic positions – as well as revisionist institutionalists who not only take an interest in broader societal processes but also in social forces and conflicts. Separately and together those scholars seek to revise and to combine vital and productive elements from the earlier perspectives. Some institutionalists of the earlier variety now speak, for instance, of a 'state-in-society approach'.[1]

Studies of Marxist theory and practice have demonstrated, in the opinion of post-Marxists, that much of conventional Marxism must be fundamentally revised and transcended.[2] Complementing and supplementing is not enough. Conventional Marxism has had particular difficulty in taking account of political factors and analysing them thoroughly. In addition, the claim goes, 'others' have made critical contributions to political analysis. To some extent this refers to scholars whose studies have focused on rent-seeking politicians, but above all to those whose efforts have illuminated the significance of institutions, people's actions and their perceptions.

Post-Marxists argue, however, that these contributions have brought with them an unfortunate result: they have caused the pendulum to swing to the other extreme. It is not enough, in the view of these theorists, to emphasise the selfish behaviour of individuals or the independent importance of institutions, and of people's actions and ideas. It is important, therefore, that we do not throw out the baby with the bathwater and reject Marxism lock, stock and barrel. On the contrary, many of its insights can help us to make our way forward.

What does this mean? When it comes to analysing rent-seeking politicians and bureaucrats, post-Marxists consider it unfruitful to reduce political behaviour to the assumption that rational self-interested individuals are just making their way in another kind of market. The analysis of rent-seeking behaviour itself, however, is not abandoned – 'only' the causal explanation in terms of self-interested individuals. Rather, it is argued, one should base the analysis on people's position in the social and economic structure and then add further explanatory factors.

Moreover, the post-Marxists continue, there are several ways – not just one – to define common interest and special interests. Egoistic individuals are not all that there is. Social and economic conflicts give rise to classes and social movements with divergent basic interests and societal projects. Similarly, one should not forget the widespread striving for the monopolisation of rent in the market – outside the narrowly defined political and administrative spheres.

Let us turn, then, to the role of institutions. Post-Marxists agree, of course, that institutions matter and that efforts at political regulation and redistribution are not, always and forever, unproductive and destructive. They add three things, however.

First, that the institutionalists neglect material resources, their mobilisation and unequal distribution, and the conflicts over them. When institutionalists consider resources (such as taxes or oil incomes) they usually disregard how said resources are accumulated, distributed, controlled and used. (Even parasitic rents, for example, can come to a productive use – as more of them did in Indonesia than Nigeria, for instance.) Accordingly, many post-Marxists claim, institutionalists forswear material explanations of how it comes to be that state institutions and organisations vary so much in efficiency and stability. For instance, they failed to analyse the new and conflicting interests and classes behind the privatisation and undermining of what seemed to be efficient institutions in East and South-East Asia.

Second, post-Marxists say, institutionalists lay too much stress on historical continuity. This disregards the fact that only some institutions survive and continue to serve certain interests under new circumstances. When, for example, 'traditional' sharecropping lingers, it may reflect less the persistence of a 'feudal element' than the fact that this institution has been adapted to contemporary capitalism and plays an important role in it. Such a pattern deserves study in its own right.

Third, post-Marxists stress the analysis of people's interests and perceptions, and of actors like social and political movements and organisations. Given the present structural and institutional arrangements, after all, it is the movements and organisations that are able to change things. Civil society, in terms of reasonably independent associational life, public communication and identity-based movements (such as those based on birth and sexual orientation), is not good in itself. Citizens may even have one vote each and certain liberties but they are not equal in other respects, and their associations and media can be conquered and characterised, for instance, by authoritarian ideas and ways of reading the society, and by narrow religious and ethnic loyalties. This calls for research into inequalities and conflicts, and into the dynamics of dominance and hegemony. Citizens' participation and co-operation in associations, moreover, are fine, and nice ideas like that of 'another' development may be added, but usually democratisation and the developing of a country require also collective identities, perceptions, imaginations, organisations, plans and actions that relate to joint interests and visions.[3]

Control of Resources, Political Dominance and Social Movements

Having situated the post-Marxists in relation to other perspectives, how do they themselves wish to proceed when investigating politics and development? No uniform collection of social scientists, let it be noted, is in question here. The tendencies are many and often new; it is hard to know which will be the most significant. Allow me, then, to zero in on the four streams that I myself find most interesting:[4] one path starts with production and class but broadens the analysis; another begins instead with institutions but situates them in the dynamics of socio-economic and political conflicts; and yet two other approaches focus on political domination and movements while similarly relating them to the wider context.

Broadened Class Analysis and Contextualised Institutions

The first tendency is, thus, to broaden the analysis of how production takes place. When studying, to begin with, people's capacity to produce more, better and more efficiently, one must also consider whether this is done in a manner that is environmentally sustainable over the long term. To get an idea of what this implies one need just recall, for instance, Union Carbide's death toll in Bhopal, India, or the plantation owner's recent slashing, burning and eclipsing of the sun in South-East Asia.

When investigating, moreover, how the division of labour is structured, who controls the means of production, or how the surplus is accumulated, distributed and utilised, one should take care to include those important processes, means of control, and factors of production missed by conventional Marxism. For example, certain groups can acquire exclusive control over vital resources by political means; resources which they may then direct to uses which are more or less profitable and developmental, and which they can use to extract monopoly rent besides – rents which, finally, may be squandered or invested productively.

In this way, then, account can be taken of how capitalism expands differently over time and in different parts of the Third World. There is not one way to accumulate capital but many. Markets vary; so does the manner in which they are regulated. State intervention, moreover, takes a variety of forms and degrees.[5]

One can also examine political institutions, organisations and actors in depth. Actually, this is the second tendency that I would like to highlight. Of course, one may simply add an analysis of institutions when one has already covered as much as possible by employing the broadened class analysis indicated above. More innovative and fruitful, however, is to place institutions at the point of intersection between, on the one hand, the fundamental social and economic conditions on which they rest, and on the other, the actors who influence such institutions and are limited by them. In this way, the interplay between actors and their circumstances can be analysed.[6]

On what resources, for example, do rent-seeking politicians or powerful organisations rely? Can these actors contribute to development? What is the institutional framework or rules of the game? On whose interests would they be based? What are the implications for democracy's prospects? To what extent does capitalist expansion depend on political monopolisation and coercion?

Those are the kind of questions that become increasingly important when we have to go beyond, for instance, the discussion of democratic institutions as such, or the elitist crafting of them, in order to study the broader dynamics of their introduction, survival and further development. One pioneering study is Rueschemeyer et al.'s *Capitalist Development and Democracy*, which stresses the importance for the emergence of democratic institutions of the new conflicts and classes under capitalism, especially the working class, rather than capitalism as such and the middle class.[7] Another illustration is the attempt by several scholars to situate their analyses of political institutions in the framework of specific sections and levels of the state *and* various social forces.[8]

Similarly, those are the kind of questions that we have to pose when studies of the institutional set-up as such are no longer enough to understand the rapid development and the driving forces involved in the current crisis in East and South-East Asia. Good examples may be found among the recent studies of the industrial policies and new interests and classes emerging with the rise of capital in East and South-East Asia.[9]

What conclusions can be drawn, then, about politics and development? Just like many institutionalists, post-Marxists claim that the importance of free and dynamic economic entrepreneurs has been overstated, while that of state intervention has been underrated (both as regards the historical development of Western Europe and the experience of developing countries today). On a general level they would also

agree that many classes in Third World societies – including businessmen and landowners – remain weaker than they were in Europe. When
it comes to explaining why the state and its leaders are not just relatively
independent but also capable of effective action, however, post-Marxists
first look for the source of the power of institutions, organisations,
politicians and bureaucrats in the control over resources. To begin with,
such actors themselves control many important resources. Moreover, in
many cases – and most clearly in connection with deregulation, privatisation and structural adjustment – they transform themselves or their
close associates into what might be called private political capitalists. In
addition to many of the earlier Third World cases of structural adjustment in Africa (and to some extent Latin America), this also applies in
cases like China, India and Indonesia, where at an earlier stage broad
and radical national movements had exercised a strong pressure from
below on behalf of state intervention to promote development but where
privatisation has then taken root. Politically injected capitalism *of this sort*
may inhibit a more advanced development of civil society, including
popular organising and politicisation in accordance with interests and
ideas. So even if de-monopolisation is an important question for large
societal groups, the prospects for a stable and thoroughgoing democratisation are not the best. In the currently crisis-ridden countries of East
and South-East Asia, for example, certain advances have been made in
South Korea and Thailand, where some popular organisations have
emerged, while the situation is more difficult in Indonesia where no
orderly transition from the old regime was possible and where there are
no popular mass organisations to build democracy on (aside from
religious movements).[10]

Political Domination

A third problem area is the more detailed study of the various forms of
political domination that emerge together with the late and often politically injected capitalist expansion.

To begin with, many comparative sociologists and historians argue
(and risk some idealisation thereby) that the early industrialisation of
Western Europe created a civil society with a broad and comparatively
uniform labour movement. This meant the people could be integrated
into politics and democratic forms of government could emerge. On the
other hand, in many developing countries (as well as in the Balkans, for
example), a process of industrialisation that is limited and delayed yields
a weak civil society characterised by popular organisations which are
likewise weak and fragmented. At the same time, restricted or elitist
forms of democratic government are often introduced among the middle
class and the ruling sectors, whereupon politicians try to incorporate the
popular classes and to gain their votes by such means as clientelism and
populism. For instance, this is the way in which Nicos Mouzelis goes

about analysing the cases of Argentina and Chile.[11] A similar framework may well make sense in countries such as India and the Philippines.[12]

Other scholars choose in a similar spirit to focus on just those institutions and organisations that link the state and society, for instance political parties and corporative arrangements. How do various sections of the state relate to actors and forces in society? In many post-colonial countries, dominating state apparatuses and ruling parties are undermined. What, then, are the new links between the state and society?[13] Will some kind of corporatist arrangements emerge in countries like China?[14] What are the role and dynamics of religious and ethnic loyalties in South Asia?[15] Paul Brass, among others, stresses the ways in which political leaders nourish and employ primordial loyalties.[16] Of Africa, Mahmood Mamdani points to the legacy of indirect late colonialism still drawn upon by rulers and contending parties.[17]

Yet another approach is to stress – together with the early Marxist revisionist Antonio Gramsci, who fought against fascism in Italy – that not only material interests but also political ideas influence and dominate people. How do people interpret reality? How are they governed by the so-called dominant discourses (interpretative patterns composed of identities, expressions, assertions and conceptions)? How do they affect these discourses in turn? What is the importance of modern mass culture and increasingly global notions of freedom, equality and democracy? How does all this interact with ethnic and religious identities? So far, theoretical writings have dominated.[18] A genuine empirical application in three volumes, however, is now available, testifying to the fruitfulness of thus analysing the growth of Hindu nationalism in India; the latter, it is argued, is less about primordial identities than the contextualisation of modern ideas of democratic rights and freedoms.[19]

Popular Movements

Many post-Marxists, finally, focus upon how the uneven (and often politically injected) capitalist expansion leads to many (and frequently overlapping) conflicts, identities and loyalties. Old social and political movements develop problems. New movements appear, rooted in the socio-economic conflicts but also in environmental and women's movements. How does all this influence society? What are the political implications? What kind of development is fostered? We shall return to these problems in the final chapter of the book, but let us point to the main schools of thought.

Two points of departure dominate. The first is sceptical of the fashionable and normative ideas about the emergence and positive impact of civil societies (dense associational life and public communication) in the West and among citizens assumed to be equal. Rather, while nobody is against civil society as such, the first tendency is rooted in the previously mentioned comparative historical and sociological approaches that stress resources, inequalities, conflicts, and more or less organised actions.[20] What is the relation between the new contradictions and problems, on the one hand, and the dynamics and behaviour of old and new movements, on the other? What are the tendencies and potential of new protests and organisations among labour, peasants, professionals, students, environmentalists and others, as well as, for instance, among community organisations?[21]

Moreover, such movements (which can be more or less organised) often meet with difficulties in forming powerful political blocs – while it is easier for unscrupulous politicians to use religion or ethnic differences to mobilise popular support. On the other hand, a degree of economic and political liberalisation may widen the space for popular movements. Perhaps it is less necessary than before to conquer the state before promoting alternative development. Democratisation from below (to foster basic forms of democracy as well as to further develop them) may therefore become a more realistic alternative. Maybe this means there is hope for a democratisation process which is thoroughgoing and popularly rooted.[22]

The second point of departure is also interested in conflicts and inequalities (and should not be confused with post-modern and institutionalist studies of civil society). Its focus, however, is more on people's own perceptions and on their framing of new movements. This relates to the previously mentioned post-Marxist interest in political and ideological domination. How do people interpret reality? How do they react against the so-called dominant discourses? When does it become possible, for example, for clients not merely to complain about an unfair patron but to break with the oppressive relationship as a whole? When do new movements emerge? Why do some become radical and others reactionary?[23]

From Substantive Theory to Analytical Framework

While scholars within the institutionalist framework have set aside much of their old explanatory basis in hard-core modernisation theories, the post-Marxists abandon much of classical Marxism's determinist perspective on politics and the state, recognising instead the explanatory power of the political and ideological spheres. Post-Marxists continue to insist, however, on situating politics and ideology and institutions in their societal context and on heeding what they regard as fundamental material interests and conflicts. In this respect the post-Marxists draw extensively on the comparative historians and sociologists who first revolted against the functionalism and harmonious aspects of the modernisation school of thought.

This post-Marxist rethinking in the main, I would argue, is done in three steps. First, the post-Marxists part with many of the substantive theories of a determinist nature characterising conventional Marxism, in particular those based on its theory of value.

Next, they concentrate on sketching a framework – a conceptual and analytical context – within which to formulate and test different hypotheses. They try in this way to retain a sense of the whole, even while immersing themselves in particulars. At the same time, they refrain from tossing material explanations on to the scrap heap just for the sake of giving political institutions and ideas the attention they are due; the one approach does not exclude the other, in their view.

Within this framework they proceed, finally, on two fronts. On the one, they seek to explain as much as possible with the help of a broadened analysis of how vital resources are controlled and surpluses are accumulated, distributed and used – and then they supplement this with analyses of institutions, politics and ideology etc. On the other, they begin instead with institutions but situate them in the dynamics of socio-economic and political conflicts.

They identify, in other words, important factors within both the state and society – and perhaps especially in the linkage between them. Politics and economics are politically firmly intertwined in developing countries. The earlier Marxist interest in how structures govern human behaviour is now complemented by a recognition of the importance of institutions. Revisionist institutionalists, meanwhile, are doing the converse. Post-Marxists also devote their attention, finally, to social and political movements and organisations, and to the importance of ideas and so-called discourses in analysing relations of power. Thus the interplay between actors and structures/institutions often assumes a central importance.

The big problem for post-Marxists is that they cannot do everything at once. Giving up on hard-core Marxist theory and determinism makes way for eclecticism and fragmentation. It is easier to say than to solve this by using the overall picture as a framework, within which one can zero in on institutions or social movements, test different explanations and yet hold the pieces together.

New Movements and an Alternative Common Interest

As mentioned earlier, post-Marxist analyses are far from uniform. Nor do they lend support to an integrated political development project. The criticisms made of earlier social and economic determinism have led, of course, to the abandonment of the old theses about a development from capitalism to socialism decreed by historical laws. Even so, I would like to highlight some important tendencies.

Nowadays post-Marxists pay attention not just to fundamental socio-economic factors but also to the scope, forms, content and ideas of politics. Thus they underline that even political changes, which by earlier standards would have counted as marginal, are in fact important. Such changes may include the introduction of elite-dominated elections, some civic rights and freedoms, and less brutal structural adjustment programmes.[24]

Second, there is a widespread interest in new social and political movements and organisations. That these are called new can be seen primarily as an expression of the fact that many complex contradictions and problems have appeared in connection with the rapid changes taking place in developing countries (and which conventional Marxist analytical tools cannot adequately capture). The implicit thesis here is that many of these movements may bear the seed of a new generation of radical and popularly rooted demands, actions and organisations. Many of the old movements and organisations, on the other hand, have become rigid and incapable of taking the new questions on. Some have even become part of the problem, in much the same way as the earlier radical nation-state projects. It may happen, according to the post-Marxists, that certain new movements – and some of the old ones – will converge and become politicised, in the sense of taking the step from channelling a variety of interests and ideas to joining together to create a common political development project.[25] And perhaps, in that case, democrat-isation from below can become both a vital instrument and a part of the goal itself.[26]

The majority of post-Marxists hold fast, finally, to the view that significant antagonisms between different groups and classes in society render it impossible to discern any self-evident common interest in development questions (in relation to which special interests can then be defined). On the contrary, there are various ways of promoting develop-ment. One can invest, certainly, in the social groups who are already strong. One can count on the likelihood, certainly, that if such persons are granted higher profits and a better business climate, some of them will also increase their investments. One could assert, certainly, that this will improve the conditions of the common people in the end. But many post-Marxists believe that the result, in terms of development, would be at least as good (and of greater benefit to the majority besides) if investment was made to the highest degree possible in the dynamic effects of a redistribution of resources. This means investing more in the popular majority, whose capacity for hard and innovative labour is not fully utilised under prevailing conditions, than in the minority who are already strong – roughly as when land is redistributed from feudal-like landlords to industrious and independent peasants, in order thereby to

increase production, reduce poverty, prepare the way for industrialisation, and create the pre-conditions for democracy.

Summary

1. The post-Marxists come from two directions. Revisionist Marxists
   abandon their determinist perspective on politics and the state,
   recognising instead the explanatory power of politics and ideology.
   They insist, however, on the continued need to take fundamental
   material factors, different interests, and conflicts into account. At the
   same time, revisionist institutionalists argue that politics in general
   and the state in particular must be analysed in the context of the
   conflicts and social forces in society.

2. While recognising the importance of rent-seeking politicians and
   bureaucrats, post-Marxists add analyses of rent-seeking among private business as well; they do not reduce the political to a question of
   individual self-interest, but start out from people's place in the social
   and economic structure – and discuss, thus, different interests as well
   as the more or less productive utilisation of rents.

3. While recognising the significance of institutions and organisations,
   post-Marxists discuss also material resources, their mobilisation and
   unequal distribution, and the conflicts over them. This, the claim
   goes, is in order to explain, for instance, why state institutions and
   organisations vary in efficiency and stability, and how they change
   over time.

4. Post-Marxists attempt to account for the different ways in which
   capitalism expands in the Third World (including through political
   means). Substantive determinist theories and narrow institutional
   studies are set aside. The object is to combine class analysis and
   institutional analysis. Simultaneously, post-Marxists stress how
   important it is to study people's interests and ideas, as well as social
   and political movements and organisations (especially those linking
   the state and society). Essentially, thus, post-Marxists draw at length
   on comparative historical and sociological approaches focusing upon
   inequalities, conflicts, and more or less organised actions.

5. The major problem for the post-Marxists is that they cannot do
   everything at once. They try to maintain a sense of the whole and
   avoid fragmentation by means of a framework which enables them
   to focus on varied situations and to test alternative explanations.

6. There is no uniform post-Marxist project. Above all, the old idea of a
   law-bound historical development from capitalism to socialism has

been set aside. The majority of post-Marxists claim, however, that
fundamental social and other conflicts make it difficult to discern
neither a self-evident common interest in questions of development
nor (in contraposition to this) a set of obviously threatening special
interests. In addition, post-Marxists argue that voluntary association
and public communication in dense civil societies are not enough.
One must pay special attention to different interests, and to social
and political movements and organisations. Old ones change; new
ones grow in step with the rapid transformation of the developing
countries. Some of these may bear the seeds of a new generation of
radical and popularly rooted demands, actions and political development projects, with the introduction and deepening of democracy in
the foreground.

Notes

1 See some of the contributions in Migdal et al., *State Power and Social Forces*.

2 For studies of politically applied Marxism, see for example Omvedt, *Reinventing Revolution*; and Törnquist, *What's Wrong With Marxism* and 'Communists
and Democracy in the Philippines'.

3 We shall return to the details of the critique of the civil society and social
capital paradigm in Chapter 13.

4 Please note here, as in this chapter in general, that it is rarely possible to
identify standard works. Usually, therefore, I only give examples of the research
I have in mind.

5 For a good example, see Bangura, 'Authoritarian Rule and Democracy in
Africa'.

6 Cf. Isaac, *Power and Marxist Theory*.

7 Rueschemeyer et al., *Capitalist Development and Democracy*.

8 See some of the contributions in Migdal et al., *State Power and Social Forces* –
the chapter by Kohli, however, is on the borderline between institutionalism and
the post-Marxist focus upon conflicts and social forces; and the same may be said
of Peter Evans' *Embedded Autonomy*, 'Introduction: Development Strategies
Across the Public–Private Divide' and 'Government Action, Social Capital and
Development'.

9 See, for example, Jomo et al., *Southeast Asia's Misunderstood Miracle*; Jomo,
Tigers in Trouble; and Hadiz, *Workers and State in New Order Indonesia*. See also the
following edited volumes: Hewison et al., *Southeast Asia in the 1990s*; Rodan,
Political Oppositions in Industrialising Asia; Robison and Goodman, *The New Rich
in Asia*; and Rodan et al., *The Political Economy of South East Asia*. Cf. also, for
example, Gibbon et al., *Authoritarianism, Democracy, and Structural Adjustment*;
and Gibbon, *Social Change and Economic Reform in Africa*.

10 For similar worries with reference to Africa cf., for example, the previously
cited works by Gibbon, his 'Some Reflections on "Civil Society" and Political
Change'; and Mamdani, *Citizen and Subject*.

11 See, in the first instance, Mouzelis, *Politics in the Semi-Periphery*. Later on
Mouzelis has tried to formulate a paradigm in which he compares the way in

which a society is dominated politically and ideologically with the way in which goods are produced. In part, then, one draws certain parallels between political activity and technical developments in production; in part, one likens control over political apparatuses to control over economic units. See Mouzelis, *Post-Marxist Alternatives*.

12 For a somewhat related and stimulating analysis of the Philippines, see Anderson, 'Cacique Democracy and the Philippines'.

13 Cf. Migdal, 'The State in Society'. Cf. also – on the borderline between institutionalism and post-Marxism – Kohli, 'Centralization and Powerlessness'.

14 Cf., for example, Shue, 'State Power and Social Organisation in China'; and Unger and Chan, 'Corporatism in China'.

15 For an overview, see Ahmed, *State, Nation and Ethnicity in Contemporary South Asia*.

16 See at first hand Brass, *Ethnicity and Nationalism*.

17 Mamdani, *Citizen and Subject*.

18 Among the theoretical classics is Laclau and Mouffe, *Hegemony and Socialist Strategy*. Among the more empirically related standard works is also Anderson, *Imagined Communities*.

19 Blom Hansen, *The Saffron Wave*.

20 Cf. Chapters 6 and 8.

21 For a few examples, see Brandell, *Workers in Third-World Industrialisation*; Andræ and Beckman, *Union Power in the Nigerian Textile Industry*; Lindberg and Sverrisson, *Social Movements in Development*; Rudebeck, *When Democracy Makes Sense*; Rudebeck and Törnquist, with Rojas, *Democratisation in the Third World*; and Mohanty and Mukherji, with Törnquist, *People's Rights*. Cf. also the efforts to develop analyses of 'Social Forces: Engaged with State Power', in Migdal et al., *State Power and Social Forces*.

22 For references, see Chapter 13.

23 Cf., for example, relevant parts of Escobar and Alvarez, *The Making of Social Movements in Latin America*.

24 See, for example, Beckman, 'Whose Democracy?'.

25 Cf., for example, Omvedt, *Reinventing Revolution*.

26 Again, we shall return to those issues in Chapter 13.

PART 3

FROM A SCHOOL TO A PERSPECTIVE AND STUDY OF ONE'S OWN: THE CASE OF DEMOCRATISATION

The purpose of the critical analysis of the schools contained in Part 2 was to help the reader form a picture of, and take a position towards, the various ways of describing and explaining the problems at hand, before making a choice about how to describe and explain, and then moving on. But how does one make this choice? And how does one move on from that point?

It bears stressing that while one ought to know about the different approaches before choosing, this does *not* mean one must embrace one or the other narrowly defined school. It suffices, rather, to stay within a given coherent framework.

To begin with, this is because there is at least one general weakness in almost all the approaches (something that first became clear to me during the course of my work and which I have been unable to consider in the manner that I wished to) – this is that the historical perspectives are even shorter and the historically oriented explanations yet more deficient than I had feared. Perhaps this is because social scientists who focus on the actors and structures of today have often predominated. A further reason may lie in the fact that research funds have for the most part come from trend-sensitive and results-oriented ministries for foreign affairs and aid agencies. For whatever reason, however, the historical proportions are often unrealistic. Ideas and projects like land reform are expected to yield the outcome desired within a few years. The anti-colonial struggle and the radical nation-state project are already dismissed and forgotten. Suddenly, rapid development is discovered in East Asia. A horde of analysts immediately connect it to factors lying closest in time (like belated state-led export drives). Until mid-1997 they even contended that the authoritarian cum market-oriented countries in South-East Asia were better than the more regulated ones further to the north. Then, a short time later, many of the very same actors flee the area and at best, like the World Bank, confess that they 'got it wrong'. Almost all development theory (dependency perspectives too) is based on comparison with an idealised and inaccurate picture of a Western developmental idyll. And those, on the other hand, who heed the facts of historical continuity are seldom able to explain what fades away and what survives.

Moreover, in some respects the various schools and theories may even complement each other – whether this is because their distinct emphases have grown out of differing contexts (for example, dependency theory out of problems of poverty in Latin America, or institutional theories often out of developmental states in East Asia), or because they focus on different factors (for example, classes and institutions).

The strategy I would recommend, then, is that after acquainting oneself with the various schools, one begins by selecting the research theme one finds to be of greatest interest: democratisation in the Third World, for example, or how the state, interest organisations, ideology or ethnicity affect the relationship between politics and development.

One can return *thereafter* to the various schools and their differing explanations, and ask quite simply whether, and if so how, earlier research has treated the theme in which one is interested. The importance of gender, for instance, has rarely been considered.[1] What theories and perspectives are on offer? If we want to test them, what are the critical empirical cases to research? If we want to describe and explain important empirical questions, which are the most fruitful categories and theories to guide us? Can they be combined? In what areas is more work needed? How can this be done?

Finally, however, one must be careful. One cannot simply pluck up, as if at a smorgasbord, whatever dishes strike one's fancy. The undogmatic approach I recommend should not be confused with spineless pragmatism. I would gladly see the iron curtains separating the old schools broken up, yet it is important, notwithstanding this, to retain a coherent overarching framework. The parts or explanations with which one is working must hold together. Elements borrowed from another perspective must therefore be related to one's 'own' framework.

Let me just take one example to clarify what I mean. If one is inclined towards structural explanations in the main, but at the same time is persuaded that neo-classical analyses of rent-seeking capture something important, one is compelled to ask how one's original view that the behaviour of individuals is governed by their place in the structure can be reconciled with the neo-classical assumption that human behaviour springs from individual rational self-interest.[2]

A framework can either be set out on the basis of the earlier (and much more uniform) schools, or one can choose to work within one of the two later ones; the institutionalist or the post-Marxist. These latter, in any case, are more in the manner of analytical frameworks than of substantive 'grand theories'.

I believe, in fact, that most researchers can agree on this nowadays. The grand substantive theories and schools – whether with Marxist or non-Marxist roots – *are* on the wane. Not even the latest attempt of this kind – the neo-classicist argument about rent-seeking politicians and bureaucrats – has wind in its sails any longer. This does not mean approaches of the opposite type – post-modernist analyses of imaginary fragments – have taken over instead. Rather, it seems to me, it is broad analytical frameworks – like the institutionalist and post-Marxist ones – that are gaining ground. They offer no simple overarching explanations, but they at any rate provide conceptual and analytical contexts. The road is then open for sketching and testing theories and hypotheses which may be more or less applicable to the developing world as a whole, but which must in any event be relevant to the country or area on which one has focused. The results obtained thereby can be compared to other cases, finally, and one can try to generalise from them.

Accordingly – since one must start with the issues one personally finds to be most interesting and important, proceeding from a knowledge of the various schools of thought to a perspective and study of one's own – Part 3 of the book can only be based on an example. The theme chosen as an example is one of the most central contemporary ones: processes of democratisation within the framework of Third World development.

I shift here, consequently, from my aim in Part 2 – to analyse the different schools critically but without pushing a thesis to the effect that one particular orientation is best – to give an example of how one can argue for a perspective and study area of one's own. In Part 3 I will argue for theses of my own.

In Chapter 12 I shall show how one can specify the problem of democratisation and take a position on the contributions of the various schools. In this example, the conclusion is that we should go beyond the preoccupation with the middle class, the rational elite and 'good governance', and focus instead on the problems of democratisation from below.

The next question, then, is how one should go about the actual study of one's own. Hence, Chapter 13 is an example of how one can argue for a specific approach and research design. In this example, the dominant paradigm of civil society and social capital is criticised. Rather, I argue, one should focus on the *politics* of democratisation in terms of political space, inclusion and politicisation.

Notes

1 For important work, see Waylen, *Gender in Third World Politics*.

2 For instance, some post-Marxists solve this by rejecting the assumption of individual rational self-interest, even while discussing how people try to collect rents on the basis of their ownership and control of productive resources, that is, their place in the structure. Cf. the section on post-Marxism above; Cf. also Törnquist, *What's Wrong with Marxism? Vols 1 and 2*.

12 Towards the Study of Democratisation in the Context of Late Development

The new buzzwords of the 1990s are democracy and democratisation.[1] It is necessary, first, to specify the concepts one is using. Like most democracy researchers, I find it most fruitful scientifically, and least dubious politically, to start off with a definition of democracy which is narrow and universalist rather than broad and culturally relativist. Most would seem to be agreed that the *core of modern democracy* is the sovereignty of the people in accordance with the principle of constitutionally guaranteed political equality among citizens or members who are independent enough to express their own will. Or, put in terms more amenable to empirical investigation: constitutional government on the basis of majority decision among adult citizens or members who have one vote each, an equal right to stand for election, and freedom of speech and association. Democratisation, in turn, may thus be defined in terms of the promotion and further development of democracy as an idea and as a method.

Universalist minimum definitions, however, do not mean that all the factors which are in some sense related to democracy and democratisation have the same general validity. On the contrary, these vary over time and between cultures and social and economic systems; and both scholars and politicians hold varying views about them.[2]

The *forms* of democracy can vary between, for example, direct and indirect popular government and control: similarly the forms of democratisation (or the means to promote democracy) include, for instance, work within or outside the established political system.

The *scope* of democracy can range from a situation in which the public sector is small to one in which the democratic public sphere embraces virtually everything people have in common (including factories, the various associations of civil society, and perhaps the division of labour within the household). Similarly we may include the extent to which actors promote democratisation beyond a narrowly defined political sphere.

The *content* of democracy is about what actors like to use democratisation and democracy for. The outcome (intended and actual) can vary in terms of efficiency and, for instance, from the promotion of social and economic equality to the establishment of neo-liberal policies (so long as the minimally defined democratic procedures indicated above are

respected). Similarly we should ask what kind of democracy the democratisers are out for and how they intend to use it.

Probably the most important question, however – the one that we
should focus upon – concerns the *pre-conditions* for democracy and
democratisation. In addition to fair elections, and freedom of speech and
association – which go with the minimum definition of democracy itself
– some actors may argue, for instance, that democratisation requires less
socio-economic inequality, while others may say that private property
rights and a capitalist market economy are vital.

The specific answer to the question of pre-conditions depends, of course,
on the scope, forms and content of democracy and democratisation – as
well as on the country or perhaps province being examined. Even so, let
us begin with the conclusions which others have reached on an overarching level.

Back again, then, to the schools in Part 2 – but this time on the basis of
the instrumental question about how earlier research has dealt with,
primarily, the pre-conditions for democracy and democratisation in the
context of Third World development. First, a small repetition of the
explanatory models which are available. Then, a discussion about how
fruitful these models are, what problems need further research, and how
such problems can best be approached.

Democratic and Authoritarian Modernisation

Just three or four decades ago, the predominant view held that capitalist
modernisation and expansion – of an idealised Western sort – was a
fundamental pre-condition for political development and democracy in
developing countries. Both Marxists and non-Marxists carried out broad
society-oriented studies. Those inspired by conventional Marxism
stressed the social and economic structure and the importance of a
domestic bourgeoisie (which could lead the fight for a nation-state and
settle accounts with feudal remnants).[3] Non-Marxists spoke of modern –
as opposed to traditional – values among groups and individuals,
particularly in the middle class.

Soon enough, others revised these perspectives. As we have seen,
Samuel Huntington was among those claiming that social and economic
modernisation did not lead automatically to political development and
democracy, but rather to new social and economic conflicts (which the
old political institutions and organisations were incapable of handling).
'Political order', therefore, had to be created through stable and modern
institutions and organisations (in the worst case, with the help of
modernising military officers), in order to enable the middle class to take
part in government and to prevent popular revolt. Similarly, Eastern-bloc
Marxists took the view that modernisation seldom produced a national

bourgeoisie or working class strong enough to push through a functioning liberal democracy. It was therefore both possible and necessary to bet
on progressive politicians and state administrators (again, in the worst
case, with the assistance of officers), in order that land reform and
industrialisation might be introduced, thus generating stronger popular
forces.

The dependency theorists, we recall, turned all this upside-down.
They argued that capitalism and modernisation did not create the pre-
conditions for democracy at all, but rather for dictatorship. The developing countries were not genuinely independent. The rulers were more
dependent on foreign capital than on the resources and citizens of their
own countries. A sort of permanent state of emergency became unavoidable. In the worst case, people had to take to armed struggle in order to
change the way of things.

Marxist class analysts soon modified this picture, certainly, by trying to
take account of how various organised interests attempted to influence
the state and take advantage of it. Some of these researchers also talked
about an 'overdeveloped' Third World state which had inherited strong
colonial institutions and organisations, and which had become unusually
autonomous in relation to the classes out in society. Yet even if this
approach could help us explain why democracy emerged and survived
in a few countries such as India, the major impact of the analysis was to
contribute to a more refined and dynamic analysis of the authoritarian
systems found in the majority of developing countries.

Finally, many scholars explained the lack of democracy more in terms
of the state (and the social forces acting within it) than in terms of classes
out in society. Neo-classicists spoke of rent-seeking politicians and
bureaucrats who monopolised state organs in their own interest. Many
institutionalists argued that the successful developmental states rested
on autonomous, efficient and authoritarian governance. The inefficiency
and decay of democratic government in such countries as India testified
to the lack of universalist administration and strong political institutions
and organisations. Post-Marxists, finally, pointed to the fact that capitalism in the Third World has often been introduced by forces which
have acquired for themselves the exclusive control of state resources and
regulatory powers – which again presupposed authoritarian governance,
or at least state-dominated corporatism or a combination of populism
and cacique(boss)-democracy.

Neo-Modernism, the Rational Elite, Civil Society and 'Good Governance'

Thus, at the end of the seventies and the start of the eighties – when
democracy began, despite everything, to sprout in the Third World – the

most advanced research was much better at explaining the absence of democracy than democratisation.

The fact that events took the course that they did had some consequences. On the one hand, we may recall, universalist political development approaches rooted in the modernisation paradigm were restored to a place of honour. According to many scholars, actual developments had proved the correctness of the harshly criticised old theses.

For one thing, non-Marxists claim that social and economic modernisation in general, and the growth of a stronger middle class in particular, clearly promotes democracy. In the mid-1980s, as we know, such grand old scholars as Seymour Martin Lipset initiated, together with others, a large-scale US research project on the basis of this approach (albeit in a manner less rigid than in the fifties and sixties, and with a particular focus on effective democratic leadership). Samuel Huntington reappeared with similar claims as well, stressing the importance – naturally – of stable political institutions, organisations and leadership.[4]

On similar grounds, moreover, Marxist theories – which argued that capitalist development is a pre-condition for democracy – attracted attention once more. Some claimed, for example, that political monopolisation and complex and arbitrary administration are an obstacle to forceful capitalist expansion. This may give rise to elite-level negotiations and a degree of liberalisation, which in turn can lead to limited democratisation.[5] In any case, these researchers argue, it is the antagonisms and structures emerging with the growth of capitalism that lay the basis for democratisation.[6] Others put a greater emphasis on the social forces active in such contexts, and on the role of the working class in particular. In this they form a contrast with more conventional modernisation theorists, with their fixation on the middle class and the national bourgeoisie.[7]

On the other hand, many of those who grew up with dependency-oriented analyses of capitalism generating authoritarian rule did not really abandon their long-term structural approaches but rather put them on hold, choosing instead to focus on the actual transitions from authoritarian to more democratic rule. They describe these transitions as an incomplete liberalisation process which takes place during periods of economic and ideological crisis and institutional disintegration.[8] Their explanations, we may recall, focus on how 'hard- and soft-liners' within the elite interact with each other, how they are influenced by the rules of the game, and how they interpret these rules and try to change them. This all varies from country to country, of course, but a common feature is that 'the bourgeoisie, or at least important segments of it, regard the authoritarian regime as "dispensable" . . . either because it has laid the foundation for further capitalist development or because it has demonstrated its incompetence for so doing'. A further common circumstance is the 'resurrection' of civil society.[9]

By contrast, those inspired by neo-classical perspectives did not content themselves with putting their old approaches to one side; rather, they held strictly to their claims about selfish, rent-seeking politicians who nourish 'overpoliticisation' and 'futile' political short cuts to development. They take the view, therefore, that democratisation presupposes the dismantling of the state – except for those functions involving the maintenance of law and order, the protection of the capitalist market economy, and the deepening of civil society (including on the international level). Structural adjustment, the claim goes, is thus a prerequisite for democratisation.

At roughly the same time, political scientists and others developed new institutional and organisational perspectives. The state, they said, is not just the extended arm of the ruling class; it is important in its own right. It has distinct functions and interests of its own (in political stability, for instance, or maintaining a favourable position *vis-à-vis* other states). This in turn requires extensive resources and popular support of some sort – which can make room for a degree of democratisation.

Other scholars, as we have seen, focused more on institutions (in the sense of rules of the game). The result has been a series of studies of how institutional conditions, including new constitutions and electoral systems, affect negotiations between different rational elites during the transition from authoritarian to more democratic rule.[10] In a parallel fashion, many researchers focus on the significance of constitutional governance, stable institutions and organisations, and effective rule, especially now that the main theme has become 'the consolidation of democracy'.[11] One basic prescription would seem to involve the ideas about 'good governance' supported by the World Bank. Another is indicated by the respect shown in the West for the (until recently) stable and efficient institutions and organisations found in the developmental states of East and South-East Asia, including the attempts made to incorporate significant interest groups through co-optation and state–corporative arrangements.

Finally, we should remember the renewed interest in how culture and institutions out in society affect governance and administration. An example may be seen in the argument that social capital – in the form of mutual trust and co-operation among citizens – promotes effective democracy.[12]

How Fruitful are the Explanatory Models of Today?

After this brief repetition of the most important explanatory models, the question before us is how relevant and vital are they?

Let us consider this question with an eye to three common situations in the developing world. The first prevails in countries where nation-state development projects and centralised democratic government are in crisis and transformation – as in, for example, India or Mexico. The second is seen in those many countries where authoritarian rule replaced limited democratic forms of government and thereafter ran aground, and where the middle class led a rebirth of the civil society and elitist democracy that had earlier existed; examples include several countries in Latin America and Africa, and the Philippines as well. The third obtains in countries where authoritarian rule contributed to rapid social and economic development, and where dominant groups claim that too much democratisation risks undermining all that has been achieved; many of the states of East and South-East Asia fit the bill here.

Modernisation and the Middle Class

Let us look first at the non-Marxist thesis that social and economic modernisation and a stronger middle class prepare the way for democracy. Naturally, this approach has much to recommend it.

However, the same processes and social forces also lie behind many of the problems democracy faces today. Much of the economic and political deregulation that has occurred may be unavoidable, but in any event it contributes to a continued weakening of institutions and organisations vital to democracy. Even the Philippines, for example – with its widely appreciated middle-class-led democratisation – continues to be stamped by the elitist boss-democracy of former times, notwithstanding the fact that the social basis of the old system (in the form of political clans and clientelism) is slowly being undermined. A solid new basis for continued democratisation is still missing (as might be provided, for instance, by popularly based organisations which stand for different interests and ideas about how society should be organised, and which keep an eye on their political representatives). And in countries where authoritarian policies have been especially important in the development process, there is often a shortage of the comparatively independent business-men and middle-class groupings that have otherwise provided the basis for the transition from authoritarian to more democratic forms of government.

On the other hand, conventional perspectives inspired by the modernisation paradigm do not always take into account the extremely important role which certain new and well-educated middle-class groups actually play in the process of democratisation. This particularly means journalists, lawyers, teachers, cultural workers, clergy and environmental experts (and female activists from among all such groups) who form independent organisations to defend their rights, their professional integrity, and/or to perform genuine development work (thereby linking up with broader popular needs and aspirations).

The Dynamics and Conflicts of Capitalism

Second, let us consider the Marxist modernisation thesis that capitalism undermines political monopoly and arbitrary rule, and in the process creates a civil society, new conflicts, and above all a working class that pushes through democratic changes. Of course there is also much in this.

At the same time, it is difficult to generalise from European experiences to the Third World, especially in the case of countries and areas where the political sphere is and has been of particular importance in capitalist development. Even if deregulation, privatisation and attempts to increase the efficiency of state administration are or have been on the agenda in the great majority of developing countries, former power-holders usually succeed in reorganising their networks and in keeping the resources they have captured. The division of labour and the patterns of subordination and exploitation are very complex. Even in the newly industrialising countries – such as those in East and South-East Asia – we are far from a classical protracted industrial and cultural transformation in general, and the emergence of a large and comparatively homogeneous working class in particular. So even if the workers will be likely to play an exceedingly important role in democratisation in the Third World, we must identify that which distinguishes these cases from the specific historical instances forming the basis for the generalisations generally accepted about the connection between capitalism and democracy.[13] This is necessary if we are to be able, in the best case, to revise perspectives and to test generalisations.

Elite-led Transitions

Third, we might take a look at the studies done of transitions from authoritarian to more democratic government which emerged from negotiations between political elites (yielding a sort of 'crafted instant democracy'). This is quite clearly a fruitful approach for analysing many developing countries. Elite horse-trading has been a prominent feature of the transition from authoritarian to more democratic rule in such countries as Chile, South Africa and even the Philippines (Marcos's forced departure and peaceful demonstrations notwithstanding) and Indonesia. Recently, moreover, the special characteristics of many African transitions have been analysed in terms of less negotiations among the elite (with their roots in extensive private business communities) and more rallying of the masses behind politicians who try to get access to the relatively extensive resources of the state and its patronage systems.[14]

Those elitist perspectives, however, disregard the lengthy and far-reaching opposition – and constructive work too – of ordinary people which had prepared the way for (limited) democratisation by way of elite negotiations and contending politicians rallying the masses. Nor do they provide us with any real help in understanding why the popular opposition has so rarely been able either to influence (still less to participate in) the transition itself, or to play an important role afterwards (as far as the so-called consolidation and deepening of democracy is concerned).

This lack of popular inclusion and influence also applies in part to countries where the nation-state development project and centralised democratic rule are in crisis and transformation (for example, India and Mexico). Here also the most significant attempts to recreate and to deepen democracy come from popular action groups and grassroots organisations – which seldom are really capable of influencing the political system, or even becoming properly integrated into it.

Finally, we must again recall that, in countries where authoritarian rule contributed (and to some extent still contributes) to rapid social and economic development, we usually cannot find that combination of businessmen and the middle class on the one hand, and a relatively independent civil society on the other, which otherwise has provided the basis for an 'instant democracy' emerging from negotiations between elites. In those authoritarian developmental states we may rather expect a combination of limited liberalisation through a combination of the Latin American horse-trading between various power-holders and the African top-down mobilising of the masses behind politicians who try to get access to state resources (often by way of nourishing ethnic and religious loyalties). At present, Indonesia is a good example; maybe Nigeria will follow.

The State versus Civil Society

Fourth, let us examine the liberal thesis of the state versus civil society. No one denies, of course, that free citizens and associations are a constituent part of democracy (or at least a pre-condition for it).

On the other hand, I would argue, theories which hold that deepening civil society in itself promotes democracy are not fruitful. Even when elite-led democratisation has been combined with the middle-class-led resurrection of civil society, this has mainly prepared the way for political boss-rule at the local level and personalised populism at the national (as, for example, in the Philippines). In countries with disintegrating nation-state projects and centralised democratic rule (for example, India), liberalisation is more likely to nourish clientelism, group-specific organising, and populist mobilisation on the basis of religious or cultural identity. And as we have seen, where authoritarian regimes still hold out, privatisation and deregulation have mainly enabled most of the old power-holders to reorganise their networks and legalise their virtually private possession of the greater part of the resources they had already earlier controlled (this is even so in so-called socialist countries like China). The separation between the state and civil society remains unclear. The special role of popular efforts in civil society, finally, are also open to criticism. To the details of this, however, we shall return in the concluding chapter of the book.

There is also an international aspect to the thesis of the state versus civil society. Many claim that globalisation and international support for human rights undermine authoritarian regimes and foster democracy – especially when associations in civil society collaborate over borders. Naturally it is easy, on the one hand, to agree to this proposition, at least if one recalls the exposed position in which pro-democracy actors still find themselves under regimes such as the Nigerian or Indonesian. On the other hand, it is important to remember that one of democracy's pre-conditions is a clearly demarcated demos – consisting of citizens or members with the right to govern themselves. As far as I know, there are no examples – at any rate hitherto –[15] of any reasonably genuine process of democratisation which has not been related to the nation-state, or to a relatively autonomous region of local government within the same.[16]

'Good Governance'

Fifth, let us look at the new institutionalism and 'good governance'. These have spread the crucial insight that the pre-conditions of democracy are not just social and economic in character – many organisational and political-institutional factors are necessary too.

Yet, even if – needless to say – no one opposes the demand for effective and unimpeachable governance, the real problem is to discover the conditions under which such governance can actually emerge. There is a shortage of such studies. As pointed out in Chapter 10, even the recent World Bank report on the state fails to identify driving social, economic and political forces. Instead, 'good governance' is offered up – at best together with 'instant democracy' – much as neo-liberal market solutions have been hawked the world over by IMF economists for quite some time now.

In other words, institutionalists who do search for the causes of 'good governance' tend, moreover, to consider the problem from above, much as Samuel Huntington did.[17] Popular opposition from below easily becomes a disturbing or 'dysfunctional' element. Effective market governance in East Asia is often explained, for instance, in terms of the autonomy of the state over troublesome groups and 'special interests' out in society. Robert Wade, we may recall, even concludes his celebrated book on this subject with the recommendation that 'effective institutions of political authority [should be developed] before, [and] corporatist institutions as or before, the system is democratised'.[18] As already indicated, moreover, such authors mainly relate ineffective governance in such countries as India to 'overpoliticisation', and to 'soft' political and administrative institutions and organisations which are unable to handle wide-ranging demands or to execute political decisions.[19] Actually, the recent World Bank report on 'good government' tends to restrict demo-cratisation to the introduction of elections. Efficient state institutions in consultation with co-operating people in civil societies are regarded as more important.

Social Capital

Sixth, we may recall the renewed interest in civic virtues, confidence and co-operation – as collected under the heading of 'social capital'. Such things are clearly an important aspect of the forms of democracy, and they are important for outcomes as well.

That a democratic culture promotes democracy is, of course, a self-evident truth. Many of the researchers in question argue, however, that they are searching for practices and attitudes which can promote demo-cratisation, deepen an already existing democracy, and render it more effective. It still remains, though, to explain the growth of social capital in a manner which is persuasive – which amounts to more than just citing contestable historical continuities. And even if social capital is seen as a pre-condition for some kind of 'good democracy' – and under certain conditions there may be a good deal in that – there is something worrying about how the social-capital school – like the Marxist capital-logic school of old – tends to explain politics in an essentially reduction-ist way, without devoting any attention worth mentioning to decisive intermediary variables such as political activity, strategic action and organisation. As already mentioned, we shall return to a critique of the civil society and social capital paradigm in the concluding chapter.

Which Research Problems Merit Continued Attention?

Against the background of the oversights and deficiencies noted in the discussion of established perspectives on democratisation, there is reason to highlight the following ten factors and circumstances as especially worthy of future study:

1. What are the pre-conditions for consolidating and deepening demo-cratisation processes led by the middle class? Even such exemplary cases as the Philippines, after all, still recall the elitist boss-democracy of former times.
2. What will happen in those countries where authoritarian regimes contributed to rapid social and economic development, while at the same time that combination of businessmen and the middle class on the one hand, and a relatively independent civil society on the

other, which have provided the circumstances for democracy else-where cannot be found? What are the pre-conditions for the emergence of a reasonably autonomous civil society alongside a politically injected type of capitalist development?

3. What is the character and importance of organisations among the new well-educated middle-class groups, especially when these connect up with broader popular aspirations and demands?

4. Is there any prospect that the workers in countries characterised by a politically injected capitalist expansion can come to play as important a role in democratisation as their counterparts once did in Europe?

5. How does widespread popular struggle pave the way for, and how does it condition, elitist mobilisation of mass support and/or elite negotiation over transition from authoritarian rule and on to further democratisation?

6. How is it the case that reasonably genuine popular forces have so rarely been able to influence, still less participate in, the transition from authoritarian to more democratic rule, or to play an important role thereafter in consolidating and deepening democracy? What are the pre-conditions that must be fulfilled, in other words, to enable popular forces to be integrated into the political system, rather than being incorporated into it by such means as clientelism, populism and state-corporatism?

7. How do globalisation and international support for human rights and democracy affect the emergence – indispensable for every process of democratisation – of a clearly demarcated demos?

8. Under what conditions can so-called 'good governance' emerge? What are the driving forces? What is the relation then between efforts to foster, on the one hand, effective institutionalisation and organisation from above, and, on the other, alternative strivings and demands from below?

9. Under what conditions does social capital develop within different societies and groups? In what ways does it affect democracy and democratisation?

10. What are the pre-conditions (structural and institutional as well as, for example, ideological) that must be fulfilled in order for popular movements to be able to converge with each other? What conditions are requisite to their generating such overarching questions, perspectives and organisations as can lead to a more effective and comprehensive politics of democratisation?

Notes

1 The following is based on Törnquist, 'Whither Studies of Asian Democratisation' *kasarinlan* and *Economic and Political Weekly.*

2 For an interesting discussion, see Markoff, *Waves of Democracy.*

3 Including Moore, *Social Origins of Dictatorship and Democracy.*

4 Diamond et al., *Democracy in Developing Countries*; and Huntington, *The Third Wave.*

5 Cf., for example, Hewison et al., *Southeast Asia in the 1990s.*

6 Cf., for example, Therborn, 'The Rule of Capital and the Rise of Democracy'.

7 See especially Rueschemeyer et al., *Capitalist Development and Democracy.*

8 O'Donnell and Schmitter, *Transitions from Authoritarian Rule.*

9 Ibid., pp. 27 and 48ff.

10 See, for example, Przeworski, *Democracy and the Market.*

11 See, for example, Mainwaring et al., *Issues in Democratic Consolidation.*

12 See Putnam, *Making Democracy Work*; and, for example, Agora project, *Democracy and Social Capital in Segmented Societies*; and Evans, 'Introduction: Development Strategies Across the Public–Private Divide' and 'Government Action, Social Capital and Development'.

13 For some recent attempt in this direction, see Brandell, *Workers in Third-World Industrialisation*; Hadiz, *Workers and State in New Order Indonesia*; and Andræ and Beckman, *Union Power in the Nigerian Textile Industry.*

14 Bratton and van de Walle, *Democratic Experiments in Africa.*

15 Not even in studies like Held, *Democracy and the Global Order.*

16 Plus, of course, democratisation within various associations with a clearly demarcated membership.

17 Huntington, 'Political Development and Political Decay' and *Political Order in Changing Societies.*

18 Wade, *Governing the Market.* My combination of Wade's recommendations 8 and 9, pp. 372–7.

19 Cf. Kohli, *Democracy and Discontent.*

13 From Civil Society and Social Capital To the Politics of Democratisation

The important but rather overlooked problems in the debate on democratisation that we pointed to in Chapter 12 have one common denominator: they all require that we look at democracy in more depth, at its basic building blocks. So the next question is, how do we actually go about studying the process of democratisation from below?[1]

As we know, the paradigm in vogue is of civil society, and of civic community generating social capital. Is this relevant and fruitful? I do not think so. I shall dispute the paradigm in four sections: first by recalling its general theoretical weaknesses; second by questioning its relevance in the Third World; third by arguing that it nevertheless does not address the most urgent problems; fourth by showing how empirical results from my own comparative studies of popular efforts at democratisation in civil society speak against the theses. Finally, therefore, I shall argue instead for an alternative approach in terms of the study of politics of the democratisation.

Before going further, the reader might wish to return to the general presentation of the paradigm in Chapter 10, in the sub-section entitled 'Civil Society and Social Capital'. Hence, it may suffice to give just a brief summary of the general theses on democracy here:[2]

- *Civil society* – or independent associations and public communication – is a pre-condition for democracy.
- The stronger (or more dense and vibrant) the civil society, the better the democracy.
- Just as civil society is threatened by 'too much politics' and an extended state, so is democracy.
- The *social capital* proponents, however, argue that civil society is not enough, rather it takes a civic community.
- Democratisation in general, and democratic performance in particular, is due to social capital.
- Social capital is roughly the same as inter-personal trust, enabling co-operation among people and their keeping track of government.
- Trust varies with unhierarchical associational life, including football clubs and bird-watching societies.
- This kind of associational life is due to historical 'path dependence'. (The original argument, for instance, is that the dense associational

life in northern Italy is rooted in the late-medieval city-state culture.)

- Therefore, if one wishes to promote democratic governance, one should support networks and, for instance, co-operative community development schemes.

General Theoretical Weaknesses

To use a common formulation, civil society and social capital may be fine as normative concepts (and personally I subscribe to most of the ideals), but I do not find them to be effective analytical tools in studies of democratisation.[3]

First, as was already pointed out in Chapter 10, this paradigm sets aside relations of power in civil society and assumes citizens to be equal. Yet most social science research indicates that conflicts over power, related for instance to class and gender, and differences, associated for instance with ethnicity and religion, are absolutely fundamental – including in processes of democratisation.

Second, hardly anyone would dispute the importance of associations and public discourse that are relatively independent of the state, and, even better, of the market as well – but the processes behind all this are also set aside by the paradigm. Historically civil society signifies a *politically created* society of citizens (excluding slaves, mobs, natives and immigrants – and, of course, distinguished from anarchy). The Greeks explicitly talked of *politike koinonia*, political community, and the Romans distinguished *societas civilis*, society of citizens, from non-citizen societies like those based on residence or kinship. Hence one should be careful in contrasting or even inciting politics and society against each other. On the other hand it is fruitful, of course, to distinguish between civil government of the society as a whole (including through parties and parliamentarians) on the one hand, and the administrative and military state apparatuses on the other. We need to allow for the power that flows out of hierarchies, legal authority, guns, common resources and the executive control of them. But even in the few cases where civil society theorists make this distinction, there is a lack of interest in the extent to which governments are in command of their state apparatuses, and citizens are in command of their governments. For instance, in the almost 800-page standard work on civil society and politics by Cohen and Arato there is hardly any theoretical or empirical reference to the pro-democratising effects of close to a century of North European co-operation between popular movements, government and state at various levels; *parts* of which have also been labelled social corporatism and associative democracy. Yet I believe most of us would agree on the difference between state/civil society relations in well-established democracies and in dictatorships like Poland under the Communists, or Latin America under the juntas.

Third, there is ambiguity on the importance of the economy. Most analysts agree that modern civil society emerges with the rise of relatively independent socio-economic relations as against the family, the feudal lord and the absolutist state. Some add the mixed blessing of capitalism in terms of its anti-social effects. But the civil society paradigm offers no precise tools to analyse these dynamics. In this field it is rather the Marxist-oriented framework that is most sharp and critical. It stresses the atomisation of people under a 'bourgeois' division of labour and a social plurality which, if not resisted politically, tends to produce bureaucratic authoritarianism rather than a political plurality. But even in Cohen and Arato's rather radical theorisation of civil society, this is hardly discussed nor made use of. On the contrary, it is *assumed* that the best way of fighting the negative effects of capitalism is to further deepen *the same civil society that capitalism is giving birth to*, and to bet on 'people themselves' and their autonomy (including their special identities) as against, and in order to influence, the state and politics.

Fourth, the existence and strength of civil society are poor historical explanations for democracy. Civil society has coexisted with very different types of regime – including fascism in Italy and Germany. To take but one additional example, the very vibrant Swedish civil society with its deep historical roots stands in sharp contrast to the country's comparatively late democratisation.

Civil rights, of course, are of vital importance for any democrat, and once the right to vote is added, rights and suffrage together form much of the basis for the particular way of governing society at large, its resources and its organs, that we call democratic. But civil rights are never the same as democracy. Before becoming part of democracy they are rather elements of constitutionalism. And even though the free 'space' of some civil rights usually turns into a hotbed for popular participation and struggle for democracy, we should remember that democracy has often come about through illegal means and despite the lack of civil rights. Anyway, democratic struggles within or outside such a liberal space are more a question of socio-economic conflicts (such as on class) and of politics aiming to alter the rules, as well as the division of labour and resources (at least to such an extent that both civil and political rights become universal), than a question of civil society associations to amuse and help each other, no matter how important, within the framework of existing rules and inequalities.

It is true that civil society activists who fought the totalitarian regimes in Poland and Latin America consciously limited themselves to the strengthening of civil society, and to the democratising of some of its associations, in order thus to influence and undermine the regimes – as it was impossible to conquer the state, fight the armies, and democratise the society and its institutions as a whole. But it is equally true that the very processes of transition to democracy soon called for political organisations and actors – and that many well-intentioned and hard-working grassroots activists were thus set aside. Some of the leading civil society theorists themselves began to write about this.[4]

What, then, of the extended ideas on the importance for democracy of a strong civil society in terms of vibrant associational life in civic communities; an associational life that is said to be due to path dependence on old city-state cultures, to generate social capital in the form of trust which facilitates interpersonal co-operation, and in the final instance to produce good democratic government as well?

First, one may question the 'big bang'[5] path dependence explanation. The thesis does not help us to analyse the reproduction of history – to explain what survives and why – and to account for the fact that seemingly similar phenomena like associations do not necessarily have the same function (for example, to promote democratic government) under different conditions. Much of the thesis, as we know, is based on Robert Putnam's argument that the successful institutional reforms in northern Italy are because it has inherited more social capital than the south.[6] In fact, however, scholars of Italy's history convincingly argue that Putnam has not accounted for changes over time, that the degree of civicness is much more fluctuating than stated, that vital norms are fairly similar in the regions, and that the critical differences between them were rather 'megaconstraints imposed by geography, location (earthquake areas in the south), economics, and politics'.[7] For instance, according to Sidney Tarrow, 'every regime that governed southern Italy from the Norman establishment of a centralised monarchy in the twelfth century to the unified government which took over there in 1861 was foreign and governed with a logic of colonial exploitation, [and] southern Italy's semicolonial status [did not] suddenly disappear with unification'.[8] The only plausible reason why a well-read scholar like Putnam could miss this, Tarrow argues, is that there is something wrong with 'the model with which he turned to history'.[9]

Second, yet other and neglected factors seem to be significant – both in order to account for the form of government (including democracy) and the very rise of social capital. How can it be explained, for instance, that Sicily, by 1922, had the 'highest number of locally constituted and operated farmer cooperatives and the second highest number of locally established . . . rural credit institutions in Italy'? Why did the labour movement in the Capitanata region of Apulia really fight fascism and why was it 'stronger and more powerful than its counterpart in Emilia Romagna'?[10] Why did fascism emerge in Putnam's northern civic and therefore inherently pro-democratic communities in the first place? What of their contemporary scandals over bad governance and corruption – and of the rise of civic associations in the south?[11] Perhaps most important of all: what of the deliberate and powerful efforts of the Italian Communists, and many Socialists and Christian Democrats too, in vital parts of the north since the late nineteenth century to constitute and work through civic associations?[12] Given the weakness of the path dependence explanation, it is plausible that this kind of politics is of vital importance both in the process of democratisation and in the creating of social capital.[13]

In other words, the critique is both concerned with the rise and the effect of social capital. Third, therefore, one may specifically question how and why social capital would translate into democratisation and efficient democratic government. In Putnam's study there are correlations but few causal chains and no agents of change. Why and how would football clubs always promote co-operation outside the clubs and in wider societal fields? What is 'the causal chain between bird watching and political activism'?[14] How far are people capable of really standing up against non-performing governments and suggesting other policies? Again, how and why do Putnam and his followers exclude other plausible explanations for all this – including the state and politics?

Finally, why would civic community demands have to be democratic? On a closer look, one finds, actually, that the dependent variable of the social capital analysts is neither democratisation nor democratic practice (despite the titles of books and applications for funds) but government performance – which is not part of the 'normal' definitions of democracy but rather used to be stressed by instrumental Leninists, among others.[15] The content or outcome of democracy, of course, has some bearing on its consolidation, but as we know from fascism in Europe or the pre-crisis East and South-East Asia, government performance is not altogether clearly related to a democratic type of regime.

Problems of Generalisation

Applying the civil society/social capital paradigm outside its primarily European framework also means that historical realities tend to be set aside. For instance, while Göran Therborn's studies on the rise of modernity and democracy point to the relevance of civil society (and even civil war) in the European framework, they also make clear that the shaping of citizen societies, or the demos, in the New World was rather directed against former colonists and natives; that the externally induced modernisation and subsequent steps towards democracy in countries like Japan was mainly carried out through the state from above; and that the initial modernisation in the colonies was first imposed by conquerors but later turned against them by nationalists, who often added initial democratisation and always made use of the state and politics.[16]

On contemporary Africa, for instance, Mahmood Mamdani has recently demonstrated forcefully the problematic usage of the civil society/social capital paradigm in view of the legacy of late colonialism.[17] 'Actually existing civil societies' were primarily in urban areas; the rest, the subjects, were under customary rule, which, however, was integrated, refined and made use of by the colonisers. Much of the nationalist struggle was about deracialising the civil societies – whereafter the lives of subjects were either governed through clientelism or 'enlightened and developmental' one-party states. Democratisation among the subjects at the grassroots level was rarely even attempted. The few real efforts are still lacking firm co-ordination with urban civil society movements. And equally isolated civil society movements, including many of the recent pro-democracy ones, either turn shallow and formalistic – or approach, again, the lives of subjects through potentially explosive clientelistic linkages based on, for instance, ethnicity or religion. Similar stories could be told of many other parts of the Third World. (Of Asia, though, one might add that there were more and stronger, but not necessarily more successful, efforts to create real citizens and promote democratisation through 'anti-feudal' rural struggles.)

Currently it is true, of course, that commerce and capitalist relations are also spreading. But this far from always comes with the kind of politically rather independent business and middle classes, and the relative separation between the state and civil society, with which modernisation is often associated. Even before the crisis in dynamic Indonesia, for instance, there was some dismantling of the state, but primarily by factions which monopolised its resources even earlier, rather than by strong new capitalists and members of the middle classes from 'outside' (who usually become partners instead). Surviving rulers and executives reorganise their 'fiefdoms' and networks, and are able to legalise the privatisation of formerly public resources which they have already laid their hands on. In fact, this privatisation is making it increasingly difficult to regulate daily transactions and conflicts, not to mention political succession. Hence this is also the background to much of the current crisis in the area.

Finally, the specific attempts to export the social capital thesis are up against additional problems, primarily the inability of the thesis to account for the legacy of late colonialism (already displayed in Putnam's study of the relations between northern and southern Italy) and its difficulties in handling social capital related to ethnicity and religion, or coexisting with authoritarian rulers like the Indonesian ones. Moreover, the adherents of the thesis do not even put it to the test for its much-criticised path dependence explanation of the rise of social capital and for its negligence of 'intermediary' variables between social capital and efficient democratic governance (including socio-economic dynamics, government intervention, and political organisation). Just about the only thing they ask is whether their thesis is better than outdated and similarly deterministic ideas about connections between economic development and democracy.[18] In fact, as already mentioned in Chapter 12, one may even equate the social capital school of the nineties with the capital logic school of the seventies.

Dubious Relevance

Social science is also about societal relevance, beyond the curiosity of applying and testing theses around the globe. Do researchers and their analytical tools really tackle existing and vital societal dilemmas? Since the eighties, the civil society paradigm (later on supplemented with the theses about social capital) has been widely acclaimed. This is not the place to discuss why,[19] but at the very least the paradigm is not particularly helpful if one considers, as many of us do, the lack of popular political organisation and representation based on interests and ideologies to be the most serious problem in current democratisation. It is seen as the most serious problem because:

- the genuine efforts at democratisation which emerged in the course of the liberation struggles were undermined both by the deterioration of the movements themselves and by the rise of new authoritarian forces which repressed the movements and reduced or redirected ambitious land reforms and health and educational programmes, all initially aimed at turning subjects into citizens;
- the then emerging civil movements which contributed to the undermining of the authoritarian regimes (as in Latin America and the Philippines during the eighties) were unable to generate efficient *political* organisations and representatives – wherefore the inevitable horse-trading associated with most transitions to democracy was captured by the traditional political elites, their clientelism, and their (sometimes) emerging state-corporatism;
- the related problems of 'consolidating' democracy may best be summarised, by Adam Przeworski et al., as 'something more profound . . . than institutional factors', namely 'the absence of collective projects, of socially integrating ideologies, of clearly identifiable political forces, of crystallised structures of interests to be represented';[20]
- still persisting authoritarian rule, even in dynamic East and South-East Asia, goes hand in hand with the rise of capitalism, general modernisation, elements of civil society, and the creation of social capital – but not necessarily with democratisation.

The Weakness of Politics Against Fragmentation

Finally, the new paradigm is not only questionable but outright insufficient if there is anything to my own results from some eight years of
'going down' to renewal-oriented popular organisations in the field;
'going down' to these organisations (since many old parties, strategies
and scholarly theories are becoming increasingly invalid)[21] in order to
study over time the processes of democratisation from below through the
movements' ways of promoting similar ideas of civil society/social
capital *and* democratisation under very different conditions;[22]

- in the till recently economically dynamic but politically repressive
  Indonesia, where the old popular movements have been eliminated
  and new ones are only beginning to appear;
- in Asia's Latin America, the Philippines, where the old Left has
  become irrelevant and new movements are trying to make their
  way;
- in the most impressive case of attempts to renew the radical and
  democratic nation-state development project from below through
  popular movements *and* government policies, that is in the south-
  western Indian state of Kerala.

The paradigm seems to be questionable and insufficient because in all
these three cases the scholarly puzzle and the societal dilemma is, that
all the organisations that I have followed have primarily had problems
with uniting fragmented interests, ideas, groups and actions. This is

- despite a relatively strong civil society in the Philippines and perhaps
  the Third World's strongest civil society in Kerala; and
- despite the organisations themselves having done their best to promote in most cases civil society and in all cases social capital.

So the decisive problem of democratisation is not one of civil society
and social capital but of weak politics of democratisation. In other words,
that is, a lack of the ability to get people to unite around common
interests and ideas and, in the process, to fight for democratisation.
Moreover, there are strong indications that social capital does not emerge
on its own in civil society but through deliberate political work and
efforts.

Let me give some general examples from the three contexts: Indonesia,
the Philippines and Kerala.

Indonesia[23]

The basic problem for the democracy movement in Indonesia is that new
dissidents are isolated from the people in general. This is because of the

destruction of the broad popular movements in the mid-sixties and the authoritarian rule during Suharto's New Order. Till recently it was even impossible to form membership-based autonomous organisations. Aside from religious organisations, there are hardly any movements among people themselves to relate to. The same holds true in terms of critical ideologies and historical consciousness. Most of the dissident groups have had to work from above and out of the main urban centres, where a certain degree of protection was and is available from friends and temporary allies in influential positions. In this way, fragmented layers of dissidents have developed over the years.

The expansion of capitalism may indirectly promote democratisation, but is a double-edged sword. On the one hand, the expansion is related both to authoritarian state intervention and to a division of labour that often breaks down old class alliances and gives rise to a multiplicity of interests and movements. On the other hand, even limited liberalisation has created some space which may allow a few people to try to partially improve their standard of living by different local efforts – rather than always having to grab political power first and thereafter rely on state intervention. For many years, this local space and this need to overcome socio-economic fragmentation have spurred on pro-democracy work from below. Despite everything, it has thus been possible for a lot of development-oriented NGOs to relate to new social classes in society, and for a new generation of radical students to relate to peasants (hard hit by evictions) and new industrial workers. Hence the new movements are potentially significant and more than a product of the global wave of democracy and some quarrels within Jakarta's political theatre – they are also conditioned by the expansion of capital and the new classes thus emerging.

Moreover, there has been a tendency since the early nineties to link up alternative development and human rights work in civil society with politics. Major groupings try their best to relate specific issues and special interests to more general perspectives. But in doing so they also tend to get stuck in either their limited kind of politicisation with some social foundation at the grassroots, or their attempts at broader perspectives without much social basis – finally even causing trouble for each other, and for their followers.

Hence, they themselves were not able to generate a democratic opening. Instead, 'external' rallying points gave and give rise to more general movements for transition from authoritarian rule. And within such a broader movement many of the outright democrats have related to legally accepted populist democrats, while others have held on to fragmented activism and development work, or insisted on 'consistent' top-down party building.

This is what happened in mid-1996 when the government ousted moderate opposition leader Megawati Sukarnoputri, while many genuine democrats tried to relate to the recognised political system by mobilising as many potential voters as possible behind her in the face of the 1997 elections. Finally the regime displayed its incapacity to reform itself by cracking down on demonstrators and the democracy movement in general with brutal force (thus ironically generating ethnic and religious riots instead). But simultaneously the basic weakness of the movement itself became equally obvious – its fragmentation and its separation between top-down activists who tend to 'run offside' and grassroots activists who have not yet been able to generate interest-based mass organisations from below.

At the time of writing, the economic and political crisis has accentuated this. Even though the market, most business leaders, the IMF, the World Bank and the international media were finally against the Suharto regime, nobody found an alternative to it. For many years they had all boosted the regime and its general policies. This helped to generate increasingly powerful semi-private vested interests, who were directly or indirectly dependent on Suharto's patronage; it undermined all attempts at building institutions and organisations that could have paved the way for social contracts, compromises among civil, religious and military reformists, and orderly succession; and it sustained the weak position of the democracy movement, making it almost impossible to build mass-based representative organisations (such as trade unions) and, of course, political parties – beyond movements based on religious and ethnic loyalties.

The Philippines[24]

Probably the most astounding breakthrough for the Third World's new democratic middle-class uprisings took place in the Philippines in February 1986. Peaceful mass demonstrations and protests against massive electoral rigging incapacitated the military and brought down the Marcos regime. The Communist-led 'national democrats' and their mainly peasant-based New People's Army, who until then had continuously gained strength, swiftly lost the initiative. Corazon Aquino became the new president. Economic and political liberties were saluted. The Philippines became in vogue in the international aid market. Almost immediately, however, the many NGOs and popular movements that had contributed to the undermining of the regime lost ground. Even today the polity continues to be almost a caricature of the individualistic, personality-oriented and ideology-resistant American settler-democracy – which was exported to the former US colony and was then conformed with and taken advantage of by feudal-like clans and bosses. Of course, much of the old socio-economic basis of the restored Philippine 'cacique democracy' is falling apart, but new solid forms are failing to appear; though there was, at least till the current crisis, some economic progress and relative political stability at the fringes of the dynamic countries of

East and South-East Asia. The widely esteemed middle-class democratisation, however, still has no solid foundation, including a reasonably clear-cut representation of different interests and ideas for societal change.

The most vital question, therefore, is whether and how new popular movements and organisations could instead become significant in anchoring democracy. For most of the old 'national democrats', political democratisation in general and electoral politics in particular were simply not meaningful. In the early nineties I decided instead to follow the experiences of renewal-oriented sections of the Left.[25] None of them were parties but rather significant groups promoting slightly different ideas about 'new politics' and linking up with like-minded cause-oriented organisations, NGOs and unions. In the face of the 1992 elections three of them formed an electoral movement which adopted an agenda generated by many different progressive groupings as its own programme. The key-words were 'people's interest', 'participatory democracy', 'sustainable development', and 'genuine structural reform'. In the spirit of realism, leading members also brokered an alliance with the liberal electoral coalition, with respected senator Salonga as its presidential candidate. It is true that most movement activists were eager to stress that the new political efforts were subordinate to their basic tasks as, for instance, unionists or NGO-workers 'in support of people's own initiatives' and various forms of extra-parliamentary pressure politics. But now they really wanted to supplement and make use of all this to mobilise votes for progressive political representatives.

The results, however, indicated that the certified capacity of the new movements and associated organisations to carry out actions, conduct alternative development work, nourish civil society and support 'ideal' community networks and co-operation could not be transformed into votes and a more widespread and dynamic politics of democratisation. For instance, most activists gave priority to their 'normal' progressive work independently of partisan and especially electoral politics. Many groupings did not link up with the new efforts at all. It was an uphill task to convince radical people, whom the Left had been telling for years and years that it did not matter which way they voted, that this time it would really make a difference. As a result, rival candidates gained a lot of votes even from people who had otherwise fought against them – for instance, within a union or an action group or co-operative. Collective interests, such as those ascribed to peasants, workers or co-operative members, were usually not strong enough to generate votes for progressive candidates. Outright vote-buying could not be resisted even in the then stronghold of the huge co-operative in Tarlac, led by the dissenting and retired legendary founder of the New People's Army, 'Dante' Buscayno. And as the electoral movement basically carried the same issues that its constituent groupings were otherwise used to emphasising in their extra-parliamentary work, and paid little attention to how one should govern public resources and implement their great general ideas, the field was open instead to populist candidates and clientelist politics.

In view of these experiences most leading activists talked of the need to institutionalise the electoral movement, but little happened. In the face of the 1995 elections, moreover, progressive groups and movements had further disintegrated. The renewal-oriented organisations were still there but limited themselves to supporting various 'reasonable' individual candidates and to local efforts where there should be more space for progressive grassroots organisations and NGOs, thanks to the decentralisation of state powers. Simultaneously, however, the implementation in the mid-nineties of the Local Government Code also paved the way for traditional bosses and their client organisations. It is true that much experience has now been gained, that civil society is stronger, and that social capital has been promoted. But the basic problem is still to transform fragmented interests, groups and actions into an extended politics of democratisation. At the time of writing (before the 1998 elections) it remains to be seen, for instance, how much work will be put into the fairly new permanent political vehicle, '*Akbayan!* – Citizens' Action Party', and what may come out of it. Many sections of the movement seem to bet instead on sectoral representation and to mobilise support behind various traditional politicians in (at best) exchange for certain 'pro-people policies'.

Kerala[26]

Kerala is different. It has won international recognition for having accomplished, in addition to stable democracy, comparatively high levels of health, education and social welfare, despite a gross national product per capita that is lower than the Indian average. This has been related to a long history of an unusually vibrant civil society (much of which would now be called social capital) with deep roots, particularly in the south, in various socio-religious reform movements and later on in many other citizen associations as well, such as co-operatives and a library movement. This Kerala model of human development, despite slow growth, is no longer valid because of stagnant growth and India's structural adjustment, among other reasons. But a new generation of civil society associations, including the impressive People's Science Movement (KSSP), has been vital in generating huge campaigns for civil action and community development co-operation. Since the late seventies there have been forceful campaigns against environmental destruction and for literacy, decentralisation, community-based group farming and resource mapping. This has also generated further democratisation and has positively effected government performance. At present, for instance, genuine decentralisation and an absolutely unique process of

planning from below is going on with extensive popular participation.[27]

This, however, is only one and a sometimes distorted side of the coin.
One must also add that the positive results vary over time – and that
they (given the economic constraints) vary much more with popular
politics and government policies than with the vibrancy of civil society
or the (roughly estimated) degree of social capital.

In a comparative Indian perspective, to begin with, Amartaya Sen and
Jean Dréze have recently concluded that 'determined public action'
explains the positive human development in Kerala as compared with
the less impressive West Bengal and miserable (but economically partly
dynamic) Uttar Pradesh. The liberation of economic initiatives, they
argue, must therefore be accompanied by more, not less, government
intervention in favour of public action.[28]

In addition to this, let us discuss Putnam's claim that it is difficult to
test the competing hypothesis mentioned earlier that radical politics
rather than path dependent social capital explains both citizen co-
operation and good democratic government – that this is difficult
because leftists have never even come to power in southern Italy, and
only then would it have been possible to study their performance.[29]
However we may now do it in Kerala and West Bengal.

In Kerala the strong leftist movement is rooted in the former British
Malabar in the north – with much less civil society and social capital than
in the subordinated princely states of Cochin and Travancore in the
south. Thanks to popular pressure and state intervention, those socialists
and Communists have not only managed to implement India's most
consistent land reform in the state as a whole, but also to create more
civic communities in the previously so feudal north than in the south
where, for instance, caste identities still play a more important role. Even
right now a new massive campaign for popular planning from below
seems to be more successful in rural than urban areas, as well as around
the Trichur district in the centre and further north than in the old civil
societies of the south.

Similarly, the Communists in West Bengal do not only have their main
base in rural areas with deep feudal roots, but have also, right there and
since the mid-seventies, managed to generate India's most impressive
democratic decentralisation, and a good deal of community co-operation
and development too (despite using some alternative patronage and
many top-down policies, as compared with Kerala). This is a bit more
than one can say of the eastern part of Bengal, Bangladesh, where, in the
late-seventies, there existed similar landlordism and ideas about democratic decentralisation, but where thereafter emerged a myriad of voluntary associations (promoted by all kinds of foreign agencies in favour of
civil society and social capital) rather than forceful democratic
Communists.[30]

Back in Kerala again, as should be clear by now, it was thus the broad, radical and politicised popular movements beyond communalism that from about the twenties and onwards generated much of the democratisation and positive human development in the state, both from outside and later on also from inside the state government and administration. Despite the otherwise impressive land reform, however, stagnant growth and civic co-operation now constitute a major problem. But this problem is primarily related to the consistently bourgeois character of the reform. A positive outcome was that there were far more independent citizens than in West Bengal – a negative one was the economically rather unco-operative individuals and families. Hence, while intensive political organisation and state intervention survived, this 'old' organisation and politicisation was increasingly affected by privatised and atomised economic activities and interests – soon extending beyond farming into commerce, real estate, etc. So even though many now talk of 'over-politicisation', this is only true in the sense that atomised economic actors often make selfish and unproductive use of state and conventional politics. The root cause is, thus, privatisation and atomisation causing a lack of co-operation among the producers and the citizens at various levels. And the remedying of such problems in turn, as we shall see in a moment, actually requires a good deal of political facilitation.

Moreover, while it is true that much of the renewal-oriented work to promote alternative development by way of further democratisation has grown out of civil society movements like the KSSP, the latter has often been accused of abstaining from the otherwise 'normal' NGO pattern of neglecting the importance of radical politics and established leftist organisations.[31] More importantly, however, my results show that the problems of extending and sustaining many of the remarkable popular campaigns from the mid-eighties to the early nineties were not because of respect for the established Left but rather the lack of efficient politics of the movements themselves.

On this point, due to lack of space, let us turn directly to the common denominators. First, in the social setting of Kerala, marked by the expansion of petty capitalist relations after the land reform and with incoming migrant money from the Gulf, there did not seem to be widespread immediate interest among the many dispersed farmers in the movements' ideas about joint democratic control and management of land and other resources to improve production. Despite the campaigns, no powerful social movement (like the one for land reform) came forward. Second, most non-party development alternatives that were suggested made little sense within the logic of the public administration and the established leftist movements and parties – aside from when such activities formed part of the Left Front government's top-down development policies. The activists were politically isolated, therefore, and left without such necessary measures as a consistent democratic decentralisation. Third, the reformists themselves found it difficult to

explicitly politicise their development actions (by which is not necessarily meant party-politicise; we shall soon come back to this concept).
Perhaps they were simply incapable of, or uninterested in, so doing.
Anyway, the reformists rather restricted themselves to creating the pre-
conditions for major social and political forces to move forward[32] –
which the latter did not do. Fourth, analytical reductionism and/or
political considerations prevented the reformists from dealing with the
origins of such problems, including the multiplicity of socio-economic
interests and conflicts, *plus* their links with vested interests within the
obstructive logic of established politics, conservative as well as leftist.

Again there was, thus, a lack of convergence of fragmented issues,
groups and actions – despite one of the most vibrant civil societies one
can think of – because in the last instance the renewal-oriented groups
could not master the politics of promoting such a convergence, while the
established parties and institutions abstained from promoting it.

Activists, however, have learnt their lesson.[33] Most of the campaigns
could not be sustained when the Left Front lost the elections in 1991.[34]
But after some time reformists managed to turn instead a decentralisation scheme imposed by New Delhi against the dubious ways in which
the new Congress-led Kerala state government tried to undermine the
same. Hence the reformists succeeded also in getting the opposition Left
Front politicians, who used to be hesitant while in office, to jump on the
bandwagon and to commit themselves to more consistent decentralisation, if and when they were voted back into office.

Interestingly, this neither caused the Left Front to really use the 1995
panchayat[35] elections to develop local demands, initiatives and visions,
nor to give decentralisation and local development top priority in the
following 1996 Assembly elections. Such an orientation, quite obviously,
would have called instead for alternative forces and pressure from
below. But thereafter this pressure was rapidly and skilfully facilitated
(as compared with the previous 'campaign period' until 1991). Once the
Left had won the elections and the Communist patriarch E.M.S Namboo-
diripad had insisted on consistent decentralisation, scholarly as well as
politically very able activists managed to get access to the State Planning
Board, to use years of experience from KSSP projects to immediately
launch a well-prepared massive popular campaign for planning from
below, *and* to simultaneously have leading politicians proudly promise
that no longer would only a few per cent of the state development
budget go to all *panchayats* that seriously involve themselves in the
programme, but rather between 35 and 40 per cent. Hence there is new
space for the previously contained popular efforts – but only thanks to
elections, political pressure and to government intervention. The local
governments have got some real powers and many fresh politicians have
been elected, particularly women. The centralised parties must produce
results in the new development arenas, which gives some elbow-room to
reformists. Supported by reformists-cum-experts, local governments may

alter the centralised and compartmentalised administration, try to co-ordinate various measures at district, block and village levels, and most importantly facilitate the coming together of the myriad of dispersed voluntary associations (and the fragmented social capital that they have come to nourish) for joint societal efforts. The earlier kind of popular movement campaigns may be more institutionalised and legitimate (including from a democratic point of view) when carried out in mutu-ally respectful co-operation with elected local governments. In Scandi-navia we may recall 'the good old' co-operation between popular movements and governments at various levels. At any rate, many obstacles still lie ahead in Kerala. I am particularly worried that politi-cians and bureaucrats with vested interests may cause the impressive planning from below not to be followed up rapidly and efficiently enough by new regulations and an equally impressive campaign to institutionalise (politically and administratively) the planning efforts and to really implement the projects.[36] Yet, a more politically developed society of citizens may stand a good chance of taking the crucial steps ahead.

Fragmentation of Interests and Democratisation

To sum up so far, the *politics* of democratisation is more decisive than a vibrant civil society with social capital. Even in such societies, the major problem of democratisation is the fragmentation of interests, groups and actions, no matter if well intended. To overcome this, links must be developed between various civil society efforts as well as between them and state or local authorities – that is, politics and a political society.

Against this conclusion on the special importance of politics, one may argue that the very fragmentation of interests and its socio-economic roots are more fundamental. The division of labour, the subordination of people and the appropriation of surplus are extremely complex and contradictory under the present expansion of capitalism. This breeds individualistic strategies of survival, clientelism, group-specific organis-ation, and mobilisation on the basis of religious and cultural identities. We are far from a classical protracted industrial and cultural transforma-tion in general, and the emergence of large and comparatively homoge-neous working-class movements in particular.

Much of this very process, however, is also politically facilitated. Many vital resources and other pre-conditions for profitable business (includ-ing the subordination of labour and the regulation of the markets) are controlled through the state and frequently monopolised by special groups and individuals. The most obvious example is the way in which the Suharto family made use of the state to get privileged access to profitable sectors of the Indonesian economy as a whole. However, much less dominating characteristics such as the semi-private political control in Kerala of a rural co-operative bank or the assignment of contractors is also important.

This political facilitation of capitalism through the monopolisation of various important resources was neglected by the old leftist movements and parties. They gave priority instead to privately controlled land and capital. Hence they could not fight effectively the simultaneous rise of economic and political monopolies, rather they sometimes even promoted this.

But things have changed, lessons have been learnt, and new realities have given rise to new conflicts, interests and movements. Close studies of many years of movements' efforts in as different contexts as the Philippines, Kerala and Indonesia show that two major reasons (among others) why they give priority to democratisation are: (a) that they need to fight politically the monopolisation of many different crucial resources and regulations, and (b) that they must find a way of mobilising and co-ordinating efficient action among people and groups whose interests are not particularly clear-cut and thus unifying as such.

For instance, displaced peasants, marginalised traders, repressed workers or frustrated students who try to improve their lives in Indonesia continue to almost immediately face the state at various levels. Land reform but also commercialism in rural Kerala make necessary new forms of co-operation over the use of scattered resources – including land, water, inputs and labour – which in turn calls for political decentralisation and improved institutions for democratic local government. Dante Buscayno's negligence of internal democratisation in 'his' huge co-operative in Tarlac (in order to move on as rapidly as possible to more advanced political tasks) proved as disastrous as the nearby eruption of Mt. Pinatubo when members did not act in accordance with the basic interests as 'genuine peasants' that he had ascribed to them.

At any rate, as the problem of socio-economic fragmentation is a general one and of similar importance in the three different contexts, it is only a fundamental background factor for studies of democratisation – but not a factor for describing and explaining *different* processes and outcomes. Rather we must first study the kinds of democratisation that the movements attempt and then analyse how they go about it.

The movements have different views of democracy and democratisation. Yet they would probably agree with the minimum definitions offered in the previous chapter (Chapter 12). They neither subscribe to the post-modernist idea of everything being culturally specific, nor to the neo-nationalistic and authoritarian idea that there is some kind of 'Asian value democracy'. They have no problems in separating democracy as a procedure from its content – that is, its content in terms of the particular alternative development which they want to decide upon and get implemented in democratic ways. Nor are there any serious problems of distinguishing between the various forms (or procedures) of democracy that they like to give priority to, such as more or less direct popular control and participation. But much of this goes for democracy as a rather static and universal method. Democratisation (or the way to democracy *and* to its further development) is something quite different. To begin with, this includes various ideas about the pre-conditions for democracy and about its extension. And these pre-conditions and this extension vary with the conditions in the different contexts and with the perspectives of the different movements. Further, some may limit democratisation to the introduction of basic civil rights, while others may argue that it also calls for land reform, total literacy, education and other basic entitlements.[37] Some may say that democratisation may be limited to the conventional political sphere, while others would like to extend it to parts of the economy and civil society. My point, however, is not to make a full list or to produce a normative definition, but rather to allow for an open and critical analysis of actors' various positions on the pre-conditions for and scope of democracy.

Towards the Study of the Politics of Democratisation

Equally important is that besides aiming at certain forms of democracy (and certain democratic decisions to promote development), and then proposing a way of getting there through the fulfilment of certain pre-conditions, as indicated above, the actors also require efficient means or forms of democratisation to be able to really travel that path. It is precisely this process of developing and applying the means of getting movements' ideas of democratisation off the ground in terms of the *politics* of democratisation that we need to concentrate upon. And the question, then, is how to approach and analyse this process, to best explain it and to help to shape discussions on how to support it.

As we have now moved beyond the paradigm of civil society/social capital, and are focusing rather on links between various movements in civil society, and between them and state or local authorities, we have to look instead for analytical tools among scholars of socio-political movements and parties,[38] and for relevant institutional linkages between the state and society.[39] I suggest that to study the process of democratisation from below by analysing movements' politics of democratisation, we should concentrate on three aspects. First, given the 'political opportunity structure' that movement analysts talk of, what is the *space* for the pro-democracy efforts? Second, as people also have to come together and affect politics, what are the 'mobilisation structures' (to use the language of the same theorists) that movements apply; that is, how are people *included* into politics? Third, as these people are included into politics to put forward their interests and ideas, how are these interests and ideas *politicised*?

Political Space

It is reasonable to distinguish four dimensions of factors which together constitute the political opportunity structure conditioning the movements' politics:

1.   the relative openness or closedness of the political system (widely defined to include not just the state and political institutions but also, for instance, groups putting forward popular demands);
2.   the relative stability or instability of the alignments among dominating groups constituting the basis for the established polity;
3.   the possibilities for movements to link up with sections of the elite;
4.   the capacity and propensity of the state in particular to repress movements.[40]

However, I am in full agreement with the conclusion that 'the core idea weaving together the disparate threads . . . is the opening and closing of political space and its institutional and substantive location'.[41] On the one hand we may then study this space as such. On the other hand we may also analyse how the movements themselves read the opportunities and what they therefore conclude in terms of the space available for their work. I myself make basic studies of the opportunity structures in the various cases, but then focus on analysing what the movements arrive at. This may be categorised along two dimensions. First whether or not they believe that there is space enough for meaningful work within the established political system. (The political system – parts of which are 'established' – is defined widely to include not only the formal political institutions but also, for example, the generation of political pressure and demands from within civil society.) Second, whether they believe that it is possible and necessary to promote democratisation directly in civil society under the prevailing conditions (including unequal division of power and resources) – or if they feel that one can and has to first create or capture political instruments such as party and state institutions, at best democratise them, and thereafter politically facilitate civil rights and a 'good' civil society.[42] In Figure 13.1 we thus we arrive at four basic positions.[43]

In *Indonesia* – until the recent fall of Suharto – there was little space for pro-democracy work within the established system, high risk of repression, few signs of real splits within the ruling coalition, and only occasional possibilities for movements to link up with limited sections of the elite. Hence, the radicals were to the left in the matrix and the moderates to the right. The explicitly politicising activists aiming at the state and the political system – including those who linked up with Megawati early in 1996 and faced repression – are found in box I. Below in box III are many other radical democrats who instead gave priority to more indirect work in civil society, for instance by promoting civil and

Space for meaningful work within the
established political system?

		No. Must work outside	Yes. Can work inside
Space for meaningful direct work in civil society?	No. Must be politically facilitated	**I** Unrecognised avant-garde policies to alter the system and then promote democratisation	**II** Recognised political intervention to adjust the system and then promote democratisation
	Yes. May be strengthened directly	**III** 'Empower' civil society and, some add, harness popular movements to promote democratisation	**IV** Vitalise movements and NGOs more or less related to **II** to promote democratisation

Figure 13.1   *Movements' basic positions on the space for political work*

human rights and alternative development. In box II, on the contrary, are the less explicitly democratically oriented persons who tried to work through the two recognised 'opposition' parties, as did Megawati before she was ousted, or within various state apparatuses and the pro-government Association of Muslim Intellectuals (ICMI) (though the latter was already at that time getting increasingly associated with the regime), like the former NGO leader Adi Sasono. In box IV, finally, are many semi-autonomous NGO workers but also the Muslim leader Abdurrachman Wahid (Gus Dur). The latter did not link up with the government but stayed within the established widely defined political system and tried to affect it indirectly with the kind of self-restrictive actions in support of a more autonomous civil society that we know from the eighties in Eastern Europe. Much of all this will change, of course, after the recent fall of Suharto. One possible scenario is that of the Philippines.

In *the Philippines* the propensity for repression has gone down and the political system is open. Yet there are few chances for renewal-oriented democrats to work within the framework of simple-majority elections in single-member constituencies characterised by 'machine politics', per-sonalities (for example, within film, sport and media), and local bosses with access to business or shady government finance. Also, ex-general and president (till 1988) Ramos was fairly successful in building a new ruling coalition among leading politicians and businessmen, including in the provinces. Democratisers may well relate to sections of the elite on specific issues, but on general issues it is probably less easy now than earlier. Since the early nineties, therefore, there have been two main tendencies among the renewal-oriented groups. One is to move from box I to box II, that is to combine extra-parliamentary work with also entering into and trying to change the established polity, for instance via electoral coalitions and a new party. The other tendency is to try to work 'part-time' in boxes III and IV respectively, for instance by harnessing autonomous community development while also occasionally relating this to electoral mobilisation behind the 'least worst politicians' and NGO representation in local government development councils.

Kerala is characterised by a non-repressive and open system but also by a deep-rooted bipolar party-politicisation of various socio-economic as well as caste and religious pillars, within which movements and their leaders can relate to factions of the elite. Unrecognised avant-garde politics in box I is now (with hardly any Naxalites left) limited to a few action groups, while certain NGOs promoting, for instance, community organisation continue work in box III. Most of the democratisers are rather within the established political forces of the Left Front and/or associated with movements like the autonomous KSSP in box IV. In the latter case they try to complement and reform progressive party and party-politicised popular organisations, as well as government and *panchayat* policies, by way of their own relatively independent actions in civil society, constantly benefiting from close contacts with sections of the political and administrative elite.

Political Inclusion

Politics, essentially, is about people coming together on what should be held in common and how this should be governed in a politically created society such as a nation-state or a municipality. Given the spheres in which actors have found that there is most space for their work, *how* do people really come together to affect and be included in the political discourse and struggles? We may label this third dimension political inclusion and (ideally) consider it in each of the boxes in the previous matrix.

In general accordance with Nicos Mouzelis, one may distinguish historically (as we know from previous chapters) between the integration of people into politics on the basis of relatively autonomous broad popular movements generated by comprehensive economic development (like in many parts of Western Europe), and the elitist incorporation of people with less solid organisations of their own into comparatively advanced polities in economically late-developing societies (like in the Balkans and many Third World countries).[44]

These concepts, of course, call for further elaboration. Following Mouzelis, one may talk of two ways of incorporating people into comparatively advanced polities: clientelism and populism. Clientelism, primarily, is associated with bosses on different levels with their own capacity to deliver patronage in return for services and votes. At present, I would add, clientelism is sometimes 'modernised' in the form of state-corporatism. Populism, on the other hand, generally goes with charis-matic leaders who are able to express popular feelings and ideas, but not necessarily interests, and whose positions are essential to the stability of adjoining leaders and their ability to patronise followers. In addition to this, I would argue, political leaders aiming at integrating people into politics have sometimes tried short cuts by adding elements of clientel-ism (and occasionally populism as well), for instance the Communists in West Bengal with access to state resources and a strong party machinery. Let us label this alternative patronage.

How, then, do movements try to integrate rather than incorporate people into politics? In general accordance with Sidney Tarrow, one may distinguish between two basic methods: one emphasising autonomous collective action and another focusing upon the internalisation of actions and movements in organisations with some leadership. Tarrow argues, and my studies confirm, that the most important but often-neglected element of movement organising is what he calls the 'mobilising struc-tures'. These link the 'centre' (in terms of formally organised leadership identifying aims and means) and the 'periphery' (in terms of the actual collective action in the field). The 'mobilising structures' are thus 'permit-ting movement co-ordination and allowing movements to persist over time'.[45] Historically, he continues, there are two solutions to the problem, one with roots in anarchist and one in democratic socialist thinking.[46] The anarchist approach emphasises people's natural and spontaneous willingness and ability to resist repression and exploitation through linked networks and federations of autonomous associations – in reality, however, through instigating organic leaders as spearheads. The social democratic concept stresses the need for political ideology, organisation and intervention through an integrated structure of parties, unions and self-help organisations.[47] As these labels often carry different and biased connotations, however, I shall talk instead of federative and unitary forms of integration.[48]

Thus we arrive at two ways of incorporating people into politics: (I) populism and (II) clientelism/state-corporatism. Moreover, the combina-tion of integration and incorporation tends towards the latter and may be called (III) alternative patronage. Finally, the two ways of integrating people: (IV) federative and (V) unitary. (See Figure 13.2.)

If we then add the positions related to space for political work within the political system and civil society respectively, we end up with the summarising matrix shown in Figure 13.2.

Politicisation of Interests and Issues

Considering how *people* are included into politics, however, is not enough. In each of our ten strategic positions in Figure 13.2 we must

	Incorporation		Integration		
	I Populism	II Clientelism (state-corporatism)	III Alternative patronage	IV Federative	V Unitary
	In/out of system	In/out of system	In/out of system	In/out of system	In/out of system
Little space for work in civil society – hence it has to be politically facilitated	1. For example, Megawati in Indonesia	2. For example, Sasono within ICMI in Indonesia – at least till recently	3. Leading radical patrons in, for example, party and NGO alliance	4. Networking avant-garde catalysts	5. General organisers
Space for work in civil society – hence this may be strengthened directly	6. For example, Gus Dur in Indonesia – at least till recently	7. For example, NGOs related to ICMI in Indonesia – at least till recently	8. Local radical patrons in, for example, a party or NGO	9. 'Independent' NGOs with grassroots activities	10. Movement organisers-cum-co-ordinators

Figure 13.2 *Basic strategic concepts among pro-democratising movements on space for work and ways of including people into politics*

simultaneously analyse also the content of the politics of democratisation in terms of how *interests* and *issues* are politicised. There is a lack of sharp analytical tools. On the basis of a Marxist-oriented understanding of civil society and democracy, Peter Gibbon, among others, has succinctly suggested some exciting propositions. These were hinted at already at the beginning of this chapter and may now serve as a point of departure. Modern civil society primarily reflects the 'bourgeois' social division of labour with its individualised and privatised entities. The plurality of groupings thus generated is not likely by itself to promote general interests and democratic forms of government. Rather the associations may turn into prisoners of the process through the deepening of civil society, thus becoming unable to combine single issues and specific interests by way of politicisation.

This way of conceptualising politicisation, however, is both too narrow (and partly normative), as it is not problematised, and too general, as it tends to include all aspects of politics. We should not rule out politicisation through, for example, development-oriented civil society organisations. And just like pluralism, of course, politicisation is not a sufficient recipe for democratisation, as recently demonstrated in the former Yugoslavia, and earlier when carried out with the very best of intentions within the framework of various socialist projects. Hence, there is a need for qualifications. Moreover, we have to be more precise. We have already discussed how people are involved in politics. So let us now reserve the concept of politicisation for the ways in which interests, ideas and issues are also included into politics – that is, put into a societal perspective by people who have come together about what should be held in common *and* how this should be organised in a politically created society such as a nation state or a municipality. Three aspects are most important: the basis, the forms and the content.

The *basis of politicisation* may be derived from the kinds of ideas and interests about which people come together and which they consider in a societal perspective. Let us distinguish between, first, single issues and/or specific interests and, second, ideologies and/or collective interests. The *forms of politicisation* are by definition related to societal organs like the state or local government (otherwise we may talk of, for example, privatisation), but vary according to whether one 'only' demands that certain policies should be carried out by these organs or also really engages in promoting similar ends through self-management, for instance by way of co-operatives. The *content of politicisation*, of course, is about different ideas, ideologies and concrete policies, plus the ways in which various movements articulate norms and ideas, such as democratic rights and equality, in different contexts. The basis and forms of politicisation may be illustrated in a simple figure, whereafter we have to add the content in each box. (See Figure 13.3.)

In this way we may distinguish four types of politicisation. In box A we find the kind of single pluralism where pressure groups, single-issue movements and special interest organisations try to affect state or local government policies; in box B, dual pluralism with various groups and organisations putting forward their demands while also self-managing issues and interests; in box C, the single social type of politicisation with organisations or corporations demanding state or local government policies on the basis of ideologies and/or collective interests; in box D, dual social politicisation through similar organisations which also, to a considerable extent, manage common interests.

| | | Forms of politicisation | |
		Via state/local government only	Also via self-management
Basis of politicisation	Single issues or specific interests	A. Single pluralism	B. Dual pluralism
	Ideology or collective interests	C. Single social	D. Dual social

Figure 13.3   *Types of politicisation*

Divisive Politicisation

Ideally we should now consider for all our cases and over time the ten strategic options and (for each of them) the four types of politicisation, but in this context a few illustrations of the fruitfulness of the venture will have to do.

In *Indonesia*, the populism that was so important during the Sukarno period has now returned to the explicitly political level with his daughter (box 1 of Figure 13.2), and to civil society with Gus Dur (box 6), leader of the world's largest and comparatively pluralist Muslim organisation Nahdlatul Ulama. Insiders like Adi Sasono, on the other hand, tried to turn pro-government ICMI into a forum for the modernisation of clientelism into Malaysian-like state-corporatism (box 2) – and under the new president Habibie he may be rather succesful. The most genuine and outspoken democrats, however, were until recently outside the system and among the myriad of groupings at the other end of Figure 13.2.

While recalling the important difference between the explicitly political activists focusing on state and government, and those working more indirectly in civil society, we now also pay attention to their ways of mobilising and organising. Ever since the liberation struggle much of the activism in Indonesia, especially among students and now also in several NGOs, is based on radical, courageous, often personalised and sometimes moral leadership that is supposed to ignite people's spontaneous ability to resist (box 4). In the late eighties, a new generation of activists began staging daring demonstrations, trying to give a voice to subordinated people. 'Action maniacs' constantly hunted for new issues that would attract media attention but did demonstrate also that there was more space for radical action than most 'established' dissidents thought.

The general organisers, on the other hand, continue to agree on the need to change state and government but draw instead on two other political traditions (box 5). First, the middle-class intellectuals who tried to build 'modern' parties but ended up in the fifties and sixties with elitist formations like that of the socialists, or elite-based parties based on conventional loyalties, like those of the Muslims and populist nationalists. Second, the reformist Communists who also made use of some conventional loyalties but still managed to build in the fifties and sixties a comparatively 'modern' party with some 20 million people in attached popular organisations. What now remains are basically leaders from the elitist tradition who first supported Suharto but then turned critics and were deprived of their organisational bases. Their main remaining asset is some integrity and legitimacy in the eyes of many people, and among Western governments and agencies. In the face of the current crisis and the possible return of mass politics, there are attempts to draw again (as during the fifties and sixties) on conventional loyalties among Muslims and populist nationalists. The reformist Communists, on the other hand, are no more – but instead a new generation of mostly young former 'action maniacs', who since 1994 put their faith in ideology and organisation to build a new socialist party by mobilising from above workers, urban poor, displaced peasants and frustrated students. Here are, thus, the roots of the People's Democratic Party (PRD), that was made a scapegoat after the riots in Jakarta in mid-1996 and then faced repression.

Finally, most grassroots groups and supportive NGOs 'empower' civil society in the federative column (of Figure 13.2), harnessing people's own protests but staying out of explicit politics and leaving it to the 'people themselves' to organise (box 9).

None of those major actors trying to integrate people into politics, however, had till recently been markedly successful. Hence, their democratising potential does not vary *directly* with their strategic positions. The important common denominator is instead their pattern of politicisation. There was a basic orientation towards single issues and specific interests (boxes A and B in Figure 13.3), especially among the comparatively firmly based grassroots workers (box 9 in Figure 13.2) and the many rather free-floating avant-garde catalysts (box 4). Moreover, when (as since about 1994) almost all the actors made efforts anyway to address general problems of democratisation they did so, first, within the framework of 'their' old strategic positions and, second, by relating 'their' issues or 'their' interests to general problems and ideologies. The end result was both conflicts between various factions and a tendency to unintentionally cause trouble for each other. This I have labelled *divisive politicisation*.

The outcome in 1996, as we know by now, was that the political activists who sensed a political opening and short cut in the conflict over Megawati 'bet' on alternative patronage and 'ran offside' (box 3), while the long-term potential of the grassroots work was left behind. Thereafter the only optimistic prospect was that the strategic perspective of the still weak and untested movement organisers-cum-coordinators (box 10) – who tried to bring initiatives at the grassroots level together from below but within a unitary mobilisational framework – would gain strength and prove more fruitful. There were hopeful experiences from co-ordinating labour activists as well as supportive organisations; and there was a desperate need of non-party partisan but interest-based mass organisations – in order both for people to put forward their demands to any regime, and for reformist politicians to be able to negotiate social contracts with reasonably representative organisations. At least in principle, moreover, the independent electoral watchdog KIPP could have been reconstructed into a non-party partisan *democratic* watch movement made up of not only daring top-down activists (as till 27 July 1996) but also those working at the grassroots level.

Box 13.1   *The Indonesian lesson*

Suharto is gone. His 'New Order' regime remains. But it is
undermined and disintegrating. Its perfidious survivors try to
relegitimate their wealth and positions. Its anti-Communist
supporters from the mid-1960s, who turned middle-class dissidents
in the '70s, try to recover their losses. Its less compromising
younger critics (and principled intellectuals) try contradictory ways of
promoting a fresh start. So while the common people suffer, various
factions of the elite quarrel, and the market and the West hesitates,
it is time to ask why it all happened, and what chances there are for
a more human order. What is the Indonesian lesson?

The thesis in vogue is that the Indonesian problem was about too
much politics and too much state; too many regulations and too little
market. While the dissidents could not beat the regime, and others
could not resist its patronage, it was only the market and the
International Monetary Fund (IMF) that finally stood up against the
dragon, brought down Suharto and created an opening for
democracy. Now there must be privatisation and deregulation and
the opening up for foreign companies.

These, of course, are but ideological half-truths. A critical analysis
indicates instead that the actions of the market and its supporters
were politically disastrous, contributed to a socio-economic
catastrophe, obstructed democratisation, and only accidentally
helped do away with Suharto.

The crisis was not because of too much politics . . .

To begin with, the economic crisis did not result from excessive
regulations but from bad regulations, and from too little popular
influence. Bad regulations that were exploited by special interests with
the state, business and international finance; and too little popular
influence capable of holding such special interests in check. As
elsewhere in East Asia, the serious problems did not develop until
private interests became stronger and deregulation increased. Then the
regime was unable to co-ordinate the new groupings and could only
hold down discontent among the new middle and working classes.

. . . but the problem was political

Further, once the Indonesian crisis had erupted, conventional
economic measures did not work. Many observers began to realise,
therefore, that the basic problem was political rather than economic.
Suddenly even conclusions drawn from critical analyses of the mid-
1996 crackdown on the democracy movement were no longer
ignored: that is, that dissidents were too poorly organised to make a
difference yet had to be supported since the regime was totally
unable to regulate conflicts, reform itself, and prepare an 'orderly'

succession. But even though it became increasingly apparent that the crisis could only be solved through fundamental political changes, little was done to support rapid development of the only alternative – the democracy movement and the moderate reformists. Suharto's monopolies were no longer appreciated – but temporary stability was.

'If you had only been able to give us an alternative', the West derogatorily told democracy activists who faced an uphill battle after a recent crackdown and decades of repression and 'floating mass' politics.

Actually, the West itself had been contributing to those difficulties of generating an alternative. Much of Sukarno's authoritarian nationalism in the late 1950s was because the Dutch refused to give up their colonial interests; because the CIA supported separatist movements; and because the West wanted to prevent the communists and their unique modern interest-based mass movements from wining liberal democratic elections. Thereafter Western powers paved the way for the military takeover and the massacres in 1965–66. Their favourite liberal and so-called socialist administrators did not have a strong enough social and economic base to make a difference, so the United States in particular turned to the army instead. According to the conventional Cold War wisdom of the West (and Professor Huntington's then forthcoming 'politics of order' theory), the army would serve in policing and containing the masses, thereby allowing liberal middle-class experts to run the country. But as we know, once the Left had been massacred, and many others jailed, harassed and domesticated, it was rather the army generals who took over – with the middle-class experts as their servants. And yet, the repression, corruption and nepotism that followed were also sustained by political and extensive economic support from the West, including loans issued on the basis of political guarantees rather than on well-founded economic evaluations. Neither the IMF and its partners nor various corporate leaders had anything decisively negative to say about Suharto's Indonesia till hours before the crisis broke out. On the contrary, Indonesia was on the World Bank's top-ten list of promising emerging economies.

Economic recipes deepen the crisis

Moreover, as the Indonesian crisis evolved from September 1997 onwards, the West not only abstained from betting on democrats and moderate reformists to tackle the basic political problems but instead referred the matter to neo-classical IMF economists. From October 1997 onwards their narrow-minded recipes diminished confidence in Indonesia's ability to avoid an economic breakdown. (Officials in the IMF and the World Bank later on admitted this themselves.) The situation deteriorated. Suharto had to look for alternatives – and to create additional problems by nominating a vice president whom nobody would prefer to himself, Habibie. By January 1998 the currency fell beyond imagination, the economy came to a standstill, people began to protest, anti-Chinese riots spread, and the regime was on the brink of collapse. According to the World Bank, no country has suffered a similarly harsh economic backlash since the Second World War.

In fact, however, the economic backlash was like the US bombing of Baghdad during the Gulf War. Suharto was just as able to turn the negative into a positive, putting the blame on the West (and on the Chinese business community), as the West was unable to find an alternative to him. He was reappointed president in the March and formed a provocative kind of combat government with his daughter 'Tutut' as *de facto* prime minister and an absolute majority of family friends and loyalists in other posts.

Concessions to stability

Faced with the threat of a new Saddam Hussein, the West retreated. Too many business interests were at stake in Indonesia. Forty per cent of the world's shipping passes through its straits. Just before Easter, the IMF adopted Australia and Japan's so-called flexible positions and postponed some of its own far-reaching demands.

This, of course, was a perfectly rational *political* decision. Given the situation and the interests of the powerful parties involved, democratisation as well as neo-liberal marketism had to give way to stability. If food and fuel subsidies had really been withdrawn by April, as the IMF initially requested, this would have been an invitation to massive riots. Meanwhile the World Bank and others tried to mobilise food and medical relief to meet immediate needs (worth 3 billion dollars), and trusted the military to keep people in check. The regime had got another temporary lease on life, it seemed.

Inconceivable price hikes and early resignation

My own analysis showed a weakness at this point. For on 10 April the Indonesian government managed to convince the IMF that essential subsidies should only be reduced step-by-step until October in order to prevent major social and political unrest. But less than a month later, on 4 May, the regime and the IMF agreed instead, quite unexpectedly, to increase the price of petrol by as much as 70 per cent and of kerosene by 25 per cent. Suharto went further than the IMF had sought – and the IMF applauded. I still cannot understand how even neo-classical economists could make such a politically irrational decision. Perhaps Suharto had lost touch altogether, while politically illiterate economists in Jakarta were short of money and wanted to impress their equally naive IMF colleagues in Washington as well as their critics in the US Congress.

Predictably, anyway, the new prices generated immediate public anger. This gave a new dimension to the student demonstrations that had hitherto been rather isolated, though increasing in number. In Medan, anti-Chinese riots and looting erupted and spread to Jakarta, where, a week later, the situation got out of hand. Demonstrating students were killed. Rioting and looting led to the burning to death of hundreds of people in shopping centres and to widespread acts of cruelty, including the rape of women of Chinese descent. Some of the excesses were aggravated by hardliners in the armed forces who wanted an excuse for more forceful intervention. But their provocations backfired. More and more people turned against the regime. The students occupied the parliament and no longer allowed themselves to be abused downtown. Suharto tried without success to win back the initiative by promising various reforms. He saved his skin only by resigning early, as the 'rats' (like the parliament speaker and several cabinet ministers) began to abandon the sinking ship.

From breakdown to democracy?

The Indonesian lesson is, thus, about the inability of the market, civil society and their proponents to prevent social and economic disaster for Indonesia's almost 200 million citizens by betting on political reform, popular representation, and democratisation. Once again the market and civil society libertarians have been proven wrong.

But does not this breakdown create an opening for democratisation? The waters we sail into with this proposition are both uncharted and rough. I see four major problems.

To begin with, most actors focus on how to alter the old regime that still remains. Everybody is busy repositioning themselves, consolidating their assets, and forming new parties and alliances. Incumbents (and their military and business allies) are delaying changes in order to be able to adapt, making whatever concessions are necessary to be able to steer their course. Established dissidents trade in their reputations and, occasionally, their popular followings, for reforms and 'positions'. Radicals try to sustain popular protests to weaken shameless incumbents who might otherwise be able to stay on. The market and the West are interested in anything that looks stable enough to permit the payback of loans and safe returns on investments. It is hard to predict the outcome – except to say that as ordinary people get hungry the conflicts are likely to continue, escalate, and, at worst, open up for more extensive military and religious involvement.

Meanwhile many donor agencies and students of society add that a weak democratic culture and civil society are equally problematic. Culture in terms of informal norms and patterns certainly becomes more important when organised institutions and rules of the game are weakened and even disintegrate. Yet I do not share the view that support for civil society is always the best way of building a democratic culture. In many cases, such as the backing of free journalists, there are no problems, but all civil society associations do not necessarily promote democracy. And what is political culture but routinely practised remnants of yesterday's rules, institutions and organised politics? Hence, it is on the latter level of formal rules, institutions and organised politics at which change and improvements have to start.

Third, therefore, the fact that giving priority to the organising of constituencies based on shared societal interests and ideas does not make much sense among leading political actors in Indonesia is a more serious problem than a weak democratic culture. Even democrats go for short cuts like charisma, populism, religion and patronage in order to swiftly incorporate rather than gradually integrate people into politics. There is a shortage of time, of course, and everybody is afraid of losing out. But a common lesson learned from other transitions away from authoritarian rule is that without well-anchored politics and unionism there will be no meaningful democracy. And the conditions today are worse than they were during Indonesia's period of parliamentary democracy in the '50s, which ended in authoritarianism – or in the Philippines after Marcos, where populist bossism now prevails.

Finally, we also know from other cases that the few genuine democrats who might be able to build such popular and well-rooted parties and unions are in desperate need of supportive rules of the game. At the same time, the progressive movements are rarely interested in such constitutional and legal formalities, until they later on have to fight uphill battles within unfavourable political systems.

In conclusion, it is difficult for the Indonesians to learn from other experiences, given the current dynamics and the weakly organised democracy movement. Right now successful betting on popular organising and more favourable rules would be possible only if the West gave as much support to democratisation as it has to Indonesia's financial recovery. This is unlikely given the fact that the West has not so far been able to break out of its vicious circle of recurrent re-creation of the authoritarian Indonesian beast rather than helping to awaken its potentially democratic beauty. The more likely outcome, therefore, is rather a 'bad-guy democracy' within which incumbent bosses on various levels are able to survive, attract military and business allies, co-opt some dissidents, and mobilise mass support through Islamic populism – all well before genuine democratic activists and ordinary people manage to organise themselves.

17 June 1998

(First published in the *Bulletin of Concerned Asian Scholars*, vol. 30, no. 3)

The *Philippine* story is, by now, less complicated, though the pattern is the same and even older. Megawati's political sister Mrs Aquino, for instance, plays no role any more. The exciting democratisers are instead among 'our' groups at the other end of Figure 13.2, aiming at the integration of people into politics. As in Indonesia, certain leading personalities do play an important role in the Philippines, but many of them are less avant-garde catalysts (box 4) than related to general organising (box 5). To put it crudely, their problem is similar to that of their fellow Indonesians – they lack an organised popular base. It is true that some of them stayed out of the rigid 'national democrats', but this did not automatically render the independents a mass following. It is also true that many more left the same disciplined but increasingly irrelevant organisations later on, but this did not cause many of the rank and file to come along.

Actually, the very basis of the new democratisers is cause-oriented groups and NGOs, related community organisations (including co-operatives), and some, but not broad-based, interest organisations, for instance among labourers (often box 9). They have all, quite naturally, a tendency to focus on specific interests and issues (boxes A and B in Figure 13.3). There were exciting attempts among the democratisers to prevent the isolation and fragmentation of progressive work at the grassroots level in civil society, for instance in co-operatives. But the fact that a few NGOs really tried co-ordination from below (box 10 in Figure 13.2), and indirectly supported electoral efforts as well, was far from enough. Nor was the electoral movement of 1992 up to much in terms of general organisation on a unitary basis (box 5) but rather, as again in 1995, an attempt to move towards alternative patronage short cuts (column III). This, however, is now much more firmly rooted at the local level than in Indonesia (box 8). Renewal-oriented action groups and NGOs hold on to their own efforts in civil society, while rallying behind reasonable politicians in elections. Many now have ample experience of the need to link their special tasks to general problems, but the pattern has mainly been to hold on to special strategic positions and different issues.

In trying to solve this, the renewal-oriented forces that I follow have refuted conventional recipes in terms of a grand theory, tight ideology and cadre-based organisation. Some visualise instead a common framework of politics and society, as well as democratically run fora for various organisations and groups, within which activists can situate themselves, analyse the various movements, and consider different problems and issues. As these things have not emerged spontaneously from below, however, the question of how to initiate them remains to be answered. For a long while, coalitions and co-ordinating bodies have been among the initiatives (boxes 5 and 10). But there have been additional concrete problems of time, space, money and a limited number of activists; the need to sustain basic groups and movements;

and the need to influence at least local policies by participating in councils and making some difference in elections by relating to reasonable politicians with a chance of winning. Hence it is tempting to go for Americanised community action, pressure politics and lobbying behind 'reasonable' politicians with access to media and moneyed bosses (boxes 3 and 8 in Figure 13.2, and A and B in Figure 13.3). In the face of the 1998 elections it remains to be seen whether it will be possible instead for the activists to co-ordinate the efforts from below (box 10), and use the new '*Akbayan!* – Citizens' Action Party' to provide an overall unitary framework (box 5). As already indicated, many activists seem to focus instead on sectoral (or regional) representation, and to trade support to the 'least worse' traditional politicians.

In *Kerala* the pattern is even more clear-cut. Populism and clientelism, of course, are also found within the Left and some of the radical grassroots organisations. But generally speaking this is confined to the Congress-led front and the many civic associations related to caste and religion. As compared with the alternative patronage found in West Bengal (column III in Figure 13.2), the Kerala Communists, as already indicated, are subject to many more checks and balances – as their party grew out of popular organisations and because of their more consistent land reform, turning so many downtrodden people into comparatively independent citizens. The Left Front, and especially the leading Communist Party (Marxist), still dominates politics and general organising (box 5).[49] The 'leftist clientelism' of today is mainly a question of commerce and semi-privatisation having crept into political and interest organisations as well as co-operatives, though the official picture remains a clear-cut one of historical traditions of focusing upon collective interests and ideology. Party-politicisation, by now, is often associated with the favouring of special interests and vested interests related to political-cum-socio-economic pillars (occasionally shaped by caste and religion as well), and with the setting aside of broad societal interests in promoting both human and economic development (boxes 5 in Figure 13.2, and A and B in Figure 13.3). When therefore, on the other hand, civil society based movements like the KSSP oppose this and proclaim the need for 'de-politicisation', the latter expression is in fact misleading since the reformists favour local organisation for common societal aims instead of private or group specific ones. Hence, they rather try a dual social type of politicisation (box D in Figure 13.3).

Having said this, however, it is also important to remember that in carrying out the re-politicisation, the reformists themselves have stumbled over how to relate special tasks such as the promotion of health, education and production to societal government. But less so than in Indonesia and in the Philippines. Over the years their programmes have become more comprehensive and linked to broad perspectives. The local resource-mapping programme, for instance, is now firmly situated within the general framework of decentralised democratic governance –

in co-operation with state as well as local governments. Till recently, the reformists' major problem has rather been the mobilisation and polit- icisation of demands for democratic decentralisation. This task was mainly left to the authorised parties (and the special interests that they harbour). And when little happened the reformists' alternative develop- ment politics only proved possible in isolated showcase villages. During recent years, however, there has been a decisive gradual shift of many KSSP members and actions from developmental, 'independent' grass- roots work (box 9) to more promotion of local organising and co- ordination among the people (box 10). The aim is thus to promote both universalistic popular politics (as against particularistic politics related to separate pillars) and to change from below the established parties and their priorities. In the recent process of decentralisation and popular planning – with the synchronisation of forceful work from above, pressure from below and movements' capacity to really get campaigns off the ground and work done – one can visualise ways of tackling these dilemmas. But there remain the uphill tasks of handling bureaucrats and politicians with vested interests, and pushing for the institutionalisation and actual implementation of the plans and projects.

Conclusion

First, if there is something to the critique of the civil society/social capital paradigm offered in this chapter, we should focus instead on the politics of democratisation – and pay special attention to the rise, potential and problems of the tenth strategic position in combination with the fourth type of politicisation (see Figures 13.2 and 13.3); that is, on movement co-ordinators-cum-organisers with a dual social way of politicising interests, issues and ideas.

Second, if there is something to this conclusion, international support for Third World democratisation should be redirected from the incon- clusive promotion of civil society and social capital to the specific support of genuine actors in real processes of democratisation – such as, to take but three examples, the genuine Indonesian pro-democracy forces' attempts to bridge the gap between top-down activists and those working at the grassroots level, the Philippine democratisers' efforts to co-ordinate movements from below and link them up with the building of a new party, or the Kerala reformists' propelling of decentralisation and popular planning from below.

Notes

1 The following analysis is based on Törnquist, 'Making Democratisation Work.

2 On civil society, see at first hand Cohen and Arato, *Civil Society and Political Theory*; and Keane, *Civil Society and the State*. Cf., for example, also Karlsson, *The State of State*; and Hadenius and Uggla, *Making Civil Society Work*.

3 I am thankful for having been able in this part of the chapter to benefit from discussions with the participants in a series of master/doctoral courses in Uppsala 1994–97 on 'State, Development and Democratisation in the Third World' (co-chaired by Lars Rudebeck) and our guest lecturers.

4 See, for example, Stepan, *Democratising Brazil*.

5 Tarrow, 'Making Social Science Work Across Space and Time' (referring in his fn. 23 to David Laitin).

6 Putnam, *Making Democracy Work*.

7 Sabetti, 'Path Dependence and Civic Culture', p. 27.

8 Tarrow, 'Making Social Science Work', p. 394

9 Ibid, p. 395.

10 Sabetti, 'Path Dependence and Civic Culture', p. 32ff.

11 Tarrow, 'Making Social Science Work Across Space and Time', p. 392, referring also in his fn. 15 to the results of Carlo Trigilia with collaborators.

12 Cf. Tarrow, ibid., p. 393ff.

13 I shall return to this on the basis of my own empirical results in Third World contexts.

14 Levi, 'Social and Unsocial Capital', p. 49.

15 Cf. Tarrow, 'Making Social Science Work', p. 395ff.

16 Therborn, 'The Right to Vote and the Four World Routes to/through Modernity'. (Cf. also Therborn's basic *European Modernity and Beyond*.)

17 Mamdani, *Citizen and Subject*. (Cf. my own analysis in Chapter 1, section on 'Third World Politics of Development: The Symbiosis of the Political and Economic Spheres'.

18 Agora Project, *Democracy and Social Capital*. On theories on economic development and democracy, see Przeworski and Limongi, 'Modernization: Theories and Facts'.

19 Cf., for example, Gibbon, 'Some Reflections on 'Civil Society' and Political Change'; Beckman, 'The Liberation of Civil Society'; and White, 'Civil Society, Democratisation and Development'.

20 Przeworski et al., *Sustainable Democracy*, p. 57.

21 See, for example, my own earlier works on the 'old tradition' and its dubious contemporary relevance, *Dilemmas of Third World Communism*; *What's Wrong with Marxism? Vols 1 and 2*; and 'Communists and Democracy in the Philippines'.

22 The project was financed primarily by the Swedish Agency for Research Cooperation with Developing Countries. (Because of the rapid developments in Indonesia since mid-1996, and the simultaneously initiated Kerala project on planning from below, the concluding book from the project is still forthcoming.) The method of comparing similar movements and ideas in different settings (and over time in the same settings) may in turn be compared with the methods discussed in McAdam et al., *Comparative Perspectives on Social Movements* – though I am not primarily looking at structural factors as such but at the way in which movements' read them and try to alter them; cf. also Tarrow, 'States and Opportunities', p. 48ff, who explains the similarities in different settings with reference to state-building. In my cases I would rather refer to the dual effects of the expansion of politically injected capitalism.

23 For background analyses, see Törnquist, *Dilemmas of Third World Communism* and *What's Wrong with Marxism? Vols 1 and 2*. For a reasonably extensive analysis of the developments since the late eighties, see Törnquist, 'Civil Society and Divisive Politicisation'.

24 For a background analysis, see Törnquist, 'Communists and Democracy in the Philippines'. For a reasonably extensive analysis of the developments during the first part of the nineties, see Törnquist, 'Popular Politics of Democratisation'. (This is a revised and updated (through 1995) summary of 'Democratic "Empowerment" and Democratisation of Politics'.)

25 The so-called *Bisig* movement and the Popular Democrats – both co-operating with *Pandayan*; plus Bernabe 'Dante' Buscayno's efforts.

26 For background analyses, see Törnquist, *What's Wrong with Marxism? Vols 1 and 2* and 'Communists and Democracy'. For full analyses of the development till the mid-nineties, see (in co-operation with P.K. Michael Tharakan) 'Democratisation and Attempts to Renew the Radical Political Development Project'.

27 For the concept of the campaign, see Isaac and Harilal, 'Planning for Empowerment'. Cf. also the reporting by Krishnakumar, in *Frontline*; Bandyopadhyay, 'People's Participation in Planning'; and Franke and Chasin, 'Power to the Malayalee People'.

28 Sen and Dréze, *Indian Development*.

29 Levi, Review of Robert Putnam et al. 'Making Democracy Work', p. 377.

30 Cf. Thörlind, *Decentralisation and Local Government Performance*.

31 See, for example, Zachariah and Sooryamoorthy, *Science in Participatory Development*.

32 Besides linking up with and then suffering from the fall of the leftist government in mid-1991.

33 The following is primarily based on a re-study in early 1996, and since then news clippings and brief updates in Kerala; the results have not yet been published.

34 The loss was mainly due to special sympathies with just-assassinated Rajiv Gandhi's Congress Party.

35 Local authorities on district, block and village level.

36 Cf. my *Marginal Notes on Impressive Attempts* and the interview with me in *Indian Express* (Kerala edition), 11 January 1997.

37 For a normative-theoretical construct in the latter direction, see Held, *Democracy and the Global Order*.

38 Including Charles Tilly, Sydney Tarrow and many others – for a recent synthesis, see McAdam et al., *Comparative Perspectives on Social Movements*. (My own studies of parties and movements may also be of some use.)

39 I have mainly been inspired by the writings of Nicos Mouzelis and studies of comparative corporatism, including by Göran Therborn. Cf. also Migdal et al., *State Power and Social Forces*.

40 McAdam, 'Political Opportunities', p. 27.

41 Gamson and Meyer, 'Framing political opportunity', p. 277.

42 Cf. above, in the initial part of this chapter, on the original idea of civil society as a politically created community of citizens.

43 The same actor often arrives at different conclusions depending on the type of issue or the sector of state or society. For instance, there may be some free space with regard to environmental questions but not to labour rights; or there

may be some room for manoeuvre at the centre but not on the local level. Here we only indicate the actors' general positions.

44 Mouzelis, *Politics in the Semi-Periphery.*

45 Tarrow, *Power in Movement,* p. 135ff.

46 In the 'anarchist' solutions Tarrow also includes, for instance, syndicalism and guild socialism; in the second he adds, for instance, European Christian Democracy. Of course, one could also add reformist Communist patterns (like in West Bengal and Kerala) to the second category.

47 Tarrow, *Power in Movement,* primarily p. 138ff.

48 Much could be added to this. Tarrow discusses intermediate solutions or more or less attractive compromises that have developed over time. For analytical purposes, and as a way of further distancing ourselves from Tarrow's European and North American context, I believe it is more fruitful to hold on to the basic ideal types and to cross-tabulate with political space and (later on) with politicisation.

49 Avant-garde catalysts remain few, aside from some intellectual personalities.

Study Questions

Most 'facts' need not be pounded into the head. The book can be used as a reference. One should commit the most important arguments to memory, however. Most of these are touched on, directly or indirectly, in the questions that follow.

1. Present the main features of the argument that the relation between politics and development is similar across developing countries with respect to one fundamental matter: the symbiosis of the political and economic spheres. Then submit your own critical comments.

2. Discuss the similarities and differences between the study of political modernisation (or political development), Third World politics, the politics of development, and politics and development.

3. On a general level, what are the major analytical approaches that one may use as an analytical tool when reviewing the various schools of thought?

4. Discuss how political and scientific conjunctures have left their mark on different descriptions and explanations of politics and development.

5. Describe and discuss how adherents of the modernisation school distinguished between traditional and modern in developing countries.

6. What were the similarities and differences between the ways in which non-Marxist and Marxist modernisation researchers described and explained politics and development?

7. Analyse the similarities and differences between the two major political development projects that emerged within the modernisation school: the Western modernisation project and the radical nation-state project.

8. What were the most important objections that modernisation revisionists had to the original modernisation perspective?

9. What were the basic arguments put forward by the comparative historians?

10. Present the main themes of the argument that clientelism and patrimonialism characterise politics and development in developing countries.

11. Summarise and analyse the following: (a) Huntington's critique of the original modernisation approach, and (b) his view of the 'politics of order'.

12. What was the thesis of non-capitalist development, and what arguments were marshalled on its behalf?

13. Discuss similarities and differences between the 'politics of order' and the 'non-capitalist development' theses respectively.

14. Identify the most important differences, as regards the view taken of the relation between politics and development, between (a) the modernisation school (including those seeking to revise it), and (b) the dependency school.

15. How did the dependency school differ from earlier Marxist perspectives in regard to its analysis of politics and development?

16. What did dependency theorists themselves have to say on the space for politics in developing countries?

17. On what two points did the dependency revisionists criticise the original arguments of their school?

18. How were new perspectives on politics generated by the theorists who stressed the importance of class politics and the relative autonomy of the state?

19. How did the researchers who applied class analysis view the relation between politics and the state?

20. Present the main features of the argument concerning the relative autonomy of the state in developing countries.

21. Why did scholars of the neo-classical school (who stressed the destructive role of rent-seeking politicians and bureaucrats) take the view that no political short cuts to development were possible?

22. What then could be done, in the view of these researchers, along political lines to foster development?

23. What were the main criticisms launched by adherents of the primacy-of-institutions school of the theory of rent-seeking behaviour?

24. Discuss what can be meant by 'institutions'.

25. What are 'transaction costs', and what do they tell us about the relation between politics and development?

26. How in general, in the view of institution-oriented political scientists, do institutions and organisations affect development?

27. What were the main characteristics of the renaissance of political development studies?

28. Compare the major ways in which the renewed studies of democracy and democratisation were carried out.

29. Characterise the new studies of governance and discuss similarities and differences in relation to, for instance, Huntington's earlier analyses of political institutions.

30. What are the main arguments (among scholars applying an institutionalist framework) about the role of civil society and social capital?

31. Discuss how institutions and institutional development are explained.

32. Discuss the meaning of 'good governance' as well as the characteristics and dynamics of the current policies in favour of it.

33. Present the main outlines of the post-Marxist critique of (a) the neoclassical theory of rent-seeking politicians and bureaucrats, and (b) the thesis about the primacy of institutions.

34. Summarise and analyse critically the post-Marxist attempt at a deepened analysis of the various ways in which capitalism expands in the Third World by political means. Then turn to their analysis of interests and of social and political movements.

35. Present and discuss critically the post-Marxists' way of analysing popular movements, and examine the hopes they place in these movements.

36. Discuss, in the light of other perspectives, the post-Marxist view of the claim that a common interest exists in respect of development questions.

37. Different schools stress the importance of civil society on different grounds, for example, the theory of rent-seeking, the claim that institutions are primary, the post-Marxist approach. Summarise and analyse the similarities and differences between these various ways of analysing civil society.

38. Discuss the author's claims about how you can move beyond informing yourself about the various schools of thought to asking your own questions, staking out your own position, and carrying out your own studies.

39. Discuss the way in which the author defines democracy and democratisation.

40. Identify the main points in the author's critique of the mainstream analyses of democratisation in the Third World – and then discuss *these points* critically.

41. The author argues, among other things, that the mainstream civil society paradigm neglects relations of power, the extent to which

civil society is politically created, and different paths to democracy? What does he mean and how would you criticise his arguments in turn?

42. The author criticises the mainstream thesis about both the rise and effect of social capital. What are his arguments and what are their weak and strong points?

43. Discuss the author's thesis that it is problematic and not very relevant to apply the civil society/social capital paradigm in the Third World.

44. Do you find the author's argument about the main importance of the *politics* of democratisation to be empirically and theoretically coherent? Moreover, does it make sense in other empirical contexts that you yourself have some knowledge about?

45. The author suggests that we should study problems of democratisation by focusing upon the political space, inclusion and politicisation. What, according to you, are the pros and cons of such an approach?

References
(and some additional textbooks)

Textbooks and review articles are marked '•'.

For standard works and examples of research related to various schools of thought, see footnotes in the relevant chapters.

Agora Project, *Democracy and Social Capital in Segmented Societies*, Uppsala: Department of Government, Uppsala University, 1996.

Ahmed, Ishtiaq, *State, Nation and Ethnicity in Contemporary South Asia*, London and New York: Pinter, 1996.

Alavi, Hamza, 'The State in Post-Colonial Societies: Pakistan and Bangladesh', in *New Left Review*, 74, 1972.

Almond, Gabriel, 'Introduction: A Functional Approach to Comparative Politics', in Almond, G. and Coleman, J. (eds), *The Politics of the Developing Areas*, Princeton, NJ: Princeton University Press, 1960.

Almond, Gabriel and Coleman, James (eds), *The Politics of the Developing Areas*, Princeton, NJ: Princeton University Press, 1960.

Almond, Gabriel and Powell, Bingham, *Comparative Politics: A Developmental Approach*, Boston, MA: Little, Brown, 1966.

Almond, Gabriel and Verba, Sidney, *The Civic Culture: Political Attitudes and Democracy in Five Nations*, Princeton, NJ: Princeton University Press, 1963,

Amin, Samir, *Accumulation on a World Scale: A Critique of the Theory of Under-development*, New York: Monthly Review Press, 1974.

Amin, Samir, *Imperialism and Unequal Development*, Hassocks: Harvester Press, 1977.

Amin, Samir, *Unequal Development: An Essay on the Social Formations of Peripheral Capitalism*, New York: Monthly Review Press, 1976.

Amsden, Alice, H. *Asia's Next Giant: South Korea and Late Industrialisation*, New York: Oxford University Press, 1989.

Anderson, Ben, 'Cacique Democracy and the Philippines: Origins and Dreams', in *New Left Review*, 169, 1988.

Anderson, Benedict, *Imagined Communities*, London: Verso, 1983.

Andræ, Gunilla and Beckman, Björn, *Union Power in the Nigerian Textile Industry*, Uppsala: Nordic Institute of African Studies and Transaction Publishers, 1998.

Athreya, V.B., Djurfeldt, G. and Lindberg, S., *Barriers Broken: Production Relations and Agrarian Change in Tamil Nadu*, New Delhi and London: Sage, 1990.

Bagchi, Amiya Kumar, *Private Investment in India 1900–1939*, Cambridge: Cambridge University Press, 1972, and New Delhi: Orient Longman, 1972 and 1980.

Bandyopadhyay, D., 'People's Participation in Planning: Kerala Experiment', in *Economic and Political Weekly*, 27 September 1977.

Bangura, Yusuf, 'Authoritarian Rule and Democracy in Africa: A Theoretical Discourse', in Rudebeck, Lars (ed.), *When Democracy Makes Sense: Studies in the Potential of Third World Popular Movements*, Uppsala: The Akut-group, 1992.

Baran, Paul, *The Political Economy of Growth*, New York: Monthly Review Press, 1957.

Beckman, Björn, 'The Liberation of Civil Society', in Mohanty, M. and Mukherji, P.N., with Törnquist, O. (eds), *People's Rights: Social Movements and the State in the Third World*, New Delhi: Sage, 1998.

Beckman, Björn, 'Whose Democracy? Bourgeois versus Popular Democracy', in Rudebeck, Lars (ed.), *When Democracy Makes Sense: Studies in the Potential of Third World Popular Movements*, Uppsala: The Akut-group, 1992.

Beckman, Björn, 'Whose State? State and Capitalist Development in Nigeria', in *Review of African Political Economy*, 23, 1982.

Bell, D., Brown, D., Jayasuriya, K. and Jones, D.M., *Towards Illiberal Democracy in Pacific Asia*, New York: St. Martin's, 1995.

Bhagwati, Jagdish N., 'Directly Unproductive Profit-Seeking (DUP) Activities', in *Journal of Political Economy*, vol. 90, no. 5, 1982.

Bhagwati, Jagdish N., in Grossman, Gene (ed.), *Essays in Development Economics*, Oxford: Blackwell, 1985.

Bhagwati, J.N. and Srinivasan, T.N., 'Revenue Seeking: A Generalisation of the Theory of Tariffs', in *Journal of Political Economy*, vol. 88, no. 6, 1980.

Binder, L., Coleman, J., LaPalombara, J., Pye, L., Verba, S. and Weiner, M., *Crises and Sequences in Political Development*, Princeton, NJ: Princeton University Press, 1971.

Blom Hansen, Thomas, *The Saffron Wave. Democratic Revolution and the Growth of Hindu Nationalism in India. Vols 1–3*, Roskilde: International Development Studies, Roskilde University, 1997.

Blomström, Magnus and Hettne, Björn, *Development Theory in Transition. The Dependency Debate and Beyond. Third World Responses*, London: Zed Books, 1984.●

Brandell, Inga (ed.), *Workers in Third-World Industrialisation*, London: Macmillan, 1991.

Brass, Paul, R., *Ethnicity and Nationalism: Theory and Comparison*, New Delhi: Sage, 1991.

Bratton, Michael and van de Walle, Nicolas, *Democratic Experiments in Africa. Regime Transitions in Comparative Perspective*, Cambridge: Cambridge University Press, 1997.

Buchanan, James, M., *Liberty, Market, and State: Political Economy in the 1980's*, New York: New York University Press, 1986.

Buchanan, J.M., Tollison, R.D. and Tullock, G. (eds), *Towards a Theory of the Rent-seeking Society*, College Station, TX: Texas A & M University Press, 1980.

Bulletin of Concerned Asian Scholars, vol. 29, nos 1 and 2.

Calvert, Susan and Calvert, Peter, *Politics and Society in the Third World: An Introduction*, Hemel Hempstead: Prentice Hall, 1996.●

Cammack, Paul, *Capitalism and Democracy in the Third World. The Doctrine for Political Development*, London and Washington: Leicester University Press, 1997.●

Cammack, P., Pool, D. and Tordoff, W. (eds), *Third World Politics. A Comparative Introduction*, Second edition, Baltimore: The Johns Hopkins University Press, 1993.●

Cardoso, Fernando Henrique, and Faletto, Enzo, *Dependency and Development in Latin America*, Berkeley, CA: University of California Press, 1979. (Revised version of the Spanish original published 1971.)

Carmen, Raff, *Autonomous Development. Humanizing the Landscape. An Excursion into Radical Thinking and Practice*, London and New Jersey: Zed Books, 1996.•

Clapham, Christopher, *Third World Politics. An Introduction*, London and Sydney: Croom Helm, 1985.•

Cohen, Jean L. and Arato, Andrew, *Civil Society and Political Theory*, London: The MIT Press, 1994.

Crook, R. and Manor, J. 'Democratic Decentralisation and Institutional Performance: Four Asian and African Experiences Compared', in *Journal of Commonwealth & Comparative Politics*, vol. 33, no. 3, 1995.

Dahl, Robert, *A Preface to Democratic Theory*, Chicago: University of Chicago Press, 1956.

Diamond, Larry, 'Economic Development and Democracy Reconsidered', in *American Behavioral Sciences*, vol. 35, no. 4/5, 1992.•

Diamond, L., Linz, J.J. and Lipset, S.M. (eds), *Democracy in Developing Countries, Vol. 2, Africa, Vol. 3, Asia, Vol. 4, Latin America*, Boulder, CO: Lynne Rienner Publishers, 1988 and 1989.

Djurfeldt, Göran and Lindberg, Staffan, *Behind Poverty: The Social Formation in a Tamil Village*, London: Curzon Press, 1975.

Emmanuel, Arghiri, *Unequal Exchange: A Study of the Imperialism of Trade*, New York: Monthly Review Press, 1972.

Engels, Friedrich, *The Origin of the Family, Private Property and the State*, New York: International Publishers, 1942 [1884].

Escobar, Arturo and Alvarez, Sonia E., *The Making of Social Movements in Latin America: Identity, Strategy, and Democracy*, Boulder, CO and Oxford: Westview Press, 1992.

Evans, Peter, 'Class, State, and Dependence in East Asia: Lessons for Latin Americanists', in Deyo, Frederic, C. (ed.), *The Political Economy of the New Asian Industrialism*, Ithaca, NY and London: Cornell University Press, 1987.

Evans, Peter, *Embedded Autonomy: States and Industrial Transformation*, Princeton, NJ: Princeton University Press, 1995.

Evans, Peter (ed.), 'Government Action, Social Capital and Development: Creating Synergy across the Public–Private Divide', Special Section, in *World Development*, vol. 24, no. 6, 1996.

Evans, Peter, 'Introduction: Development Strategies across the Public–Private Divide' and 'Government Action, Social Capital and Development: Reviewing the Evidence on Synergy', Special Section, in *World Development*, vol. 24, no. 6, 1966.•

Evans, Peter, 'Predatory, Developmental, and Other Apparatuses: A Comparative Political Economy Perspective on the Third World State', in *Sociological Forum*, vol. 4, no. 4, 1989.

Evans, P.B., Rueschemeyer, D. and Skocpol, T., (eds), *Bringing the State Back In*, Cambridge: Cambridge University Press, 1985.

Findlay, R., 'Is the New Political Economy Relevant to Developing Countries?', *PPR Working Papers* (WPS 292), Washington, DC: The World Bank.

Frank, Andre Gunder, *Capitalism and Underdevelopment in Latin America: Historical Studies of Chile and Brazil*, New York: Monthly Review Press, 1967.

Frank, Andre Gunder, 'Dependence is Dead, Long Live Dependence and the Class Struggle: An Answer to Critics', in *World Development*, vol. 5, no. 4, 1977. •

Frank, Andre Gunder, 'The Development of Underdevelopment', in *Monthly Review*, September, 1966.

Frank, Andre Gunder, *Latin America: Underdevelopment or Revolution. Essays on the Development and the Immediate Enemy*, New York: Monthly Review Press, 1969.

Frank, Andre Gunder, *Lumpenbourgeoisie – Lumpendevelopment: Dependence, Class, and Politics in Latin America*, New York: Monthly Review Press, 1972.

Franke, Richard, W. and Chasin, Barbara, H., 'Power to the Malayalee People', in *Economic and Political Weekly*, 29 November 1997.

Fröbel, V., Heinrichs, J. and Kreye, O., *The New International Division of Labour. Structural Unemployment in Industrialised Countries and Industrialisation in Developing Countries*, Cambridge: Cambridge University Press, 1980 [1977].

Gamson, William A. and Meyer, David S. 'Framing Political Opportunity', in McAdam, D., Mc.Carthy, J.D. and Zald, M.N. (eds) *Comparative Perspectives on Social Movements. Political Opportunities, Mobilizing Structures, and Cultural Framings*, Cambridge: Cambridge University Press, 1996.

Gerschenkron, Alexander, *Economic Backwardness in Historical Perspective*, Cambridge, MA: Harvard University Press, 1962.

Gibbon, Peter (ed.), *Social Change and Economic Reform in Africa*, Uppsala: The Scandinavian Institute of African Studies, 1993.

Gibbon, Peter, 'Some Reflections on "Civil Society" and Political Change', in Rudebeck, L. and Törnquist, O., with Rojas, V. (eds), *Democratisation in the Third World: Concrete Cases in Comparative and Theoretical Perspective*, Uppsala: The Seminar for Development Studies, 1996. (Second edition forthcoming from Macmillan, 1998.) •

Gibbon, P., Bangura, Y. and Ofstad, A. (eds), *Authoritarianism, Democracy, and Structural Adjustment: The Politics of Economic Reform in Africa*, Uppsala: The Scandinavian Institute of African Studies, 1992.

Gunnarsson, Christer, 'Development Theory and Third World Industrialisation: A Comparison of Patterns of Industrialisation in 19th Century Europe and the Third World', in *Journal of Contemporary Asia*, vol. 15, no. 2, 1985. •

Gunnarsson, Christer, 'Dirigisme or Free-Trade Regime? A Historical and Institutional Interpretation of the Taiwanese Success Story', in Hansson, Göte (ed.), *Trade, Growth and Development: The Role of Politics and Institutions*, London: Routledge, 1993.

Gunnarsson, Christer 'Mercantilism Old and New: An Institutional Approach to the Study of Developmental States in Europe and East Asia', in Lauridsen, L. (ed.), *Institutions and Industrial Development: Asian Experiences*, Roskilde: International Development Studies, Roskilde University, 1995.

Hadenius, Axel, *Democracy and Development*, Cambridge: Cambridge University Press, 1992.

Hadenius, Axel (ed.), *Democracy's Victory and Crisis*, Cambridge: Cambridge University Press, 1997.

Hadenius, Axel and Uggla, Fredrik, *Making Civil Society Work. Promoting Democratic Development: What Can States and Donors Do?* Uppsala Studies in Democracy, No. 9, Uppsala: Department of Government, Uppsala University, 1995. •

Hadiz, Vedi, *Workers and State in New Order Indonesia*, London: Routledge, 1997.

Haynes, Jeff, *Third World Politics: A Concise Introduction*, Oxford: Blackwell, 1996.•

Held, David, *Democracy and the Global Order: From the Modern State to Cosmopolitan Governance*, Cambridge: Polity Press, 1995.

Heryanto, Ariel, 'Discourse and State-Terrorism: A Case Study of Political Trials in New Order Indonesia 1989–1990'. PhD dissertation, Department of Anthropology, Monash University, 1993.

Hettne, Björn, *Development Theory and the Three Worlds: Towards an International Political Economy of Development*, Harlow, Essex: Longman, 1995.•

Hewison, K., Robison, R. and Rodan, G. (eds), *Southeast Asia in the 1990s: Authoritarianism, Democracy and Capitalism*, St. Leonards: Allen and Unwin, 1993.

Higgot, Richard and Robison, Richard (eds), *Southeast Asia: Essays in the Political Economy of Structural Change*, London: Routledge, 1985.

Huntington, Samuel, 'After Twenty Years: The Furture of the Third Wave', in *Journal of Democracy*, vol. 8, no. 4, 1997.

Huntington, Samuel, *The Clash of Civilizations?*, New York: Council on Foreign Relations, 1993.

Huntington, Samuel P., 'Political Development and Political Decay', in *World Politics*, vol. 17, no. 3, 1965.

Huntington, Samuel P., *Political Order in Changing Societies*, New Haven, CT: Yale University Press, 1968.

Huntington, Samuel P., *The Third Wave: Democratisation in the Late Twentieth Century*, Norman, OK and London: University of Oklahoma Press, 1991.

Hydén, Göran, *Assisting the Growth of Civil Society: How Might it be Improved?*, Uppsala Studies in Democracy, No. 10, Uppsala: Department of Government, Uppsala University, 1995.•

Hydén, Göran, 'Governance and the Study of Politics', in Hydén et al. (eds), *Governance and the Politics in Africa*, Boulder, CO and London: Lynne Rienner Publishers, 1992.

Hydén, Göran and Bratton, Michael (eds), *Governance and the Politics in Africa*, Boulder, CO and London: Lynne Rienner Publishers, 1992.

Isaac, Jeffrey C., *Power and Marxist Theory: A Realist View*, Ithaca, NY and London: Cornell University Press, 1987.

Isaac, Thomas and Harilal, K.N., 'Planning for Empowerment: People's Campaign for Decentralised Planning in Kerala', in *Economic and Political Weekly*, vol. 32, nos 1–2, 1997.

Jackson, R.H. and Rosberg, C.G., *Personal Rule in Black Africa. Prince, Autocrat, Prophet, Tyrant*, Berkeley, CA: University of California Press, 1982.

Johnson, Chalmers, *MITI and the Japanese Miracle. The Growth of Industrial Policy, 1925–1975*, Stanford, CA: Stanford University Press, 1982.

Johnson, Chalmers, 'Political Institutions and Economic Performance: The Government–Business Relationship in Japan, South Korea, and Taiwan', in Deyo, F. (ed.), *The Political Economy of the New Asian Industrialism*, Ithaca, NY and London: Cornell University Press, 1987.

Jomo, K.S., with Yun Chung, Chen, Folk, Brian C., ul-Haque, Jrfan, Phongpaichit, Pasuk, Simatupang, Batara and Tateishi, Mayuri, *Southeast Asia's Misunderstood Miracle: Industrial Policy and Economic Development in Thailand, Malaysia, and Indonesia*, Boulder, CO and Oxford: Westview Press, 1997.

Jomo, K.S., *Tigers in Trouble: Financial Governance, Liberalization and the Crisis in East Asia*, London: Zed Books, 1998.

Karl, Terry Lynn and Schmitter, Philippe C., 'Modes of Transition in Latin America, Southern and Eastern Europe', in *International Social Science Journal*, no. 43, 1991.

Karlsson, Nicke, *The State of State. An Inquiry Concerning the Role of Invisible Hands in Politics and Civil Society*, Uppsala: Almqvist & Wiksell International, 1993.

Keane, John (ed.), *Civil Society and the State*, London: Verso, 1988.

Kohli, Atul, 'Centralization and Powerlessness: India's Democracy in a Comparative Perspective', in Migdal, J., Kohli, A. and Shue, V. (eds), *State Power and Social Forces – Domination and Transformation in the Third World*, Cambridge: Cambridge University Press, 1994.

Kohli, Atul, *Democracy and Discontent: India's Growing Crisis of Governability*, Cambridge: Cambridge University Press, 1990.

Kohli, Atul, *The State and Poverty in India: The Politics of Reform*, Cambridge: Cambridge University Press, 1987.

Kornhauser, William, *The Politics of Mass Society*, London: Routledge and Kegan Paul, 1960.

Krishnakumar, R., in *Frontline*, 28 June 1996, 23 August 1996, and 7 March 1997.

Laclau, Ernesto, 'Feudalism and Capitalism in Latin America', in *New Left Review*, no. 67, 1971.

Laclau, Ernesto and Mouffe, Chantal, *Hegemony and Socialist Strategy*, London: Verso, 1985.

Lauridsen, Laurids S., 'The Debate on the Developmental State', in Martinussen, John (ed.), *Development Theory and the Role of the State in Third World Countries*, Occasional Paper No. 2, Roskilde: International Development Studies, Roskilde University, 1992.•

Lauridsen, Laurids S. (ed.), *Institutions and Industrial Development: Asian Experiences*, Occasional Paper No. 16, Roskilde: International Development Studies, Roskilde University, 1995.

Leftwich, Adrian, 'Governance, Democracy and Development in the Third World', in *Third World Quarterly*, vol. 14, no. 3, 1993.

Leftwich, Adrian, 'Bringing Politics Back In: Towards a Model of the Developmental State', in *Journal of Development Studies*, vol. 31, no. 3, February 1995.•

Leftwich, Adrian, 'On Primacy of Politics in Development' and 'Two Cheers for Democracy? Democracy and the Developmental State', in Leftwich, Adrian (ed.), *Democracy and Development. Theory and Practice*, Cambridge: Polity Press, 1996.•

Lenin, V.I., *Imperialism: The Highest Stage of Capitalism*, Moscow: Progress Publishers, 1966 [1916].

Levi, Margaret, Review of Robert Putnam et al. 'Making Democracy Work', in *Comparative Political Studies*, vol. 26, no. 3, October 1993.•

Levi, Margaret, 'Social and Unsocial Capital: A Review Essay of Robert Putnam's "Making democracy Work" ', in *Politics and Society*, vol. 24, no. 1, March 1996.•

Leys, Colin, 'Capitalist Accumulation, Class Formation and Dependency: The Significance of the Kenyan Case', in R. Milliband and J. Saville (eds), *Socialist Register*, London: Merlin Press, 1978.

Lindberg, Staffan and Sverrisson, Arni, *Social Movements in Development: The Challenge of Globalisation and Democratisation*, London: Macmillan, 1997.

Linz, Juan J. and Stepan, Alfred, *Problems of Democratic Transition and Consolidation: Southern Europe, South America, and Post-Communist Europe*, Baltimore and London: Johns Hopkins University Press, 1996.

Lipset, Seymour Martin, *Political Man: The Social Basis of Politics*, (expanded edition), Baltimore: Johns Hopkins University Press, 1981 [1960].

Lipset, Seymour Martin, 'Some Social Requisites of Democracy: Economic Development and Political Legitimacy', in *American Political Science Review*, vol. 53, no. 1, 1959.

Mainwaring, S., O'Donnell, G. and Valenzuela, J.S. (eds), *Issues in Democratic Consolidation. The New South American Democracies in Comparative Perspective*, Notre Dame, IN: University of Notre Dame Press, 1992.

Mamdani, Mahmood, *Citizen and Subject: Contemporary Africa and the Legacy of Late Colonialism*, Princeton, NJ: Princeton University Press, 1996.

Manor, James (ed.), *Rethinking Third World Politics*, London and New York: Longman, 1991.

March, James G. and Olsen, Johan P., 'The New Institutionalism: Organizational Factors in Political Life', in *The American Political Science Review*, vol. 78, pp. 734–49, 1984. •

March, James G. and Olsen, Johan P., *Rediscovering Institutions: The Organisational Basis of Politics*, New York: Free Press, 1989.

Marcussen, Henrik Secher and Torp, Jens Erik, *Internationalisation of Capital: Prospects for the Third World. A Re-examination of Dependency Theory*, London: Zed Books, 1982.

Markoff, John, *Waves of Democracy: Social Movements and Political Change*, Thousand Oaks, CA: Pine Forge Press, 1996.

Martinussen, John, 'General Introduction to the Theme in the Context of Development Studies', in *Selected Approaches to the Study of Institutions in Development*, Occasional Paper No. 1, Roskilde: International Development Studies, Roskilde University, 1990. •

Martinussen, John, *Society, State & Market. A Guide to Competing Theories of Development*, London and New Jersey: Zed Books, 1997. •

Martinussen, John, *Staten i Perifere og Post-koloniale samfund: India og Pakistan*, Vols I to IV (in Danish with a summary in English: 'The State in Peripherial and Post-Colonial Societies: India and Pakistan') Åarhus: Politica, 1980.

Martinussen, John (ed.), *The Theoretical Heritage from Marx and Weber in Development Studies*, Roskilde: International Development Studies, Roskilde University, 1994. •

Marx, Karl, *The Eighteenth Brumaire of Louis Bonaparte*, New York: International Publishers, 1963 [1869].

McAdam, Doug, 'Political Opportunities: Conceptual Origins, Current Problems, Future Directions', in McAdam, D., McCarthy, J.D. and Zald, M.N. (eds), *Comparative Perspectives on Social Movements. Political Opportunities, Mobilizing Structures, and Cultural Framings*, Cambridge: Cambridge University Press, 1996. •

McAdam, D., McCarthy, J.D. and Zald, M.N. (eds), *Comparative Perspectives on Social Movements. Political Opportunities, Mobilizing Structures, and Cultural Framings*, Cambridge: Cambridge University Press, 1996.

Meillassoux, Claude, 'A Class Analysis of the Bureaucratic Process in Mali', in *Journal of Development Studies*, vol. 16, 1970.

Migdal, Joel, S., 'The State in Society: An approach to Struggles for Domination', in Migdal, J., Kohli, A. and Shue, V. (eds), *State Power and Social Forces – Domination and Transformation in the Third World*, Cambridge: Cambridge University Press, 1994.•

Migdal, J., Kohli, A. and Shue, V. (eds), *State Power and Social Forces – Domination and Transformation in the Third World*, Cambridge: Cambridge University Press, 1994.

Mohanty, M. and Mukherji, P.N., with Törnquist, O. (eds), *People's Rights: Social Movements and the State in the Third World*, New Delhi: Sage, 1998.

Moore, Barrington, *Social Origins of Dictatorship and Democracy: Lord and Peasant in the Making of the Modern World*, New York: Harper and Row, 1965.

Mouzelis, Nicos, *Politics in the Semi-Periphery. Early Parliamentarism and Late Industrialisation in the Balkans and Latin America*. London: Macmillan, 1986.

Mouzelis, Nicos, *Post-Marxist Alternatives: The Construction of Social Orders*, London: Macmillan, 1990.

Myrdal, Gunnar, *Asian Drama: An Inquiry into the Poverty of Nations*, New York: Pantheon, 1968.

North, Douglass, C., *Economic Performance Through Time*, Prize Lecture in Economic Science in Memory of Alfred Nobel, December 9, 1993. Stockholm: Nobelstiftelsen, 1993.

North, Douglass C., 'Institutions and Economic Growth: An Historical Introduction', in *World Deveopment*, vol. 17, no. 9, 1989.

North, Douglass C., *Institutions, Institutional Change and Economic Performance*, Cambridge: Cambridge University Press, 1990.

O'Donnell, Guillermo A., *Modernisation and Bureaucratic-Authoritarianism: Studies in South American Politics*, Berkeley, CA: Institute of International Studies, University of California, 1973.

O'Donnell, Guillermo, 'Transitions, Continuities, and Paradoxes', in Mainwaring, S., O'Donnell, G. and Valenzuela, J.S. (eds), *Issues in Democratic Consolidation. The New South American Democracies in Comparative Perspective*, Notre Dame, IN: University of Notre Dame Press, 1992.

O'Donnell, Guillermo and Schmitter, Philippe C., *Transitions from Authoritarian Rule. Tentative Conclusions about Uncertain Democracies*. Baltimore and London: The Johns Hopkins University Press, 1986.

OECD, *DAC Orientations on Participatory Development and Good Governance*, vol. 2, no. 2, OECD Working Papers, Paris: OECD, 1994.

Olson, Mancur, *The Rise and Decline of Nations: Economic Growth, Stagflation, and Social Rigidities*, New Haven, CT: Yale University Press, 1982.

Ominami, Carlos, *Le tiers monde dans la crise*, Paris: La Découverte, 1986.

Omvedt, Gail, *Reinventing Revolution: New Social Movements and the Socialist Tradition in India*, New York and London: M.E. Sharpe, 1993.

Palmberg, Mai (ed.), *Problems of Socialist Orientation in Africa*, Uppsala: Scandinavian Institute of African Studies and Stockholm: Almqvist & Wiksell International, 1978.•

Parsons, Talcott, *Structure and Process in Modern Societies*, Glencoe IL: The Free Press, 1960.

Poulantzas, Nicos, *Political Power and Social Classes*, London: New Left Books, 1973 [1968].

Przeworski, Adam, *Democracy and the Market: Political and Economic Reforms in Eastern Europe and Latin America*, Cambridge: Cambridge University Press, 1991.

Przeworski, A. and Limongi, F., 'Modernization: Theories and Facts', in *World Politics*, no. 49, January 1997.•

Przeworski, Adam, et al., *Sustainable Democracy*, Cambridge: Cambridge University Press, 1995.

Putnam, Robert D., *Making Democracy Work: Civic Traditions in Modern Italy*, Princeton, NJ: Princeton University Press, 1993.

Pye, Lucian, *Aspects of Political Development*, Boston, MA: Little, Brown, 1966.

Randall, Vicky and Theobald, Robin, *Political Change and Underdevelopment. A Critical Introduction to Third World Politics*, London: Macmillan, 1985.•

Robison, Richard and Goodman, David S.G. (eds), *The New Rich in Asia: Mobile Phones, McDonald's and Middle-Class Revolution*, London: Routledge, 1996.

Rodan, Garry (ed.), *Political Oppositions in Industrialising Asia*, London: Routledge, 1996.

Rodan, G., Hewison, K. and Robison, R. (eds), *The Political Economy of South East Asia: An Introduction*, Oxford and New York: Oxford University Press, 1997.

Rostow, Walt W., *The Stages of Economic Growth: A Non-Communist Manifesto*, Cambridge: Cambridge University Press, 1962.

Rudebeck, Lars, 'Traditional/Modern in Modernised Modernisation Thinking: The Development of a Weberian Dichotomy', in Martinussen, John (ed.), *The Theoretical Heritage from Marx and Weber in Development Studies*, Roskilde: International Development Studies, Roskilde University, 1994.

Rudebeck, Lars (ed.), *When Democracy Makes Sense: Studies in the Potential of Third World Popular Movements*, Uppsala: The Akut-group, 1992.

Rudebeck, L. and Törnquist, O., with Rojas, V., *Democratisation in the Third World: Concrete Cases in Comparative and Theoretical Perspective*, Uppsala: The Seminar for Development Studies, 1996. (Second revised edition, Macmillan, 1998.)

Rudolph, Lloyd I. and Rudolph, Susanne, *The Modernity of Tradition: Political Development in India*, Chicago: University of Chicago Press, 1967.

Rueschemeyer, D.D., Huber-Stephens, E. and Stephens, J.D., *Capitalist Development and Democracy*, Cambridge: Polity Press, 1992.

Sabetti, Filippo, 'Path Dependence and Civic Culture: Some Lessons From Italy About Interpreting Social Experiments', in *Politics and Society*, vol. 24, no. 1, March 1996.•

Sachs, Wolfgang (ed.), *The Development Dictionary. A Guide to Knowledge as Power*, London and New Jersey: Zed Books, 1992.•

Sandbrook, Richard, *The Politics of Africa's Economic Recovery*, Cambridge: Cambridge University Press, 1993.

Sandbrook, Richard, *The Politics of Africa's Economic Stagnation*, Cambridge: Cambridge University Press, 1985.

Schumpeter, Joseph A., *Capitalism, Socialism and Democracy*, London: Unwin Paperbacks, 1987 [1942].

Schuurman, Frans J. (ed.), *Beyond the Impasse. New Directions in Development Theory*, London: Zed Books, 1993.•

Sen, Amartya and Dréze, Jean, *Indian Development: Selected Regional Perspectives*, Oxford and Delhi: Oxford University Press, 1996.

Shin, Doh Chull, 'On the Third Wave of Democratisation: A Synthesis and

Evaluation of Recent Theory and Research', in *World Politics*, vol. 47, no. 1, 1994. •

Shivji, Issa G., *Class Struggles in Tanzania*, London: Heinemann, 1976.

Shue, Vivienne, 'State Power and Social Organisation in China', in Migdal, J., Kohli, A. and Shue, V. (eds), *State Power and Social Forces – Domination and Transformation in the Third World*, Cambridge: Cambridge University Press, 1994.

Sirowy, Larry and Inkeles, Alex, 'The Effects of Democracy on Economic Growth and Inequality: A Review', in *Studies in Comparative International Development*, vol. 25, no. 1, 1990. •

Skocpol, T. and Somers, M., 'The Uses of Comparative History in Macrosocial Inquiry', in *Comparative Studies in Sociology and History*, vol. 22, pp. 174–97, 1989. •

Smith, B.C., *Understanding Third World Politics: Theories and Political Change and Development*, London: Macmillan, 1996. •

Srinivasan, T.N., 'Neoclassical Political Economy, the State and Economic Development', in *Asian Development Review*, vol. 3, no. 2.

Stepan, Alfred (ed.), *Democratising Brazil*, Princeton, NJ: Princeton University Press, 1989.

Sørensen, Georg, *Democracy and Democratization: Processes and Prospects in a Changing World*, Boulder, CO: Westview Press, 1993.

Sørensen, Georg, *Democracy, Dictatorship and Development: Economic Development in Selected Regimes of the Third World*, London: Macmillan, 1991.

Tarrow, Sidney, *Power in Movement. Social Movements, Collective Action, and Politics*, Cambridge and New York: Cambridge University Press, 1994.

Tarrow, Sidney, 'States and Opportunities: The Political Structuring of Social Movements', in McAdam, D., McCarthy, J.D. and Zald, M.N. (eds), *Comparative Perspectives on Social Movements. Political Opportunities, Mobilizing Structures, and Cultural Framings*, Cambridge: Cambridge University Press, 1996.

Tarrow, Sidney, 'Making Social Science Work Across Space and Time: A Critical Reflection on Robert Putnam's "Making Democracy Work"', in *American Political Science Review*, vol. 90, no. 2, June 1996. •

Therborn, Göran, 'The Rule of Capital and the Rise of Democracy', in *New Left Review*, no. 103, 1977.

Therborn, Göran, 'The Right to Vote and the Four World Routes to/through Modernity', in Thorstendahl, R. (ed.), *State Theory and State History*, London: Sage, 1992.

Therborn, Göran, *European Modernity and Beyond*, London: Sage, 1995.

Thorner, Alice, 'Semi-feudalism or Capitalism: Contemporary Debate on Classes and Modes of Production in India. Part I–III', in *Economic and Political Weekly*, 4, 11, and 18 December 1982. •

Thörlind, Robert, *Decentralisation and Local Government Performance: Questioning the Civil Society/Social Capital Paradigm through a Comparison of Different Types of Politicisation in West Bengal and Bangladesh*. Uppsala and Copenhagen: Seminar for Development Studies and the Nordic Institute for Asian Studies, 1988.

Tilly, Charles (ed.), *The Formation of the National States in Western Europe*, Princeton, NJ: Princeton University Press, 1975.

Toye, John, *Dilemmas of Development: Reflections on the Counter-Revolution in Development Theory and Policy*, Oxford: Basil Blackwell, 1987.

Turner, Mark and Hulme, David, *Governance, Administration and Development: Making the State Work*, London: Macmillan, 1997.•

Törnquist, Olle, 'Civil Society and Divisive Politicisation: Experiences from Popular Efforts at Democratisation in Indonesia', in Özdalga, E. and Persson, S. (eds), *Civil Society, Democracy and the Muslim World*, Istanbul: Swedish Research Institute and Curzon Press, 1997.

Törnquist, Olle, 'Communists and Democracy in the Philippines', in *Economic and Political Weekly*, 6–13 July and 20 July 1991; (and in *Kasarinlan*, vol. 6, no. 1–2, 1990).

Törnquist, Olle, 'Communists and Democracy: Two Indian Cases and One Debate', in *Bulletin of Concerned Asian Scholars*, vol. 23, no. 2, 1991.•

Törnquist, Olle, with Tharakan, P.K. Michael, 'Democratisation and Attempts to Renew the Radical Political Development Project: The Case of Kerala', in *Economic and Political Weekly*, vol. 31, nos 28–30, 1996. (Also published by the Nordic Institute for Asian Studies.)

Törnquist, Olle, *Dilemmas of Third World Communism: The Destruction of the PKI in Indonesia*, London: Zed Books, 1984 [1982].

Törnquist, Olle, Interview in *Indian Express* (Kerala edition), 11 January 1997.

Törnquist, Olle, 'Making Democratisation Work: From Civil Society and Social Capital to Political Inclusion and Politicisation. Theoretical Reflections on Concrete Cases in Indonesia, Kerala, and the Philippines', in Rudebeck, L., Törnquist, O., with Rojas, V. (eds), *Democratisation in the Third World*, London: Macmillan, 1998.•

Törnquist, Olle, *Marginal Notes on Impressive Attempts*, International Conference on Kerala, New Delhi, 9–11 December 1996.

Törnquist, Olle, 'Popular Politics of Democratisation: Philippine Cases in Comparative and Theoretical Perspective', in Mohanty, M. and Mukherji, P.N., with Törnquist, O. (eds), *People's Rights: Social Movements and the State in the Third World*, New Delhi: Sage, 1998. (Revised and updated summary of 'Democratic "Empowerment" and Democratisation of Politics: Radical Popular Movements and the May 1992 Elections in the Philippines' in *Third World Quarterly*, vol. 14, no. 3, 1993, or *Kasarinlan*, vol. 8, no. 3 and vol. 9, no. 3, 1993.)

Törnquist, Olle, *What's Wrong with Marxism? Vol. 1: On Capitalists and State in India and Indonesia; Vol. 2: On Peasants and Workers in India and Indonesia*, New Delhi: Manohar, 1989 and 1991 respectively.

Törnquist, Olle, 'Whither Studies of Asian Democratisation', *Kasarinlan*, vol. 12, no. 1, 1996, and *Economic and Political Weekly*, 17 January 1998.•

Unger, Jonathan and Chan, Anita, 'Corporatism in China: A Developmental State in an East Asian Context', in McCormick, Barrett and Unger, Jonathan (eds), *China After Socialism: In the Footsteps of Eastern Europe or East Asia?*, Armonk, NY/London: M.E. Sharpe, 1996.

Valenzuela, J. Samuel, 'Democratic Consolidation in Post-Transitional Settings: Notion, Process and Facilitating Conditions', in Mainwaring, S., O'Donnell, G. and Valenzuela, J.S. (eds), *Issues in Democratic Consolidation. The New South American Democracies in Comparative Perspective*, Notre Dame, IN: University of Notre Dame Press, 1992.

Wade, Robert, *Governing the Market. Economic Theory and the Role of Government in East Asian Industrialisation*, Princeton, NJ: Princeton University Press, 1990.

Wade, Robert, 'Japan, the World Bank, and the Art of Paradigm Maintenance:

The East Asian Miracle in Political Perspective', in *New Left Review*, no. 217, 1996.•

Wallerstein, Immanuel, *The Capitalist World Economy*, Cambridge: Cambridge University Press, 1979.

Warren, Bill, *Imperialism, Pioneer of Capitalism*, London: Verso, 1980. (Original article published in *New Left Review*, no. 81, 1973.)

Waylen, Georgina, *Gender in Third World Politics*, Buckingham: Open University Press, 1996.•

White, Gordon, 'Civil Society, Democratisation and Development: Clearing the Analytical Ground', in *Democratisation*, vol. 1, no. 3, 1994.•

White, Gordon (eds), *Developmental States in East Asia*, London: Macmillan, 1988.

White, Gordon, 'Developmental States and Socialist Industrialisation in the Third World', in *Journal of Development Studies*, vol. 21, no. 1, 1985.

World Bank, *The East Asian Miracle: Economic Growth and Public Policy*, Oxford: Oxford University Press, 1993.

World Bank, *Governance and Development*, Washington, DC: World Bank, 1992.

World Bank, *Governance: The World Bank's Experience*, Washington, DC: World Bank, 1994.

World Bank, *World Development Report 1997: The State in a Changing World*, Oxford: Oxford University Press, 1997.

Wuyts, M., Mackintosh, M. and Hewitt, T. (eds), *Development Policy and Public Action*, Oxford: Oxford University Press with the Open University, 1992.•

Zachariah, Mathew and Sooryamoorthy, R., *Science in Participatory Development. The Achievements and Dilemmas of a Development Movement: The Case of Kerala*, London and New Jersey: Zed Books, 1994.

Index

Index compiled by
J.B. McDermott